ISRAEL
IN THE PLAN OF GOD

ISRAEL
IN THE PLAN OF GOD

DAVID BARON

PUBLICATIONS

Grand Rapids, MI 49501

Israel in the Plan of God
by David Baron

© 1983 Kregel Publications, a division of Kregel, Inc., P.O. Box 2607, Grand Rapids, MI 49501. Reprinted under special arrangements with Hebrew Christian Testimony to Israel, London.

Library of Congress Cataloging-in-Publication Data
Baron, David.
   Israel in the plan of God / by David Baron.
      p.   cm.
   Reprint. Originally published: The History of Israel. London: Morgan & Scott, 1925.
   1. Covenants (Theology)—Biblical teaching. 2. Bible—History of Biblical Events. 3. Israel (Christian theology)—Biblical teaching. 4. People of God—Biblical reaching.
5. Typology (Theology). I. Title.
BS680.C67B37   1983   221.9'5   82-18678
                                                         CIP

ISBN 978-0-8254-2089-4

Printed in the United States of America

9 10 11 12/ 14 13 12 11

CONTENTS

FOREWORD

Although these expository addresses by David
Baron were delivered over fifty years ago, they are as
relevant and significant today as they were then.
Mr. Baron was a Jew, well versed in Hebrew customs
and literature. After his conversion to Jesus Christ as
Savior and Messiah he enjoyed a remarkable insight into
the Scriptures and, under the unction of the Spirit, exercised an effective ministry, both as a missionary to his
own people and as a Bible teacher.

Although he only lived to see a trickle of Jewish
immigrants return to their own land, we have seen the
establishing of the State of Israel with a growth in
population to over three million. Nevertheless the majority of Jews (estimates put the figure around eleven
million) are still scattered among the nations; many are
suffering privation and hardship. After several wars with
her Arab neighbors, the future of Israel remains an ex-
plosive issue and her existence remains precarious.

In this volume, originally published under the title,
The History of Israel — Its Spiritual Significance, Mr.
Baron looks at Israel's checkered past, considers her
present condition, and, assured that God has not cast off
His people despite their many failures, anticipates her
final glory. Mr. Baron foresaw from the Scriptures a partial return in unbelief, which has taken place. He speaks
with deep feelings of the trials that still lie ahead and
with glowing enthusiasm of Israel's spiritual conversion
and blessing, when the Lord Jesus comes again.

May this exposition, which warms the heart and
feeds the mind as it dwells on the faithfulness of God, stir
the hearts of Christians, to praise the Lord for the unchanging Covenants of God, and quicken interest for the
people still "beloved for the fathers' sakes."

Director, The Messianic Testimony   ALAN TOMS

PREFACE

THE series of expositions which are included in this volume appeared in fragmentary form in the pages of *The Scattered Nation*, the quarterly organ of the Hebrew Christian Testimony to Israel. They have all been carefully revised and some parts have been slightly altered.

The Scriptures which are here handled are among the richest and sublimest of the Old Testament, and set forth in continuous and systematic form the great fact of the self-manifestation of God in the history of the Jewish people, in which the glorious attributes of His character are displayed for the benefit of the whole of mankind.

There is something unique—something wonderful about the history of Israel. It has been described as " the paradox of the world's history " ; and philosophers and metaphysicians like Hegel have confessed that while they understood the philosophy of the history of other nations, the history of the Jews is an enigma which they could not solve. But what is beyond the solution of philosophy is fully explained in the Word of God, and it is my conviction that it is impossible for any one with an honest mind and a love for the truth, to ponder over the great Scriptures which are here imperfectly unfolded without being deeply impressed with the divine character of the forecasts which they contain, or fail to perceive the guiding, controlling hand of God in the history of the peculiar people, which He has designed from the beginning to be a witness and object-lesson to all nations.

These are days of doubt and unbelief, more particularly in relation to the Old Testament Scriptures. Many books—some of them very excellent—have been written in their defence ; but I fully share the sentiment expressed in the oft-quoted words of the late Dr. Pusey, who, in the preface of his masterly work on Daniel, says :

" This has been for some thirty years a deep conviction of my soul, that no book can be written on behalf of the Bible like the Bible itself. Man's defences are man's words : they may help to beat off attacks ; they may draw out some portion of its meaning. The Bible is God's Word, and through it God the Holy Ghost who spake it speaks to the soul which does not close itself against it."

The Scriptures carry their own divine seal, and the more we seek to penetrate to the wonderful inner depths which they contain, the more deeply is the conviction wrought in us that they are not of man's origination, but are God-breathed.

It has always been my aim therefore, not to dispute or argue about the Bible, but to show, however inadequately, some of the wonderful things which it contains, and to make the Word of God of spiritual profit to the reader.

In these chapters in particular, in which the whole history of the peculiar people—from the call of Abraham to the dispersion and final restoration—is, so to say, expounded and set in its true light by inspired prophets and psalmists with a view to vindicate the ways of God in His dealings with men, and to show forth the divine perfections of His character, there are many great and important lessons for Christians to learn. But what stands out most prominently in them are Jehovah's infinite grace and faithfulness to sinful men. Well might Micah sum up all the dealings of God with Israel with the words: " Who is a God like unto Thee, that pardoneth iniquity, and passeth by the transgression of the remnant of His heritage? He retaineth not His anger for ever, because He delighteth in mercy."

There remains only to be added that, while at the beginning of each of the sections the whole scripture is, for convenience sake, given from the American " Standard Edition," which I regard as the most satisfactory among English versions ; in the expositions I have had only the Hebrew Bible before me, and have endeavoured to bring out the true meaning of these divine oracles from the original.

DAVID BARON

Part 1

THE NATIONAL SONG OF ISRAEL: JEHOVAH'S DEALING WITH ISRAEL FORETOLD

Deuteronomy 32

Deuteronomy 32

Give ear, ye heavens, and I will speak ;
And let the earth hear the words of my mouth.
My doctrine shall drop as the rain ;
My speech shall distil as the dew,
As the small rain upon the tender grass,
And as the showers upon the herb.
For it is the Name of Jehovah that I proclaim :
Ascribe ye greatness unto our God.
The Rock—His work is perfect ;
For all His ways are judgment :
A God of faithfulness and without iniquity ;
Righteous and upright is He.
They have dealt corruptly with Him, they are not His children,
   it is their blemish :
They are a perverse and crooked generation.
Do ye thus requite Jehovah, O foolish people and unwise ?
   Is not He thy Father that hath bought thee ?
He hath made thee, and established thee.
Remember the days of old, consider the years of many genera-
   tions : ask thy father, and he will show thee ; thine elders,
   and they will tell thee.
When the Most High gave to the nations their inheritance, when
   He separated the children of men,
He set the bounds of the peoples according to the number of
   the children of Israel.
For Jehovah's portion is His people ; Jacob is the lot of His
   inheritance.
He found him in a desert land,
And in the waste howling wilderness ;
He compassed him about, He cared for him,
He kept him as the apple of His eye.
As an eagle that stirreth up her nest,
That fluttereth over her young,
He spread abroad His wings,
He took them,
He bare them on His pinions.
Jehovah alone did lead him,
And there was no foreign God with him.

He made him ride on the high places of the earth,
And he did eat the increase of the field :
And He made him to suck honey out of the rock,
And oil out of the flinty rock ;
Butter of the herd and milk of the flock,
With fat of lambs,
And rams of the breed of Bashan, and goats
With the finest of the wheat ;
And of the blood of the grape thou drankest wine.
But Jeshurun waxed fat, and kicked :
Thou art waxed fat, thou art grown thick, thou art become sleek ;
Then he forsook God who made him,
And lightly esteemed the Rock of his salvation.
They moved Him to jealousy with strange gods ;
With abominations provoked they Him to anger.
They sacrificed unto demons, which were no God,
To gods that they knew not,
To new gods which came up of late,
Which your fathers dreaded not.
Of the Rock that begat thee thou art unmindful,
And hast forgotten God that gave thee birth.
And Jehovah saw it, and abhorred them,
Because of the provocation of his sons and his daughters.
And He said, I will hide My face from them.
I will see what their end shall be ;
For they are a very perverse generation,
Children in whom is no faithfulness.
They have moved Me to jealousy with that which is not God ;
They have provoked Me to anger with their vanities ;
And I will move them to jealousy with those that are not a
    people ;
I will provoke them to anger with a foolish nation.
For a fire is kindled in Mine anger,
And burneth unto the lowest Sheol,
And devoureth the earth with its increase,
And setteth on fire the foundations of the mountains,
I will heap evils upon them ;
I will spend Mine arrows upon them ;

They shall be wasted with hunger, and devoured with burning
    heat
And bitter destruction ;
And the teeth of beasts will I send upon them,
With the poison of crawling things of the dust.
Without shall the sword bereave,
And in the chambers terror ;
It shall destroy both young man and virgin,
The suckling with the man of grey hairs.'
I said I would scatter them afar,
I would make the remembrance of them to cease from among
    men ;
Were it not that I feared the provocation of the enemy,
Lest their adversaries should judge amiss,
Lest they should say, Our hand is exalted,
And Jehovah hath not done all this.
For they are a nation void of counsel,
And there is no understanding in them.
Oh that they were wise, that they understood this,
That they would consider their latter end !
How should one chase a thousand,
And two put ten thousand to flight,
Except their Rock had sold them,
And Jehovah had delivered them up ?
For their rock is not as our Rock,
Even our enemies themselves being judges.
For their vine is of the vine of Sodom,
And of the fields of Gomorrah :
Their grapes are grapes of gall,
Their clusters are bitter :
Their wine is the poison of serpents,
And the cruel venom of asps.
Is not this laid up in store with me,
Sealed up among my treasures ?
Vengeance is Mine, and recompense,
At the time when their foot shall slide :
For the day of their calamity is at hand,
And the things that are to come upon them shall make haste

For Jehovah will judge His people,
And repent Himself for His servants :
When He seeth that their power is gone,
And there is none remaining, shut up or left at large.
And He will say, Where are their gods,
The rock in which they took refuge ;
Which did eat the fat of their sacrifices,
And drank the wine of their drink-offering ?
Let them rise up and help you,
Let them be your protection.
See now that I, even I, am He,
And there is no god with Me :
I kill, and I make alive ;
I wound, and I heal ;
And there is none that can deliver out of My hand.
For I lift up My hand to heaven,
And say, As I live for ever,
If I whet My glittering sword,
And My hand take hold on judgment ;
I will render vengeance to Mine adversaries,
And will recompense them that hate Me.
I will make Mine arrows drunk with blood,
And My sword shall devour flesh ;
With the blood of the slain and the captives,
From the head of the leaders of the enemy.
Rejoice, O ye nations, with His people :
For He will avenge the blood of His servants,
And will render vengeance to His adversaries,
And will make expiation for His land, for His people.

1

INTRODUCTION
DID MOSES WRITE THE SONG ?

THIS sublime song, which for loftiness of style and sublimity of language has scarcely anything to equal it, even within the range of sacred Scripture, has been described by an old German writer as " God's Manifesto " in relation to the Jewish nation. It is, indeed, a condensed but very comprehensive prophecy, setting forth all the dealings of God with that nation—both past, present, and future. In a very ancient Midrashic work, older than the Talmud, the exposition of this chapter closes with the exclamation : " How great is this Song ! In it is to be found the present, the past, the future, and the events of the age to come." [1]

A prominent Jewish Rabbi in the eleventh century [2] says of it : " This song is God's accusation against Israel. In it He shows them the end from the beginning, and foretells all that would ever befall them throughout the whole course of their history ; therefore it begins with creation (' Give ear, O ye heavens ; hear, O earth '), and goes on to the days of the Messiah (verse 43)."

The occasion of its composition and its history

---

[1] *Sifre*, known also as *Sifre debe Rab*, often quoted in the Talmud; The words are : גדולה שירה שיש בה עכשיו ויש בה לשעבר ויש בה לעתיד לבא ויש בה לעולם הבא.

[2] Bachya Ibn Pekuda, author of *Choboth ha-Lebaboth*—" Duties of the Heart."

we have recorded for us in the preceding chapter.[1]
God tells Moses, " *Behold, the days approach that thou
must die ; call Joshua, and present yourselves in the
tent of meeting, that I may give him a charge : and Moses
and Joshua went and presented themselves in the tent of
meeting.*"

Then God tells Moses what will happen after his
death : " *Behold, thou shalt sleep with thy fathers, and
this people will rise up and play the harlot after the
strange gods of the land whither they go to be among
them, and will forsake Me, and break My covenant
which I have made with them. Then My anger shall be
kindled against them in that day, and I will forsake
them, and I will hide My face from them, and they shall
be devoured, and many evils and troubles shall come
upon them ; so that they will say in that day, Are not
these evils come upon us because our God is not among
us ? . . . Now therefore write ye this song for you,
and teach thou it the children ; put it in their mouths,
that this song may be a witness for Me against the children
of Israel. . . . So Moses wrote this song the same day
and taught it the children of Israel.*"

Let us note, just in passing, that this Divine forecast, given at the very beginning of Israel's history,
has very fully verified itself. This is exactly what *has*
happened. Jewish history contradicts in the most
positive manner the evolutionary theory which is at
the basis of modern criticism. These critics would have
us apply the Darwinian principle to the history of
Israel ; and, according to them, the conception of one
true and living God and the sublime spiritual truths
embodied in the Bible were evolved by the Jewish
people, who are credited with possessing " a genius
for monotheism." But this theory, as I have had

[1] Deut. xxxi. 14–30.

occasion to show elsewhere,[1] is disproved by history and experience. And not only does Jewish history prove the fact that man cannot by his own searching find God, but it teaches also the fact that, apart from Divine grace and power, man is incapable of *retaining* the knowledge of the true and living God, even after it has been divinely communicated to him.

In spite of the manifestation of the God of glory in their midst ; in spite of the audible Voice out of the fire on Mount Sinai : " *I am Jehovah thy God, who brought thee out of the land of Egypt, out of the house of bondage : thou shalt have no other gods but Me* "—in spite of warnings and remonstrances of inspired prophets and teachers, and of severe premonitory judgments which came upon them while they were yet in the land, there was a growing and increasing tendency in the Jewish nation towards idolatry, and they were more and more fascinated by " the strange gods " of the heathen around them, until they became utterly corrupt, and the land became polluted by their abominable practices. It required the breaking up of the Jewish national polity and the seventy years' captivity in Babylon to cure the Jews of the grosser form of idolatry. And because of sin and progressive apostasy, which began with idolatry and culminated in the rejection of their Messiah, God's face *has* been hid from them for a very long time, and " many evils and troubles " *have* come upon them, as on no other people—even as it was recorded in advance in these inspired utterances of Moses.

Now in the unique and peculiar circumstances in which, according to this Divine forecast, they would find themselves, and throughout their sad history, this

[1] See *A Divine Forecast of Jewish History : a Proof of the Supernatural Element in Scripture.*

sublime poem was to form their national song. The purpose it was to serve is expressed in the words : *" Put it in their mouths, that this song may be a witness for Me against the children of Israel."* It is, so to say, a standing witness in their midst *to* the righteousness, justice, faithfulness, and goodness of God on the one hand, and *against* the unfaithfulness, rebellion, and ingratitude of Israel on the other hand. This twofold testimony this sublime Scripture continues to bear *to this day*, before all who have ears to hear and eyes to see.

Let us note also, before proceeding to the analysis and exposition of this inspired national song of the Jews, the certainty and definiteness with which Moses is declared to be the writer of it. *" Moses therefore wrote this song the same day and taught it the children of Israel."* *" And Moses spake in the ears of the assembly of Israel the words of this song until they were finished."* [1]

Now compare with these definite, solemn declarations of the Scripture itself the assertion of modern criticism that Moses had nothing to do with the writing of it, and that in fact it could not have been written at so early a date. " Nothing in the poem," coolly observes Canon Driver, " points to Moses as the author " ; and the grounds on which this positive assertion is made are these : " The period of the Exodus and of the occupation of Canaan lies in the distant past (verses 7–12) ; Israel is settled in Palestine, has lapsed into idolatry, and been brought in consequence to the verge of ruin (verses 13–30) ; all that is future is its deliverance (verse 31 ff.). The thought and the style of composition exhibit also a maturity which point to a period considerably later than that of Moses ; the theme

[1] Chap. xxxi. 22, 24, 30.

is developed with great literary and artistic skill ; the images are varied and expressive ; the parallelism is usually regular and very forcible." [1]

This sounds very plausible, but it is in reality a begging of the question, and it reveals the underlying principle upon which the whole system, known as the Higher Criticism, is based. *It utterly ignores the supernatural element in Scripture and denies the possibility of such a thing as prediction.* If this sublime song came down to us merely as an anonymous historic narrative in a poetical dress, of the great and solemn events of Israel's unique history, there would of course be force in the argument that it must have been written by some one much later than Moses, since it contemplates not only the Exodus and the settlement in Canaan, but Israel's apostasy and consequent ruin and misery, as already in the past.

But the Scripture itself most solemnly declares that it is *not an historical retrospect* of events after they had transpired, *but a Divine Forecast*—an inspired *prophecy* uttered by Moses *of what would befall Israel after his death and in the course of a long, indefinite future.* Of course it is open to rationalistic critics to assert that such a thing is impossible—and many do boldly assert it ; but that is just the point on which believers are at issue with unbelievers.

Christians believe in a personal living God to whom the end is known from the beginning, who has been pleased from time to time to inspire holy men of old to speak as they were moved by the Holy Ghost, and that there is no inherent impossibility in the oft-reiterated claim of the Scriptures that God not only commissioned prophets and apostles to be witnesses and preachers of righteousness to their own genera-

[1] *Introduction to the Literature of the Old Testament*, p. 96.

tions, but that He also revealed to them things to come. This indeed is one of the chief glories of Jehovah, the living God of Israel, in contrast to the false gods of the heathen. " *I am Jehovah*," He says ; " *that is My Name, and My glory will I not give to another, neither My praise to graven images. Behold, the former things are come to pass, and new things do I declare ; before they spring forth I tell you of them.*" Again : " *Remember this and show yourselves men ; bring it again to mind, O ye transgressors. Remember the former things of old ; for I am God and there is none like Me, declaring the end from the beginning, and from ancient times things that are not yet done ; saying, My counsel shall stand and I will do all My pleasure.*" [1]

To Moses especially—the greatest of all prophets, with the exception of Him of whom he was pre-eminently a type—who has left the deepest impress not only on the " traditions " and records, but on *the inmost consciousness* of the Jewish nation, as their law-giver and " teacher," did God reveal in advance the whole history of the people which He was instrumental in leading out of Egyptian bondage. This is stated in the Mosaic writings again and again, for the forecast unfolded in this sublime song is only an enlargement and setting in poetic form of what, in substance, had already been foretold by Moses in briefer form in chapters iv. 25–31, xxviii. 15–58, xxix. 14–24, and xxx. 1–10 in this same book, and in the 26th chapter of Leviticus, viz., that after his decease, " when thou shalt begat children and children's children, and ye shall have been long in the land, they would ' corrupt themselves ' and fall into idolatry." That in consequence they would be driven out of the land and be scattered among the nations " from one end of the

[1] Isa. xiii. 8, 9, xlvi. 8–10.

earth even unto the other," and great and terrible evils, such as no other people had ever suffered, and " of long continuance," would come upon them.

Yet they would not be destroyed or cease to exist as a separate people, as might have been supposed, and as has been the lot of other expatriated races, but would be preserved, and in the " latter " or " last days," after all these things shall have come upon them, they would return and seek Jehovah their God and should find Him, " *when thou searchest after Him with all thine heart and with all thy soul* "; that then Jehovah would interpose on their behalf and have compassion upon them, and gather them from all the peoples whither He had scattered them, " *and Jehovah thy God will bring thee into the land which thy fathers possessed, and thou shalt possess it, and He will do thee good and multiply thee above thy fathers, and Jehovah thy God will circumcise thy heart and the heart of thy seed, to love Jehovah thy God with all thy heart and with all thy soul, that thou mayest live* "—all which could not possibly have been foreseen except by revelation.

For even if we could accept the theory of the critics (for which I can see no basis in fact) that the book of Deuteronomy was practically a forgery of the time of Manasseh or Josiah, and is the " Book of the Law " referred to in 2 Kings xxii. 8–13, which Hilkiah the priest (who, if not himself the real author, was in the plot) pretended to find stowed away somewhere in the Temple—these forecasts in chapters iv., xxviii., xxix., and xxx. would still, for the most part, be prophecies of events in Israel's history, which even from that much later point of time were still in the future. Their settlement in the land and progressive apostasy from Jehovah would indeed by then have become history. But the beginnings of it were already

present in Moses' time. The destruction of the northern
kingdom of Israel would already by that time have
taken place, and the breaking up of the southern
kingdom, and a deportation of the remnant of Judah
into Assyria or Babylon might possibly have been
foreseen by a shrewd observer of the times, but the
universal dispersion among all nations, " from one end
of the earth even unto the other " ; their restless
condition among the nations whither they would be
scattered, so that they would " find no ease nor would
the sole of their foot find rest " ; their *preservation*,
in spite of their being universally scattered, and of
the many plagues and calamities, and " of long continuance " that would come upon them, and *the certainty
of their final restoration* to the land from which they
had been for so long cast out, and to the favour of
God, all which are definitely announced in these prophetic passages, of which the sublime song is the
climax, who—even in the reign of Manasseh or of
Josiah, except one speaking by the Spirit of God—
could have foreseen or foretold all that ?

And if it was possible for some unknown author
in the seventh century B.C.,[1] who, according to these

---

[1] I am aware that some of the critics would assign a much later
date still for this song, viz., the Maccabean period. In the large edition
of *Die Heilige Schrift des Alten Testaments*, by Kautzsch and others,
in the notes and appendices to which are embodied all the " assured
results " of the German criticism, this sublime Scripture is labelled
under " R ? " which stands first for " Redactor " No. 1, who first
patched together the " Jahvistic " and " Elohistic " codes into one
continuous though not very consistent narrative, at a time not quite
defined ; and then for another "Redactor," No. 2, who, at the "final
editing " of the Pentateuch, about the middle of the second century
B.C., took the opportunity of adding many new things by himself
and other unknown writers.

But beyond the biassed guesses of the authors there is no basis of
truth for these assertions either in history or philology.

" Everything in the Old Testament upon which men in these days

modern critics, only impersonated the great Law-giver, to utter such prophecies in relation to the future which have wonderfully verified themselves in history, could not God have revealed it all to Moses, who stood in such special relationship to Him and to Israel, as the Mediator of the Covenant, seven or eight hundred years before ?

As to the contention that " the thought and style of composition exhibit a maturity which points to a period considerably later than that of Moses " ; that, in fact, the whole lofty style and " dominant theological ideas " of Deuteronomy " presuppose a relatively more advanced stage of theological reflexion " [1] than could have been reached at so early a period, our answer is that this, too, is a begging of the whole question, on

want to throw doubt," observes Canon Girdlestone, " is credited to the unfortunate Maccabean period." But as a matter of fact the Maccabean period is the most unlikely of all for these sublime Scriptures to have originated in.

Canon Driver—in support of his assertion that " the internal evidence (in this song), though it does not absolutely preclude its being by the same author as the writer of the body of Deuteronomy, does not favour such a supposition, and the context hardly leaves it a possibility "—proceeds to state that " If chap. xxxi. 14–30 be examined carefully, it will be seen that there are really *two* introductions to the song, viz., verses 16–22 and verses 24–30 . . . which are evidently by different hands."

All I can say is, *let* the reader " examine carefully " these seventeen verses, and what he will find is that, instead of two different introductions, verses 16–22 record *God's command* to Moses to write the song, and the purpose it is to serve ; and verses 24–30 tell us that *Moses actually did* as he was commanded ; and that besides " speaking in the ears of all the congregation of Israel the words of this song until they were ended," he also handed over this song, together with the whole " book of the law," to the Levites, to be put into the ark of the Covenant, that it may be for a witness against the people.

It is upon such misconceptions and misrepresentations of the text that many of the theories of the critics are based.

[1] Driver, *Introduction to the Literature of the Old Testament*, p. 88.

which those who believe in a Divine Revelation and those who do not are at issue.[1]

We do not think it justifiable, even on historical and philological grounds, to attempt to explain the Hebrew Scriptures and to reconstruct the records of Israel's history on the Darwinian principle of evolution in the religious sphere, according to which all that may appear to the critic too " advanced " or too " mature " in any particular period, must, *ipso facto* —whatever the evidence to the contrary—belong to later stages of " theological reflexion." We believe that these Scriptures, though they bear upon them the stamp of the human mould through which they passed, did not originate with man, but that holy men of God, who were the prepared organs for Divine communications, spoke as they were moved by the Holy Ghost.

Beside, who was this Moses whom the critics declare incapable to have written the law, and particularly so sublime a Scripture as this song ? He was no obscure person brought up in the elementary class of some village school ; he was a very great man, " mighty in his words and works " [2] whose personality towers high through all the centuries—" A man cast in colossal mould, with traces of noblest character and loftiest capacity," highly cultivated, and " instructed in all

---

[1] " It has been thought strange," observes Franz Delitzsch, in his introduction to his *Commentary on the Psalms*, " that the very beginnings of the poesy of Israel were so perfect, but the history of Israel and also the history of its literature comes under a different law from that of a constant development from a lower to a higher grade. The redemptive period of Moses, unique in its way, influences as a creative beginning every future development. There is a constant progression, but of such a kind as only to develop that which had begun in the Mosaic age with all the primal force and fulness of a divine creation."

[2] Acts vii. 22 (R.V.).

the wisdom of the Egyptians," and a great leader, as is shown by his bringing Israel out of Egypt.

And it is too late in the day also to represent the time and environment in which Moses lived as being so illiterate and altogether backward. It was an age of writing and of literature—a time when the Tel-el-Amarna tablets were written in the cuneiform character, which must have been read at any rate by the scribes in Egypt, and which Moses, who was well educated as the adopted son of Pharaoh's daughter, must have understood.[1] This man, thus trained and fitted, who,

---

[1] Flinders Petrie, during his investigation of the region of Serabit-el-Khadem, made certain remarkable discoveries (see his *Researches in Sinai*, 1906). He found a number of rocks carved roughly to simulate eight Egyptian Stelæ, which were, nevertheless, covered with a script that was neither hieroglyphic nor hieratic Egyptian. A figure of the god Ptah was evident, but not a word of ordinary Egyptian. The marks were not mere scribbles, but showed some organised attempt at orthography, for they were found at mines a mile and a half distant from the Sphinx, near the temple of Serabit, where similar markings are to be seen. The direction of the writing is from left to right, contrary to the Semitic (and most Egyptian) script. Judging by the fragments of pottery found near, the date of the inscription must be ascribed to the XVIIIth Dynasty, and probably to the reign of Thothmes III. Petrie considered the writing to be one of the many alphabets in use in the Mediterranean lands long before the fixed alphabet was selected by the Phœnicians. Some of the workmen employed by the Egyptians, probably the Aamu or Retennu (Syrians), had this system of linear signs mixed with hieroglyphs borrowed from their masters. He sums up his discovery in these striking words : " Here we have the result at a date some five centuries before the oldest Phœnician writing that is known. The ulterior conclusion is very important, namely, that common Syrian workmen, who could not command the skill of an Egyptian sculptor, were familiar with writing at 1500 B.C., and this a writing independent of hieroglyphics and cuneiform. It finally disproves the hypothesis that the Israelites, who came through the region into Egypt and passed back again, could not have used writing. Here we have common Syrian labourers possessing a script which other Semitic peoples of this region must be credited with knowing."—*Nile and Jordan*, by G. A. Frank Knight, p. 166.

above all his natural qualifications, was known pre-eminently as " the man of God," [1] God could well use, not only to communicate to Israel His law, but to reveal to him in advance the great events of their unique and wonderful history. This man also—from all we know of him—was fitted, perhaps more than any one else, to express and put on record what had been divinely communicated to him, even in the loftiest style and sublimest language.

A Brief Analysis

From this not altogether unnecessary digression about date and authorship we return to the Scripture itself ; and first let us take a brief glance of the contents as a whole. It is not always possible to indicate with certainty the divisions and transition points in this sublime song ; but, as far as I can see, the whole divides itself into six strophes of unequal length.

(1) After the exordium (in verses 1, 2) the inspired singer sets forth the theme (verses 3–6), viz., the absolute perfection of Jehovah in His character and all His ways, and the perversity and ingratitude of His people.

(2) This theme is illustrated by what Jehovah did for His people, viz., (a) in their election and high calling (verses 7–9) ; (b) what He did for them in the wilderness (verses 10–12) ; (c) what He did for them in the land (verses 13, 14).

(3) In the third strophe the theme—especially the second part, viz., the perversity and apostasy of Israel —is illustrated by what Israel did against God (verses 15–18).

(4) The fourth strophe sets forth the fearful

---

[1] Deut. xxxiii. 1 ; Ps. xc., *title*.

judgments which would come upon Israel in consequence of their apostasy (verses 19–25).

(5) The fifth strophe sings of mercy and of judgment. God's wrath against His people will not burn
for ever, nor will He suffer them to be utterly destroyed. From the pleadings in this section God's
unceasing yearning for His disobedient, gainsaying
people may be inferred (verses 26–33).

(6) The last strophe (verses 34–43) is *apocalyptic* in
character, and sings of the last solemn events of the
present age, viz. God's final interposition on behalf
of His people ; the judgments to be poured out on the
enemies of God and of Israel—all culminating in the
great climax to the whole :

" *Rejoice, O ye nations, with His people ;*
For He will avenge the blood of His servants,
And will render vengeance to His adversaries,
And will make expiation for His land, for His people."

2

THE EXPOSITION

" Give ear, ye heavens, and I will speak,
And let the earth hear the words of my mouth.
My doctrine shall drop as the rain ;
My speech shall distil as the dew," etc.

THE heavens and the earth had already, again and again, been called upon by Moses in this book as witnesses of God's righteous dealings with Israel, and of the sorrows and calamities which would come upon them in consequence of their apostasy. Thus in the fourth chapter he said : *" I call heaven and earth to witness against you this day that* (when ye shall have turned away from God into idolatry) *ye shall soon utterly perish from off the land whereunto ye go over Jordan to possess it."* [1]   And in chapter xxx. 19 he says : *" I call heaven and earth to witness against you this day, that I have set before thee life and death, the blessing and the curse."*   So also in chapter xxxi. 28 we read : *" Assemble unto me, all the elders of your tribes, . . . that I may speak these words in their ears, and call heaven and earth to witness against them."*   In like manner does the prophet Isaiah, echoing the words of Moses, begin his inspired lament against Israel in the first chapter of his prophecy : *" Hear, O heavens, and give ear, O earth, for Jehovah hath spoken : I have nourished and brought up children, and they have rebelled against Me."*

The word for " my doctrine " in the second verse, is לִקְחִי—*liq'chi*—literally, *" that which I receive."*   This is

[1] Deut. iv. 26.

very significant. It indicates that what he is about
to declare is not his own, but is first communicated to
him from above. On this a learned writer has well
observed, that " Everything that comes down from the
' Father of Lights ' is handed on by one heavenly
messenger to another, until it falls upon the heart of
man, in just that form in which he can best receive it.
Thus the Son of God says : ' *My doctrine is not Mine,
but His that sent Me.*' Of the Holy Spirit He says :
' *He shall receive of Mine and shall show it unto you,*'
while the Apostles teach in ' *words which the Holy Ghost
teacheth.*' "

There is fitness in the Word of God being likened to
" rain " and " dew," because, like the refreshing
showers, it also comes from above to revive and to
fructify the hearts of those who are ready to receive it.

But the second verse stands in closest relation to
the third, and ought, I think, to be rendered as an
invocation : " *Let* my doctrine drop as the rain, and my
speech distil as the dew, . . . *for it is the Name of
Jehovah that I proclaim.*" It is the glorious theme
which inspires him with the longing desire and with a
certain enabling to be eloquent.[1]

THE GLORIOUS NAME

The " NAME " of God, which is so often spoken of
in Scripture, reminds us first of all of the great and

---

[1] A parallel is to be found in the 1st verse of the 45th Psalm, which
rendered literally, reads : " *My heart overfloweth* (or ' *bubbles over* ')
with a good word (or ' *matter* ') *; say I* (*to myself*) *my work* (*my composition*) *is for* (or ' *touching* ') *the King—my tongue is the pen of a ready
writer.*" There, too, it is the *theme* of his song, viz. the manifold
excellences and glory of the heavenly Bridegroom and all-victorious
King, which inspires the Psalmist first with the longing desire and
then also with the power to be eloquent. See the exposition of that
Psalm in *Types, Psalms, and Prophecies*.

glorious fact of *His self-revelation*. To quote words of
mine from elsewhere: " There is much about God
which men might learn from nature. The heavens
declare His glory, and the firmament showeth His
handiwork. But nature, though it testifies of His
existence, and of His infinite power and wisdom, does
not reveal to us His character or His *moral* glory.

" Natural religion has no name for God which can
bring any hope or comfort to frail, mortal man ; nor
could man by his own wisdom and searching have
attained to the knowledge of any name for the infinite
Creator of all things, which could in any adequate
measure set forth *His moral character* or His special
relationship to those whom He has endowed with in-
telligence and with the sense of moral responsibility."
The Name had to be *revealed* ; God had to *make Himself known,* and He did so progressively, and ever more
fully, in the history of His peculiar people—not only in
the *words* which He spoke through His chosen vehicles,
but by the *deeds of power and grace* which He wrought
before their eyes, and which make up the story of
Redemption. " The Name " stands therefore in
Scripture *as the embodiment of God's character, as He
Himself has revealed it.*

And it is particularly meet that *Moses* should proclaim " *the Name Jehovah,*" for it is to him first of all
that the *significance* of this particular Name (which
is the *personal* Name of the God of the history of
Redemption) was first made known.[1] And not only
so, but God Himself first " *proclaimed* the Name
Jehovah," with all the glorious attributes which apper-
tain to it, to Moses—on that memorable day when,
after he was safely put in a cleft of the rock, God
" *descended in the cloud and stood with him there,* . . .

[1] Ex. iii. 13–15, vi. 1–8.

*and Jehovah passed by before him and proclaimed—
Jehovah, Jehovah, a God merciful and gracious, slow to
anger, and abundant in lovingkindness and truth ; keeping mercy (or ' lovingkindness ') for thousands, forgiving
iniquity, transgressions, and sin ; and that will by no
means clear the guilty, visiting the iniquity of the fathers
upon the children, and upon the children's children, upon
the third and upon the fourth generation* " (Ex. xxxiv.
5–7).

Now all these great foundation attributes of God's
character which are summed up in " this *glorious and
fearful Name Jehovah* " [1]—His infinite mercy, His
marvellous grace and everlasting faithfulness, but
also *His righteousness*, justice, and truth, are displayed
in a most conspicuous manner in His dealings with the
Jewish nation, and it is this " Name," with its Divine
perfections, which God first " proclaimed " to him,
that Moses now proclaims and unfolds in this wonderful
song, which forecasts the whole history of this unique
people.

And as Moses, on that memorable occasion when
this " holy Name " was proclaimed to him, " *made
haste and bowed his head toward the earth and worshipped*," [2] so now he also calls upon us to do the
same ; for, after saying : " *It is the Name Jehovah that
I proclaim*," he adds, " *Ascribe ye greatness unto our
God*."

And as we think of all that the blessed " Name "
stands for—especially in the light of the perfected
revelation of it in our Lord Jesus Christ—who not
only " declared " or expounded it, but was Himself
the living embodiment of God's Name—we would indeed
bow our hearts in worship, and " render unto Jehovah
the glory that is due unto His Name."

[1] Deut. xxviii. 58.   [2] Ex. xxxiv. 8.

The fourth verse is a wonderful unfolding of the blessed " Name," or character, of God. It is inter-jectional in its style, and expresses something of the holy emotion of Israel's law-giver as he thinks on, and seeks to set forth, the glorious perfections of our God. To render literally :

> " *The Rock!—perfect is His work ;*
> *For all His ways are judgment (or 'justice'):*
> *A God of faithfulness, and without iniquity ;*
> *Righteous and upright is He.*"

" No such combination," observes another writer, " of all the words for *uprightness, sincerity, equity, and reliability,* is to be found elsewhere in all Scripture."

This is the first time that this word צוּר (*Tsur*,[1] which in this case has the definite article) is used as a name for God, and may be said to be one of the characteristics of this sublime song, for it is repeated in it five times. Subsequently it became a very favourite name for God. David, in his last words, calls Jehovah " The Rock of Israel," [2] while in the Psalms he frequently speaks of God as " my Rock," or " the Rock of my salvation." A direct echo or paraphrase of the words of Moses in this song we find more particularly in the 92nd Psalm (which in the Temple ritual was the Psalm sung on the Sabbath day), which ends with the words : " *To show*

---

[1] The word *Tsur*—" Rock "—itself, though not used as a name of God till Deut. xxxii., first occurs in the Hebrew Bible in Ex. xvii., when the Rock in Horeb was smitten—which Rock, we are told in the New Testament, " was (or signified) Christ." " From that time," observes Dr. Waller in Ellicott's *Commentary,* " we find that the many names of the leaders of Israel embody this confession. *Elitsur*, my God is a Rock ; *Tsurishaddai*, the Almighty is my Rock ; and *Pedatsur,* redeemed by the Rock (Num. i. 5, 6, 10), are examples." The LXX, in this song and in many other places, do not translate it at all, but give it as *God* (Θεός).

[2] 2 Sam. xxiii. 3.

that Jehovah is upright ; He is my Rock, and there is no unrighteousness in Him."

But what a grand emblem we have here presented to us of God ! He is " *The* Rock " (not " *a* rock "), for He alone is *solid, strong, firm, immovable, and unchangeable*—a sure and certain foundation, therefore, upon whom to build our hope, both for time and for eternity. Well might therefore Isaiah exclaim : " *Trust ye in Jehovah for ever ; for in Jehovah, even Jehovah,*[1] *is an Everlasting Rock* (or the ' *Rock of Ages* ')."

" *His work is perfect.*" This also, in the absolute sense, is only true of God. It is manifested first of all in His work in creation. The highest and the best that man can produce in any sphere—however *relatively* perfect it may seem—has still the mark of imperfection upon it, and cannot bear *too close* a scrutiny. But not so with anything which has come from the hand of God ; the more closely and minutely we examine it, the more overwhelmed we become, with the mark of perfection which is stamped upon it.

But it is more particularly when we contemplate His wonderful plan of Redemption, as unfolded in the Scriptures and foreshadowed in the history of Israel, that we are constrained to exclaim : " *His work is perfect !* " " In it," as an old divine observes, " there is not only a display of all the Divine perfections, but it is complete in all its parts. The law is perfectly fulfilled, justice is fully satisfied, a perfect righteousness is wrought out, a complete pardon is procured, perfect peace is made, full atonement of sins obtained—and the whole work is finished, and is so perfect, that nothing is wanting in it, nor can be added to it, nor can it be undone again."

And His work of providence, too, is perfect, although

[1] Literally, " in Jah Jehovah." Isa. xxvi. 4.

this may sometimes be difficult for us to believe now, because at present we see only part of His ways ; but when the drama which is unfolding itself in this fallen creation shall have ended, and we look back upon the whole and not merely upon a part, we shall be constrained adoringly to confess that He "*hath done all things well*," and that although His " judgments " may have seemed to us in their process unfathomable as " the great deep," and His ways inscrutable to our finite minds, the words of the Psalmist have been true all along : "*Jehovah hath established His throne in the heavens, and His Kingdom ruleth over all*" ; and that He has ever, by His almighty power and wisdom, caused *all things* to work together for the good of them that love Him—to them that are called according to His purpose.

Another glorious characteristic of the " Rock of Israel " is that : "*All His ways are judgment.*" This word *mish'pat* (" judgment " [1])—stands in the Hebrew Bible not only for God's *acts* of judgment, but for His just and righteous *decisions*, as the Judge and Moral Governor of the Universe. There is no possibility of any caprice or the least *flaw* in the judgment which *He* pronounces on any matter. " All *His* ways," *i.e.* all His dealings with man—here primarily with Israel —are therefore absolutely just and right.[2]

And He is " *A God of Truth*," or, more literally, as in the R.V., " *of faithfulness* "—one who is absolutely and eternally reliable—a God whose word of promise can never fail, nor will His threatenings remain unaccomplished, as the history of the Jewish nation solemnly testifies.

---

[1] Rendered in the R.V., " Justice."

[2] Luther is not far wrong in rendering this sentence : *Denn alles was er thut, das ist recht*—" All that He does, that is right."

"And without iniquity" (*ain 'avel*—literally,
"without unrighteousness")—a God of light, in whom
there is no darkness at all ; who cannot lie or deceive, or
act in any way which is not in accord with the strictest
principle of equity, but, on the contrary—"*Righteous
and upright is He.*"

This, dear reader, is the character of the God of
Israel, whose "Holy Name" is unfolded to us in the
pages of the Old Testament ; the God and Father of
our Lord and Saviour Jesus Christ, with whom *we* have
to do. Now His character is often brought into
question, and the justice of some of His actions im-
pugned, by wicked and foolish men ; but soon the
time of His long-suffering shall be ended, and when He
finally arises to judge the earth, "*The heavens shall
declare His righteousness,*" [1] while the whole redeemed
family "who have come off victorious from the beast,
and from his image, and from the number of his name,
. . . sing the Song of Moses, the Servant of God, and
the Song of the Lamb, saying : *Great and marvellous are
Thy works, O Lord God the Almighty ; righteous and true
are Thy ways, Thou King of the ages. Who shall not
fear, O Lord, and glorify Thy name ? For Thou only art
holy ; for all the nations shall come and worship before
Thee ; for Thy righteous acts have been made manifest*"
(Rev. xv. 2–4, R.V.).

[1] Ps. l.

3

ISRAEL'S PERVERSITY AND INGRATITUDE

FROM the sublime description of the Divine perfections of Jehovah's character, as revealed in His holy Name, which he proclaims in verses 3 and 4, Moses turns to the people, which, from among all the nations of the earth, He had called to be peculiarly His own. And how terribly sad is the contrast between Israel and Israel's God !

The first five words of the 5th verse have been variously rendered and interpreted, and by some commentators have been given up as almost hopeless, because of the great variety of possible interpretations. Yet they are in themselves simple enough. First we will translate them literally word for word :

(1) שִׁחֵת *shicheth*—" *he hath corrupted* " ; (2) לוֹ *lo*— " *to-him* " ; (3) לֹא *lo*—" *not* " ; (4) בָּנָיו *banav*—" *his sons* " ; (5) מוּמָם *mumam*—" *their spot* " or " *blemish*."

The preposition לוֹ *lo*—" *to him* "—denotes either *direction* or *reference* to some object, and I think the meaning is not only that Israel corrupted *himself*, but that he corrupted himself *in relation to God*, the " Incorruptible One," who had brought them into covenant relationship with Himself, and called them to be holy, because He, Jehovah their God, is holy.

The verb שִׁחֵת *shicheth* (from שָׁחַת *shachath*) means not only " to corrupt," but to " *ruin* " or " *destroy*." It is the word used, for instance, in Hos. xiii. 9 :

" *O Israel, thou hast destroyed thyself, but in Me is thine help* " ; or, as perhaps more correctly rendered in the Revised Version, " *It is thy destruction, O Israel, that thou art against Me, against thy help* " ; and in Ps. ciii. 4, " *Who redeemeth thy life from destruction.*" The two ideas are related, for to corrupt our moral nature is to destroy it.

The phrase *lo-banav*—" *not His sons* "—reminds us almost of the expression " *Lo-ammi* "—" *not my people,*" [1] and sets forth the fact that, whatever their high calling and position, they cannot claim really to stand in such a relationship to God so long as they are in a condition of disobedience and apostasy. The chief difficulty arises in connection with the last of these five words, not in rendering it, for that is simple enough, but as to its relation to the preceding words. The Authorised Version connects the last three words together, and renders " Their spot is not the spot of His children," while the Revised Version translates *mumam* (" their spot ") separately, and renders the last three words, " *they are not His children, it is their blemish.*"

Both these versions approximate the true meaning, which I think is this : " *They are not His sons* (or ' *His children* ')—*their blemish,*" *i.e.*, their *mum* (spot, blemish, or moral deformity) shows that they are not His sons, for children bear at least *some* resemblance to their father, and there is none between Israel in apostasy and his Father in heaven.

The utter unlikeness is brought out forcibly in the last three words of this verse when compared with the last three words which are used of God in the previous verse : " *Righteous and upright is He.*" " *A perverse and crooked generation* "—*they.* Could there be any stronger contrast ?

This then, in brief, is the charge formulated against

[1] Hos. i. 9.

Israel in the first strophe, which, as shown in the analysis, sets forth the *theme* which is fully developed in the following strophes of this sublime song—Israel would corrupt himself in relation to God, and would bear less and less moral resemblance to Him who hath called him into covenant relationship with Himself, and whom it was his boast and glory to call his " *Father in heaven.*"

The tense used is indeed not the future, but the preterite ; but that is only because, from the prophetic Pisgah to which Moses is lifted by the Spirit of God in this great prophecy, the whole history of the people is, so to say, spread before him (even as the whole land was from the top of the actual Mount Pisgah, to which he ascended by God's command before he died), and even the distant future is viewed (as is often the case in prophecy) as already past, or as actually then present.

I have already in the introductory remarks pointed out how this, as well as every other item in the Divine forecast, has verified itself in history. Israel *did* corrupt himself. Already at the foot of Mount Sinai —scarcely had the voices of thunder in which God had spoken the " Ten Words " died away, and while Moses was still in the Mount receiving the Tables of the Law, which " were the work of God,[1] with the writing of God graven upon them "—God had to say to Moses, " *Go, get thee down ; for thy people which thou broughtest up out of the land of Egypt have corrupted themselves ; they have turned aside quickly out of the way which I commanded them.*"[2] And this was the beginning of the self-corrupting process. Later on, in his farewell words before his death, Moses could say from experience : " *I know thy rebellion and thy stiff neck : behold, while I am yet alive with you this day,*

[1] Ex. xxxii. 16.   [2] Ex. xxxii. 7, 8.

ye have been rebellious against Jehovah ; and how much more after my death ? " And again : *" I know that after my death ye will utterly corrupt yourselves, and turn aside from the way which I have commanded you."* [1]

And this went on and on, as far as the great *mass* of the people was concerned, until Isaiah, seven or eight centuries later, echoing in his inspired lament the words of Moses in this sublime song, exclaims : *" Hear, O heavens, and give ear, O earth, for Jehovah hath spoken : I have nourished and brought up children, and they have rebelled against Me. . . . Ah, sinful nation, a people laden with iniquity, a seed of evil-doers, children that deal corruptly ! they have forsaken Jehovah, they have despised the Holy One of Israel, they are estranged and gone backward : . . . from the sole of the foot even unto the head there is no soundness in it, but wounds and bruises and fresh stripes ; they have not been closed, neither bound up, neither mollified with oil."* [2] And this process of progressive self-corruption or self-destruction did not stop even in the days of the prophets and of the kingdom, but continued until the final breaking up of their national polity.

But be not too ready, dear Christian reader, to take up stones to cast at the Jews, as if Christendom were in a condition to glory over them in this respect. Alas ! as I have tried to show elsewhere,[3] the apostasy of the Jewish nation finds its parallel in the still greater apostasy of the professing Church. And the story of the self-corruption of Israel, and their progressive departure from the living God who had made Himself known to them, is also in miniature the history of the whole human race.

[1] Deut. xxxi. 27–29.   [2] Isa. i. 1–6.
[3] See the section, " The Greater Apostasy," in *A Divine Forecast of Jewish History.*

" It can, I think, be proved "—to use words of
mine from elsewhere—" that the great nations of
antiquity originally started with a more or less pure
knowledge of one true and living God ; but that, as
time went on, their minds became more and more
darkened, so that they perverted and distorted the
fragments of Divinely-revealed truths which had been
handed down to them ; and, commencing perhaps with
personifying the different attributes of God, they
gradually introduced many gods, and proceeded to
deify the heavenly bodies, the works of God's hands.
Thus they wandered further and further, ' changing
the glory of the Incorruptible God into an image made
like to corruptible man.' Nor did they stop even at
so low a stage of degradation, but went on to worship
birds and four-footed beasts and creeping things."
This is the progress natural to man in relation to God,
as attested by the histories of Egypt, Assyria, Babylon,
etc., and more or less also by the history of the religions
of the pagan world of the present.

ISRAEL'S ELECTION AND HIGH CALLING

The second strophe (verses 7–14), as shown in the
analysis, illustrates the theme (in verses 3–6) by
setting forth the great things God did for Israel.
It begins with a touching expostulation, which is
designed to show up their ingratitude. To take the
words literally, and in the order in which they stand
in the Hebrew :

" *It is* (or ' *is it* ') *Jehovah that ye requite thus !*
A people foolish and unwise !
Is He not thy Father Who hath gotten (or ' *bought* ')
    thee ?
He hath made and established thee."

The first and third lines in this verse are exclamatory questions. O think of it ! It is JEHOVAH—the everlasting, self-existent God, Who, in His grace and condescension, has made Himself known to you by this covenant name as your Redeemer and Friend—that ye thus requite with ingratitude and rebellion. Truly " a *foolish* and unwise " people ! For it is not only *criminal*, but the height of *folly*, and equivalent to self-destruction, for man to depart from the living God ; and the history of the Jews in apostasy has demonstrated to the full that it is not only an evil, but a " *bitter* thing," [1] to forsake Jehovah, the " Fountain of living waters," and the only source of blessedness.

But how beautiful is this verse, and how full of grace, as well as of truth ! The people are an utter failure—they have corrupted themselves ; they are a perverse and crooked generation, and their moral blemish (or deformity) testify against them that they are not at all like His children. But " Jehovah " ever remains the same and never changes. " *Is He not thy Father ?* " They are lo-banav—" not His sons," in the same way as they are at present " *Lo-ammi* " —" not My people " ; but the broken communion between God and Israel on account of sin does not imply severed union, for the covenant relationship into which He entered with them is an indissoluble one, and His original purpose in the call and election of this nation shall yet be realised. Yes, in spite of all their sins and degradation, and the fearful judgments which their apostasy has brought down upon them ; in spite of the fact that multitudes of individual Jews in every generation may through unbelief exclude themselves from " the favour " which God bears unto His people,[2] and fail through disobedience from

[1] Jer. ii. 19.   [2] Ps. cvi. 4.

entering into the rest which He has prepared for them [1]—they are not as a nation cast off utterly and for ever.

" *Whose is the adoption,*" writes the Apostle Paul after Israel's guilt reached its climax in the rejection of their Messiah, and proceeds to demonstrate in that wonderful section of his Epistle to the Romans,[2] that, in spite of all that has happened, God's purpose in the election of this nation stands ; that the blindness or hardness which has befallen Israel is only a *partial* one—both as to its extent and in its duration—that " all Israel shall be saved," when " the Redeemer " is manifested to them a second time in accord with what " is written " in the Prophetic Scriptures of the Old Testament ; " for the gifts and the calling of God are without repentance " or change of mind on His part, *i.e.* IRREVOCABLE. " *Is He not thy Father ?* " At the very beginning of their national history, when God sent Moses to bring them out of Egypt, His word to Pharaoh was, " *Israel is My son, My firstborn, and I say unto thee, Let My son go, that he may serve Me.*"

[3] Thus Jehovah avouched them in a special sense as His peculiar people—His firstborn from among the nations ; and all His subsequent self-revelations to them, and all His dealings with them, were designed to teach them what is implied in this blessed relationship ; what it means in spirit and in truth to pronounce the word " Abba." Hitherto, though Israel has had this most precious Name of God much on their lips, they have not as a nation entered experimentally into its meaning, nor have they as yet corresponded to the character of " children of the living God." There

---

[1] Heb. iii. 17–19.   [2] Rom. ix.–xi.

[3] These remarks—set here in different type—are quoted from my booklet, *Israel's Inalienable Possessions.*

has, indeed, always been the little remnant according
to the election of grace, who worshipped God in spirit
and in truth, and who by the spirit of adoption which
was in them, cried, " *Doubtless Thou art our Father,
though Abraham be ignorant of us, and Israel acknowledge
us not ; Thou, O Jehovah, art our Father, our Redeemer ;
Thy Name is from everlasting* " ; [1] but to the people as
a whole the words uttered by Malachi to the priests
may well be applied : " *A son honoureth his father,
and a servant his master ; if then I be a father, where is
mine honour ? and if I be a master, where is my fear ?
saith Jehovah of Hosts.*" [2]

One of the most pathetic complaints of God against
Israel in this connection is to be found in Jeremiah iii.
In the first verses of that chapter He reminds them of
their many grievous sins and apostasies from Him—
of their spiritual adultery, which, if He dealt with them
according to law, would be sufficient to separate them
from Him for ever ; but being full of compassion, He
is willing to forgive all the past, and cries, " Yet return
again to Me, saith Jehovah."

Then follow these wonderful words in the fourth
verse, which give us a glimpse into the yearning and
love of His heart for His people, and show us His
longing that they should at last understand and enter
experimentally into the relations in which He stood to
them according to His covenants and promises : " *Wilt
thou not from this time (Wilt thou not now at last) cry
unto Me, Abhi (' my Father ')—Thou art the Guide of
my youth ?* " The word, " Alluph," translated
" guide," is the same as in Prov. ii. 17, where it is used
of the " strange " adulterous woman who forsaketh
" *the guide of her youth,* and forgetteth the covenant of
her God "—a truer rendering, however, of which would
be : " Who forsaketh the *mate,* or friend (or *husband*)
of her youth " ; and so, by this act, forgetteth or
breaketh the covenant of her God.

Now these were the two great and blessed relationships into which God had entered with His people—

[1] Isa. lxiii. 16.   [2] Mal. i. 6.

that of a father to his son, and that of a husband to his wife. In both of these Israel has thus far proved unfaithful. As a Father, God has to complain of His disobedient and gainsaying people, that they are "children who have corrupted themselves": and as a Husband He has to pour out His heart's grief and pain ever so many times at Israel's spiritual adulteries, because she "*had played the harlot with many lovers.*" [1] But, blessed be His holy Name, He abides faithful and true, though all men prove false, "He will ever be mindful of *His covenant*"; [2] and in spite of all their disobedience and apostasy He has never ceased to be "a Father to Israel," or to call Ephraim His "first-born." [3] And in the end Israel will at last enter *experimentally* into the blessedness of both these relationships.

It is beautiful to note in that same third chapter of Jeremiah, where, in the second part, a glimpse is given us of the future—when Jerusalem shall be called the throne of Jehovah, to which all nations shall be gathered—we read, "*But I (Jehovah) said, How shall I put thee among the children, and give thee a goodly heritage of the hosts of the nations? and I said, Ye shall call Me, Abhi ('my Father'), and shall not turn away from following Me.*" [4]

"*And I said*"—it is His irrevocable purpose— "*ye shall call Me, Abhi*"—for He who has *called* them to be "His son, His first-born," will pour the spirit of adoption—the spirit of filial fear and of love, into their hearts, so that they shall be *obedient* children and shall "*no more turn away from following after Him.*"

So also that other near and precious relationship of the Bride to the Bridegroom, or of the Wife to the Husband, to which Israel was called, shall yet become an actual experimental reality in their history; for after Israel repents of her past unfaithfulness and returns to her "first (or lawful) husband" (Hos. ii.),

[1] Jer. iii. 1.   [2] Ps. cxi. 5.
[3] Jer. xxxi. 19, 20.   [4] Jer. iii. 17, 19.

we read : " *Thou shalt no more be termed Forsaken,
neither shall thy land any more be termed Desolate ; but
thou shalt be called ' My Delight is in her,' and thy land
' Married ' ; for Jehovah delighteth in thee, and thy
land shall be married. For as a young man marrieth
a virgin, so shall thy Builder* [1] *marry thee ; and as the
bridegroom rejoiceth over the bride, so shall thy God
rejoice over thee* " (Isa. lxii. 4, 5).

But to return more directly to our context. Not
only is He " thy Father," but " *He hath gotten thee.*"
The verb קָנָה—*qanah*—means " to *get*," " to *acquire*,"
" to *possess* " with absolute right, either by *originating*
a thing, or by purchase, or by victorious conquest.
It is the word used by Eve (in Gen. iv. 1) when, on
the birth of her first child, she thought that the Promised Seed, who was to bruise the serpent's head, and
thus redeem them from the consequence of the fall,
had already arrived, and exclaimed, " *I have gotten* "
(קָנִיתִי—*qanithi*) a man—the Lord." It is used also by
personified Wisdom (in Prov. viii. 22), " Jehovah begat
(or ' possessed ') me in (or ' as ') the beginning of His
way." Thus also by *right of birth*, so to say,[2] Israel
belonged to God.

But it is most probably the idea of right *by redemption*, or *purchase*, which is expressed in this passage,
for it is in this sense that the word was already used
by Moses in his song of triumph after the overthrow
of Pharaoh and his host in the Red Sea (Ex. xv. 16):
" *Till Thy people pass over, O Jehovah, till Thy people
pass over that Thou hast redeemed* " (or " *purchased* "
—קָנִיתָ—*qanitha*)—an inspired echo of which we find

---

[1] An ancient alternative reading for " thy son." The word for
" sons " and " builder " is the same in Hebrew.

[2] See verse 18 in this Song, " The Rock that begat thee. . . . God
that gave thee birth."

in Isa. xi. 11, 12, where we read in reference to Israel's future, " *And it shall come to pass in that day that Jehovah will set His hand again the second time, to recover* (לִיקְנוֹת *liq'noth*—literally, ' *to redeem* ' or ' *purchase* ') *the remnant of His people that shall remain from Assyria and from Egypt and from Pathros and from Cush . . . and from the four corners of the earth.*"

And not only had God every right to Israel's obedience and love as his Father who had begotten him, and his Redeemer who had ransomed him out of Egyptian bondage, but " *He hath made thee, and established thee.*" It was to Him—to His infinite power and grace—that they owed their very origin and their unique and peculiar position as a nation. But instead of loving Jehovah their God with all their heart, and soul, and might, and rendering to Him the filial obedience which they were under every obligation to do, they requited Him with ingratitude and rebellion !

And is there not a message in this touching remonstrance addressed to Israel, to us too as individual believers ? All that God was and did for them as a nation, He is and does for us. Yea, He does much more for us than He had done for them nationally. In Christ Jesus our Lord He has manifested Himself to us more fully as " Jehovah," the faithful, unchangeable God of promise and covenant.

And is He not " *thy* Father," dear fellow Christian ? Yea, in the light of that fuller revelation of Himself in the person of His only begotten Son, there is deeper and fuller meaning in the cry, " Abba, Father," as it proceeds from the hearts of those who have received the spirit of adoption, than it could have had before.

And has He not " gotten," or " acquired " *you* at infinite cost, and redeemed you with precious blood to be His very own ? And has He not *made* and *established* you ? Is it not to His infinite grace and power that you owe all that you are and have ? And how do you requite Him for all His great love and kindness ? Do you seek to show your love and gratitude in holiness of life and filial obedience to His will ?

But to proceed to the following verses of this second strophe. In confirmation of what he had just set forth in the sixth verse, viz. God's wonderful grace to Israel in exalting them as His first-born among the nations, and His special favour to them as their " Father," who had bought them and established them, they are exhorted to ponder God's dealings with them and the nations, from the very beginning.

" *Remember* " (or, *bring to mind*) *the days of old* (*y'moth 'olam*—which might perhaps be better rendered " past ages ") : " *Consider* " (בִּינוּ, *binu* — literally, " understand "—try to grasp the meaning of) " *the years* " (as they have unrolled) " *through many generations.*" Here we have inspired counsel to apply ourselves to a careful study of history, with a view to trace God's hand in it. Turn over and ponder carefully the records of the past, especially as they are preserved in the inspired pages.

" *Ask thy father, and he will show thee ;*
Thine elders, and they will tell thee."

Consult the sacred traditions in the nation which, in addition to the written records, have been handed down through the generations from father to son, and you will find the great truths set forth in this inspired song abundantly confirmed.

" When the Most High gave (or *apportioned*) *to the nations*
  their inheritance,
When He separated the children of men,
He set the bounds of the peoples
According to the number of the children of Israel :
For Jehovah's portion is His people ;
Jacob is the lot of His inheritance."

Here we may learn the great truth, confirmed also
in many other Scriptures, that the land and people of
Israel were from the very beginning the appointed
centre in the counsel of God for His governmental
dealings with the nations of the earth.

The Jews regarded Palestine and Jerusalem as the
very centre of the globe.   This, in particular, is carried
to absurd lengths in the legends which are gathered
around the Church of the Holy Sepulchre, where, as
any tourist to Palestine knows, a circle of marble
pavement and a short column are pointed out by the
Greek priests as marking the exact physical centre of
the earth as attested by the Lord Himself.   Yet there
is a great truth in this ancient Jewish and Christian
tradition.   Palestine, if not exactly the physical centre,
was certainly intended by God to be the moral and
spiritual centre of the world.   But even geographically
the position of Palestine is most central, and we cannot
but trace definite design and a Divine purpose in
selecting this land as the habitation of the people who
were ordained to carry the knowledge of the One true
and living God to all nations.
    In olden times it stood midway between the three
greatest nations of antiquity—Assyria, Egypt, and
Greece ; and it not only remains " the key between
the East and West," but commands equal facilities
of access to Europe, Africa, and Asia.   There is no
country which holds such an important and central
place in the world's history, or which has exercised
such an influence on the destiny of mankind.   From
earliest times the strip of coast-land known as Palestine

proper was a special factor in the politics of the great
world-empires which lay on the banks of the Nile
and the Euphrates, and it was only as the movements
of Egypt, or Assyria, or Medo-Persia, or Greece, or
Rome, or of any other of the Gentile nations, affected
that land—or as they were brought into touch with it
—that they are brought within range of sacred history,
which is the only truthful record of events which are of
permanent importance to mankind.

And the beneficent aim and reason for this are set
forth by the great Apostle in that sublime discourse
on Mars' Hill, recorded in the seventeenth chapter of
the Acts of the Apostles, which might almost be
described as *God's manifesto to the pagan Gentile world*,
showing up the folly and futility of their idolatrous
worship and vain philosophies, and proclaiming that
" the times of ignorance," which God had in His grace
overlooked, were now passed, and that now " *He commanded men that they should all everywhere repent, as
He hath appointed a day in which He will judge the world
in righteousness by the Man whom He ordained.*"

It is in that connection, and on that famous spot
and memorable surroundings, that he proclaims that
God " *had made of one every nation of men for to dwell
on all the face of the earth, having determined their
appointed seasons, and the bounds of their habitation,
that they should seek God, if haply they might feel after
Him, and find Him, though He is not far from each one
of us.*" And as the particular times or seasons in
which nations rise, fulfil their course, and then crumble
away, are not due to blind chance, but are " appointed "
by the Creator of the universe, who is also the Con-
troller of history, so also is there a purpose with regard
to " the bounds of their habitation." These latter
are determined by Him with the beneficent end " that
they should seek after God, if haply they might feel
after Him, and find Him."

And since in His infinite wisdom it pleased Him to
choose one people as the medium of His self-revelation
to the whole of mankind, in accord with His original

promise to Abraham—" In thee shall all the families of
the earth be blessed "—He placed that people in the
most central position possible, and set " the bounds "
of all other peoples " according to the number of the
children of Israel." [1]

But, we may ask, has the purpose of God in the
choice of this people, and in placing them in this
central position, been realised ? Alas ! history, and
the confessions of their own inspired prophets and
psalmists, bear witness to Israel's rebellion and
apostasy. " *This is Jerusalem* "—is God's lament
through the prophet Ezekiel—" *I have set her in the
midst of the nations and countries that are round about
her, and* "—instead of being a light and blessing to the
nations, as He had intended by putting her in this
conspicuous position—" *she hath rebelled against Mine
ordinances in doing wickedness more than the nations,
and against My statutes more than the countries that are
round about her.*" [2]
Let it not be forgotten, however, that though the
nation as a nation failed so utterly to apprehend that
for which it was apprehended of God, yet there was
always a remnant in the nation in and through whom
the original purpose of God in the election and call of
Israel was carried out. " It is a remarkable fact,"
observes an eminent writer,—" a fact which every
thoughtful student of history must admit, that during
the whole period of Jewish history, light—intellectual,
moral, and religious—radiated from Palestine, and
from it alone. The farther one receded from that
land, the more dim the light became ; and the nearer
one approached, it shone with purer radiance. The

----

[1] These paragraphs in different type are quoted here from an article
of mine on Palestine, which appeared in *The Scattered Nation* in 1915.
[2] Ezek. v. 5, 6.

heavenly knowledge communicated in ' sundry times
and in divers manners ' through the Jewish patriarchs
and prophets, was unfolded and perfected by our Lord
and His Apostles.   In their age Palestine became the
birthplace of intellectual life and civil and religious
liberty.   From these have since been developed all the
scientific triumphs, all the social progress, all the moral
greatness and grandeur of the civilised world."

But so far the blessing that has come to the other
nations through Israel and Palestine has been only
partial. *It is in the future*—after repentant and converted Israel is once more in their land, under the sway
of their long-rejected Messiah—that Palestine will
become the centre whence light, and truth, and
universal blessing shall proceed for all nations, even
unto the utmost limits of the earth.   For " *it shall come
to pass in the latter days, that the mountain of Jehovah's
house shall be established on the top of the mountains, and
shall be exalted above the hills ; and all nations shall
flow unto it.   And many peoples shall go and say, Come
ye and let us go up to the mountain of Jehovah, to the
house of the God of Jacob ; and He will teach us of His
ways, and we will walk in His paths ; for out of Zion
shall go forth the law, and the word of Jehovah from
Jerusalem.*" [1]

Before passing on to the next verse I may be permitted a word of practical application.   Not only has
God foreordained the times and " bounds of habitation " of nations, but of each individual.   The day in
which *we* live on earth, dear fellow-Christian, and the
place and circumstances in which we find ourselves, are
not the result of blind chance, but are appointed for us
by the will of God—a will guided by infinite wisdom and
infinite love.

[1] Isa. ii. 2, 3.

And the purpose God has in our individual lives, by placing us when and where we are, is first that we ourselves should seek after the Lord, and make sure that we find Him ; and then, that we in turn should become a centre of light and blessing to others, even as Israel was intended to be to the nations round about them. Is this double purpose of God being accomplished in us ?

But to return to our context. The highest height of privilege to which Israel was exalted—if they had only realised it—is set forth in the ninth verse :

" *For Jehovah's portion is His people ;*
Jacob is the lot of His inheritance."

Wonderful and mysterious words ! For it is comprehensible enough that man whom He has created, and subjected to Himself in hope, should find his everlasting and all-satisfying portion in his Maker, but that the infinite, eternal God, the possessor of heaven and earth, should find *His* special portion and peculiar inheritance in man—this is something which passes our understanding. But this is the blessed mystery which is unfolded to us in His Word, and is the key which unlocks the true meaning, not only of creation, but of redemption.

Now let me repeat, first of all, that it is of Israel primarily that these words are spoken. Whether men like it or not, the Jewish nation not only *was*, but *is* God's people—" not only the *ancient* nation "—as Adolph Saphir used to say—" but the *present*, yea, the ' *everlasting nation* ' " ; and His word to them when He first brought them into covenant relationship with Himself, " *Ye shall be Mine own possession from among all peoples.*" And again, " *Thou art a holy people unto Jehovah thy God : Jehovah thy God hath chosen thee to be a people for His own possession above all peoples that are upon the face of the earth* [1]—*is still true*, and God never has, and never will, change His mind in reference to His choice of them—in spite of all their sins and apostasies.

But while Israel as a nation is and remains God's portion from among the nations of the earth, the Church of Christ, made up of individuals out of all nations and kindreds and peoples and tongues, is His special inheritance from among men. Yes, in Christ Jesus those who formerly were " no people " are now the people of God "—a chosen generation, a royal priesthood, a holy nation, *a people for God's own possession.*" [2]

It is for a fuller comprehension of this mystery on the part of believers that the Apostle prays in the first chapter to the Ephesians : " *That the God of our Lord Jesus Christ, the Father of Glory, may give unto you the spirit of wisdom and revelation in the knowledge of Him, having the eyes of your heart enlightened, that ye may know what is the hope of His calling, what the riches of the glory of His inheritance in the saints.*"

[1] Ex. xix. 5 ; Deut. vii. 6.   [2] 1 Pet. ii. 9, 10.

4

WHAT JEHOVAH DID FOR ISRAEL

FROM the great favour which God manifested toward Israel in choosing them from among all the nations of the earth to be a people for His own peculiar possession, the sublime song proceeds (in verses 10–12) to set forth what He did for them in the wilderness. The lines in the tenth verse are in the "pictorial present"—"He *findeth* him; He *compasseth* him; He *instructeth* him; He *keepeth* (or 'guardeth') him"—the inspired singer thus realistically describing the great acts of Jehovah's loving-kindness to His people at the beginning of their national history with the vividness of one who is a witness and sharer of it all.

The word *yim'tsa-ehu* ("He found," or "findeth him") is an idiom descriptive of His self-revelation and interposition in grace, whether to individuals, or, as in this case, to His people as a whole. Thus *"He found"* Hagar by a fountain of water in the wilderness, when she fled from the face of Sarai [1] and made Himself known to her so that she called the place "*Beer-lahai-roi,*" *i.e.,* "The well of the Living One Who seeth me." Thus also "He found" Jacob in Bethel, when he fled from the face of Esau,[2] and revealed Himself to him as his protector and friend, and constituted him the depositary of the Messianic promise of blessing for all the families of the earth which He first made to Abraham and then to Isaac.

[1] Gen. xvi. 7–14.   [2] Hos. xii. 4 ; Gen. xxviii. 10–17.

And he called the name of the place "Bethel"—
because, as he said, "This is none other than the
house of God, and this is the gate of heaven."

And thus "He found" the people of Israel when
fleeing from the face of Pharaoh in their helpless, defenceless condition, and in danger, as the Egyptians thought,
of being "entangled" and destroyed in the wilderness. And the literal "desert land" of Sinai, where
He made Himself known to them as a people, is
symbolical also of the great moral and spiritual desert
—the "waste howling wilderness" of universal idolatry,
corruption, and sin, in the midst of which He "found"
their fathers, when He first revealed Himself to them,
and called into being the peculiar people through whom
He intended to make His grace and power known to
all mankind.

And having "found" them, and adopted them as
His own peculiar possession, He took them under His
own special care and instruction. "*He encompassed
him*"—He closed them in as a man closes in a garden,
or a vineyard,[1] Himself constituting, as it were, an
invisible wall of fire round about them, and thus
separating them from all the other nations of the
earth. And having thus closed him in He began to
train and educate him.

The verb יְבוֹנְנֵהוּ—*y'bhon'ne-hu*—is, I think, rightly
rendered in the Authorised Version "He *instructed
him*," which is the translation given also in the LXX
and other ancient versions. Modern scholars, however,
take it to be another form of the same verb (בִּין—*bin*),

---

[1] The verb יְסֹבְבֶנְהוּ—*Yeso'bhebhen'hu*—from סָבַב, "to turn about,"
"to go round," "surround," either with hostile purpose, as in
besieging an enemy, or with a view to "shut off," or protect. In
2 Chron. xiv. 2, the hiphil-future of this verb is used of surrounding
with a wall.

which would mean " *He attentively considered him*," or, as the Revised Version has it, " *He cared for him.*"

A brief summary of what that Divine care and consideration for them in the wilderness included, we have in the ninth chapter of Nehemiah, which is in some respects a parallel scripture to this sublime song, inasmuch as it also confesses God's manifold goodness to His people and Israel's great and many sins and ingratitude. After recounting what God did for them in Egypt, and at the Red Sea, we read :

" *Moreover in a pillar of cloud Thou leddest them by day ; and in a pillar of fire by night, to give them light in the way wherein they should go. Thou camest down also upon Mount Sinai and speakest with them from heaven, and gavest them right ordinances and true laws, good statutes and commandments, and madest known unto them Thy holy Sabbaths . . . and gavest them bread from heaven for their hunger, and broughtest forth water for them out of the rock for their thirst. . . . Yea, when they had made them a molten calf, and said, This is thy God that brought thee up out of the land of Egypt, and had wrought great provocations ; yet Thou in Thy manifold mercies forsookest them not in the wilderness. . . . Thou gavest also Thy good spirit to instruct them, and with-heldest not Thy manna from their mouth, and gavest them water for their thirst. Yea, forty years didst Thou sustain them in the wilderness, and they lacked nothing ; their clothes waxed not old, and their feet swelled not.*" [1]

Thus His gracious care and manifold goodness extended not only to their outward bodily needs, but to their *moral* and *spiritual* need. " He *instructed* them " by giving them His law, and by appointing His ordinances and divinely ordered " service of God " [2] in their midst, and by sending His

[1] Neh. ix. 12–21.   [2] Rom. ix. 4.

"Good Spirit" among them to be their guide and teacher.

The climax of God's tender care for them—which, alas! they so ill requited—is expressed in the bold and beautiful figure in the last line of this 10th verse : "*He kept* (or '*guarded*') *him as the apple of His eye.*" The "apple" of the eye which is surrounded by the iris is called in the Hebrew by the diminutive and endearing term אישׁון—*ishon*—"the little man," because a picture in miniature of one's self is seen as in a glass, when looking into another person's eye. The same beautiful figure, echoed from this fundamental passage in Deuteronomy, is found also in Ps. xvii. 8, and Zech. ii. 8, only there it is *bath 'ayin*—"the *daughter*," or "*little girl*" of the eye, from which, through the Latin *pupilla* comes our English "pupil."

This "apple," or "pupil," through which rays pass to the retina, "is the tenderest part of the eye—the member which we so carefully guard as the most precious of our members, the one which feels acutely the slightest injury, and the loss of which is irreparable." With this same constant and tender care did Jehovah "keep" or guard His people. But there follows yet another striking figure in the 11th verse, which sets forth very graphically not only God's tender love, but His care *in the training* and *disciplining* His people, so as to fit them to take possession of the inheritance which He had appointed for them, and to which He was leading them :

"*As an eagle stirreth up her nest,*
Fluttereth over her young,
Spreadeth abroad her wings, taketh them, beareth them
    on her wings."

This is the quite possible rendering adopted in the

Authorised Version, but it may be more literally
rendered thus :

" As an eagle stirreth up her nest,
Fluttereth over her young,
(So) He spread abroad His wings ; He took him ;
He bare him on His pinions.
Jehovah alone did lead him, and there was no strange
god with Him "—

which is substantially the translation given in the
Revised Version.   The tender care and solicitude of the
mother bird for her young is a fact of natural history,
and is true also of the otherwise fierce and powerful
eagle.   Though very attentive to the young eaglets while
they are helpless, she does not, for their own good,
encourage them long in indolence, but teaches them, as
soon as she considers it safe, to fly, and find food for
themselves.   To this end she " *wakens,*" as it is idiom-
atically expressed in the Hebrew, or " *stirs* " up, her
nest, so as to make it uncomfortable for them to abide in
it, and " flutters " or " hovers " over them in order to
incite them to the effort of flying—a process which may
seem at first cruel to the eaglets, who might perhaps
prefer to remain undisturbed in their comfortable bed,
but which is absolutely necessary if they are to become
strong and fully developed eagles.   But they are not
left to face the dangers of their first attempts of flying
all by themselves—the mother eagle is there to watch
over them, and " spreadeth abroad her wings " in
readiness to render assistance if needed ; and should
there be any danger of their falling, she interposes with
remarkable dexterity by flying under them : " She
taketh them ; and beareth them (safely) on her
pinions."

Thus also in tender care, and with their highest
good ever in view, did Jehovah seek to train His people

in the wilderness. He would not allow them to settle
too long in one place, but kept on, as it were, stirring
up their nest, to remind them that that was not to be
their permanent resting-place. And He brought them
face to face with trial and danger, and humbled them,
and suffered them to hunger, in order to prove what
was in their heart, and to teach them the one great
lesson of *faith in Him*, and that man doth not live by
bread only, but that by everything that proceedeth
out of the mouth of Jehovah doth man live.[1] Oh, if
they had only learned fully to trust Him, how well
would it have been with them, even in the wilderness !

But even in spite of their forwardness and their
manifold provocations, He watched over them, and
was ever ready to interpose on their behalf. Did
danger threaten, as when pursued by the Egyptians,
or attacked by Amalekites ? It was He who fought
for them. Did they hunger, and there was no bread
to be had in the wilderness ? He fed them with
manna which neither they nor their fathers knew. Did
they thirst and there were neither springs nor wells ?
He gave them waters out of a flinty rock. True indeed
was His word to them through Moses, already in
Ex. xix. 4 : " *Ye have seen . . . how I bare you on
eagles' wings and brought you unto Myself.*"

And it was " *Jehovah alone,*" by His own all-
sufficient power and in infinite grace, who " *did lead
him* " through the " great and terrible wilderness,"
and lavished all that tender care upon him ; " *and
there was no strange (or 'foreign') god with Him* "—
none of those false gods of the nations to whom Israel
became so prone to render, at any rate, part of that
allegiance and worship which is due to " Jehovah
alone." [2]

[1] Deut. viii. 2–4.   [2] Ps. lxxxi. 8–10.

Before passing on to the next two verses, which set forth what God did for them in the land, I pause for a moment to remind you, dear Christian reader, that the beautiful Scripture which we have been considering has its application also to individual believers now.

We, too, were " found " of Him.   Illumined by the light of the New Testament, all these expressions receive fuller significance and become still more precious.   " Ye have not chosen Me," He says, " but I have chosen you " ; and with thankful hearts we confess that if He had not *first* sought and found us, we would never have found Him.

And He found us where He found Israel—" *in a desert place, and in the waste howling wilderness,*" for, as already observed, the literal desert of Sinai is also a type of the moral and spiritual wilderness of this present evil world.   Yes, *in the wilderness* — the place of desolation, of need, and of danger, where we had wandered away from the Good Shepherd—He found His sheep which were lost.

And the tender care and faithfulness of Jehovah to His unworthy Israel should remind us of His tender mercies and unchanging love to us, who are not more worthy.   We, too, are " compassed " about—not indeed with the visible pillar of cloud and of fire—but with His own invisible presence, of which it was but the symbol.   And having separated us to be His own peculiar possession, He has taken us, as it were, into His school for training, and is " instructing " and " teaching " us through His Word and " Good Spirit " ; and also through the experiences of life in the wilderness, that we may learn to know and trust Him more fully, and be fitted for the inheritance which He has reserved for us.   And we, too, though so unworthy in ourselves, are " in Christ," and for His sake, as precious and indispensable to Him as the dearest member of our bodies is to us, and may therefore apply the beautiful figure used here first of Israel to ourselves individually, and pray with David :

> " *Keep me as the apple of Thine eye ;*
> *Hide me under the shadow of Thy wings.*" [1]

And we, too, cannot be spared the discipline to which He subjected Israel in the wilderness. It is hard and painful to the flesh to have our nest " stirred " up, and to be so constantly reminded that " here we have no abiding city," [2] and that there is no permanent resting-place for us in this world, but though some of His providences may be inscrutable, and " His ways past finding out," we know and believe that in all He does, or permits, He has not only His own glory, *but our highest good* in view, viz. that we may be fully conformed to the image of His Son, and be fitted for the glorious destiny He has appointed for us " from the foundation of the world."

Therefore we will not murmur, as Israel did, at the trials of the way, but seek to glory, even in tribulation ; and all the more because of the assurance that we are not left to face trial alone, and that God will not suffer us to be tempted above what we are able to bear, but that He watches over us with the same tender care that the eagle watches over her young, and is ever ready to " spread abroad His wings " and to " take us " up, when we are ready to fall, and to " bear us on His pinions."

WHAT JEHOVAH DID FOR ISRAEL IN THE LAND

From what He graciously did for them in the wilderness, the inspired singer passes on to speak in the last two verses of this strophe to what God did for them in

---

[1] Ps. xvii. 8.   [2] Heb. xiii. 4.

the land. The style is that of vision and prophecy, for the verses are still in " the pictorial present."

First, " *He made (or ' maketh ') him ride on the high places of the earth.*"

The noun אֶרֶץ—*erets*—may mean either " earth " or " land," and here, as in very many places in the Hebrew Bible, it undoubtedly stands for " *the land.*" בָּמֳתֵי—*bam'athei*—" high places " in this connection stands for " battlefields," or " chief places," or, as we might express in modern terms, the strategic positions, the conquest of which assures possession of the land. To " ride " therefore on the " high places " is an idiomatic expression for *victory* and dominion. Thus we read also of God in His might and majesty " *treading* " or " *riding* " (the word being the same) " *on the high places of the earth,*" while in Isa. lviii. 14 we have the promise in reference to Israel's future : " *I will make thee to ride upon the high places of the earth (or land), and I will feed thee with the heritage of Jacob thy father* " —which is an inspired echo of the fundamental passage in Deut. xxxii.

And it was *He* who gave Israel victory and brought him triumphantly into his promised possession, for—

" *They got not the land in possession by their own sword,*
 Neither did their arm save them ;
 But Thy right hand, and Thine arm, and the light of
  Thy countenance ;
 Because Thou wast favourable unto them." [1]

" By their own might "—to quote words of my own from elsewhere—" they could never have conquered Palestine. All modern historical and monumental discoveries confirm the Scripture account, and go to show that Palestine was at the time inhabited by a

---

[1] Ps. xliv. 3.

number of warlike nations stronger and mightier than
they.

" What the probabilities were in reference to Israel's
taking possession of the land with their own sword was
well stated by the ten spies : ' *The people that dwell in
the land are strong, and the cities are fortified and very
great ; and moreover we saw the children of Anak there :
. . . We are not able to go up against the people, for they
are stronger than we.*' [1]

" This was all true.   The sin of those spies consisted
in the fact that they left God and His promise out of
account.   Caleb and Joshua put the matter in the true
light.   They did not underestimate the difficulties ;
they saw the fortified cities and the giants, but they also
saw God, and remembered His promises, and therefore
said : ' *If Jehovah delight in us, then He will bring us
into this land and give it unto us.*' " [2]

And thus it actually was in the end.   " *He*, by His
right hand," and His strong arm, made them " ride "
in triumph " on the high places of the land," so that
neither the Anakim nor the strongly fortified cities
could withstand their onslaught, and brought them
safely into their promised inheritance.

And it was a glorious land into which He thus
victoriously brought them, and a land of plenty.   This
is brought out in the lines which follow :

" *And he did eat the increase of the field,
    And He made him to suck honey out of the rock,
    And oil out of the flinty rock ;
Butter of the herd, and milk of the sheep,
With fat of lambs ;
And rams of the breed of Bashan, and goats,
With the fat of kidneys of wheat,
And the blood of the grape thou didst drink wine.*"

[1] Num. xiii. 28–31.   [2] Num. xiv. 8.

Well might He say through Moses : "*Jehovah thy God bringeth thee into a good land, a land of brooks of water, of fountains and springs, flowing forth in valleys and hills ; a land of wheat and barley, and vines and fig trees, and pomegranates ; a land of olive trees and honey ; a land wherein thou shalt eat bread without scarceness ; thou shalt not lack anything in it ; a land whose stones are iron, and out of whose hills thou mayest dig copper.*" [1]

Palestine has for many centuries been thought and spoken of as " the land that is desolate," but it was not so originally, and is not so naturally. It *became* barren and desolate because of the sin of the people that dwelt therein, and it is now what it is in fulfilment of the word of God.[2] As I have pointed out elsewhere, there is a parallelism between creation as a whole as having been involved in the sin of Adam, and Palestine as being involved in the sin of Israel.   When Adam sinned, God said : "*Cursed is the ground for thy sake ; in sorrow shalt thou eat of it all the days of thy life, thorns and thistles shall it bring forth unto thee* " ; and the same is true of Palestine.   Because of the sin of Israel, a special curse descended also on the land which, during the whole period of Israel's dispersion and Gentile domination, has been given over, more or less, to misrule and neglect.

But even while still under the curse the land retains many traces of its ancient beauty and fertility, and is capable of being made very productive.   In the course of my seven visits to Palestine at different intervals, extending over a period of thirty-four years, I have myself witnessed wonderful changes taking place, and it is a striking fact that quite large districts which up to twenty or thirty years ago were, owing to the neglect of centuries and the blight of Turkish misrule—wilder-

[1] Deut. viii. 7–9.
[2] Deut. xxix. 22–29 ; Jer. xxv. 11 ; Mic. vii. 13.

ness places, covered to a depth of sometimes several feet with the yellow sand of the desert which had been allowed to encroach—are transformed by the labours of enthusiastic colonists into fruitful fields and vineyards and orchards. And when at Israel's conversion the blight is removed and the finger of God once again touches the land, it will become manifest to the whole world that Palestine is not only a land of beauty, but a most fertile land, " flowing with milk and honey."

To return to the beautiful lines in the Song (verses 13 and 14), which describe the natural fertility of the land, some of the expressions may be metaphorical, but they are also literally true. Thus the sucking " honey out of the rock " may refer to the " wild honey " which is still to be found in crevices of rocks where bees often swarm, and which in early times was probably found in greater abundance ; while the " oil out of the flinty rock " may refer to the fact that " in the fertile state of Canaan olive trees abounded, even on rocky eminences."

The " herds " of cattle, and " flocks " of sheep and goats " of Bashan," were famed in the ancient world, while " the finest of wheat " is still grown in the high tableland on the east side of the Jordan known as the Hauran.[1]

Indeed, under the blessing of Jehovah, the natural products of the land were not only abundant, but of the *choicest* that the earth can yield, and the provision He made for them included some of the richest delicacies —especially in the estimation of the Easterns—and is represented in this passage by the " honey," the " oil,"

[1] The rendering in the A.V., "kidneys of wheat," is a literal translation of the Hebrew phrase, and the figure is to be explained not only by the fact that " a grain of wheat is in shape somewhat like a kidney," but because in animals the kidneys are enclosed *in the very best of the fat*, which, by the Levitical law was reserved strictly for the sacrificial altar. It stands thus for something very choice.

the choice " fat," and the " wine."   How well contented
and happy Israel ought to have been, and what great
cause they had for love and gratitude to Him who had
done so great things for them !   But instead, as we
have already seen, and as is set forth in fuller detail
in the next strophe, they requited Him for it all with
ingratitude and rebellion.

5

ISRAEL'S APOSTASY

IN the preceding eight verses (7–14), which make up the second strophe of this sublime Song, the inspired singer had set forth the great and wonderful things which God did for Israel—the grace and favour He manifested towards them in choosing and separating them from all the nations of the earth to be His own peculiar possession, and in what He did for them in the wilderness, and then in the rich and beautiful land which He assigned to them as their special inheritance. Now he proceeds to set forth more fully the charge against Israel already contained in the introductory strophe (verses 1–6) that they " corrupted " themselves, and have shown themselves to be " a perverse and crooked generation," by requiting all the great love and kindness of Jehovah with rebellion and ingratitude.

" But Jeshurun waxed fat and kicked "

" Jeshurun," as a name for Israel, occurs here for the first time, and is used only four times altogether in the Hebrew Bible—three times by Moses in these last chapters of Deuteronomy, and once by Isaiah.[1] Some scholars have taken it as a *diminutive* from

[1] Deut. xxxii. 15, xxxiii. 5, 26 ; Is. xliv. 2. As will be seen by comparing the contexts, "Jeshurun " is used in the other three passages as the *ideal prophetic* name for the Jewish nation when, by the grace and the power of God, Jacob shall at last be turned into Israel.

Yashur or *Yashar* (" straight," " just," " upright ")
and think it expresses endearment. It has been
rendered the " good little people," and the LXX translates it " the beloved one," but there is no evidence
that the נ—*un* (the last two letters of the word) has
a diminutive force. It simply means " the upright
one," and is a poetic designation of Israel under its
ideal character. This is what Israel was *called* to be
—and what it shall yet be one day—a just, " upright,"
or righteous nation ; but, alas ! how different its
actual condition. True indeed is the observation of
another writer that in the use of this name, in this
connection, " lies the keenest reproach of apostate
Israel " which is seen by Moses as falling into a state
the very opposite of that to which it was destined ;
or, in the words of Calvin, " By using the name Jeshurun
instead of Israel, Moses ironically censures those who
had swerved from rectitude. By recalling to memory
with what dignity they had been endowed he the
more sharply rebukes the perfidy which was their
crime."

    That *Jeshurun*, the people called with so high a
calling, and on whom so many favours were lavished
—instead of being constrained by the mercies of Jehovah
to bless His holy Name, and to seek to show forth
their thankfulness to Him by bringing forth the fruits
of righteousness, should have become spoilt and " *waxed
fat and kicked* " [1] in rebellion at God's law and com-
mandment, like an overfed ox who becomes unmanage-
able—this was the sin and guilt into which Moses saw
Israel falling, and over which he laments.

    The next line is best understood as a parenthetical

---

[1] The only other place where this verb is used is in 1 Sam. ii. 29,
in the Divine sentence against Eli and his house : " *Wherefore kick ye
at My sacrifices and Mine offering ?* "

ejaculation of the inspired singer, and the whole verse
may be read thus :

" *But* (*or ' and '*) *Jeshurun waxed fat and kicked ;*
    (*Thou art waxed fat, thou art grown thick, thou art
        become sleek !*)
Then he forsook God who made him,
And lightly esteemed the Rock of his salvation."

He "*forsook*," and "he lightly esteemed." The
Hebrew verbs are stronger, and there is something of
gradation expressed in them, for the first וַיִּטֹּשׁ—*vayitosh*
—has the sense of abandoning, or a putting away from
one's self with indifference, or even *with contempt*,
while the second verb, וַיְנַבֵּל—*va'ynabel*—means to
" esteem lightly," to the point of "*treating one as a
fool*." And whom was it that Israel thus treated ?
It was " *the God that made him*," and " *the Rock of his
salvation*." These two names for God are also very
significant.

אֱלוֹהַ—*Eloah*—is a form of *Elohim*—the plural form
of *El*, a name of God which is used nearly three thousand
times in the Hebrew Bible. It occurs first in this
passage, and is repeated twice in this Song. Altogether
Eloah is found fifty-seven times in the Hebrew Scriptures—chiefly in Job and in the Psalms. Elohim
stands for the God of *might* and majesty, and may be
said in a general way to be His Name as the *creator*
and *upholder* of all things. But in addition to the
essential ideas expressed in the name Elohim, *Eloah*
sets Him forth as the *living* God, *who alone is worthy
to be worshipped*, in contrast to the false gods or idols
of the Gentiles, while " *The Rock* " (which, as shown
in the exposition of the 4th verse, also occurs first
as a name of God in this song) proclaims Jehovah as
the *everlasting, unchangeable* One—the firm, immovable

foundation upon which man may safely ground his hope for time and eternity.

And not only did they "forsake" or turn away with contempt from Him who "made them" as a nation, and who was the Rock of their salvation, to whom alone they ought to have rendered adoring worship and joyous obedience, but they fell still deeper into apostasy and degradation. Unlike the Thessalonian Christians, who through Christ turned *from idols* "*to serve a living and true God*," [1] Israel in his folly and madness turned *from* the living and true God to serve idols.

" *They moved Him to jealousy with strange* (*or* ' *foreign* ')
    gods ;
With abominations provoked they Him to anger."

Cavillers may stumble, if they like, at the anthropomorphisms in the Bible, and the ascription to God of attributes which pertain to man. The believer, on the other hand, sees in them marks of God's condescension in stooping down to the level of our comprehension and experience in His desire to communicate to us His infinite thoughts, and to open up to us *His heart.*

Holy jealousy is one of the Divine *perfections*, and it is an attribute of His character, which, if properly understood, ought to be very precious to man. By it Jehovah—"the only true God"—is distinguished from the false gods of the nations. Already at His self-revelation on Sinai He spake these words, saying : "*I am Jehovah, thy God, who brought thee out of the land of Egypt and of the house of bondage. Thou shalt have no other gods besides Me. . . . Thou shalt not bow down thyself to them, nor serve them, for I, Jehovah thy God, am a jealous God.*" The nations may have their

[1] 1 Thess. i. 9.

Pantheons in which " the vanities of the Gentiles "—
as the prophets call their false gods—may be content
to share their honours with other " foreign " gods,
who were only idols like themselves. But Jehovah,
the only true and living God, must have the full and
undivided love and worship of His people. " *Hear,
O Israel : Jehovah our God is one Lord ; and thou
shalt love Jehovah thy God with all thy heart and with
all thy soul, and with all thy might.*" [1] " *I am
Jehovah,*" He says, " *this is My Name ; and My glory
will I not give to another, neither My praise to graven
images.*" [2]

And He was jealous for the whole-hearted love and
devotion of Israel because of the covenant relationship into which He had entered with them. He
betrothed them to Himself as a man betroths a woman,
and Israel became " the dearly beloved of His soul," [3]
whom He loved with an infinite and everlasting love.
But instead of reciprocating His great love and finding
her chief joy in communion with her Husband, who
was also her Maker,[4] Israel became faithless to her
marriage vow and committed spiritual adultery by
lavishing her affections upon idols.

And the character of the false gods by which
they provoked Jehovah's holy jealousy is expressed in
the terms used of them. (1) They were זָרִים—*zarim*—
" *strange* " or " *foreign* "—the underlying idea in the
word being *lack of affinity ; without sympathy*—the
very opposite of Jehovah, " our Maker," who " knoweth
our frame," and is infinite in His compassion toward
them that fear Him. (2) And they are rightly described as " *abominations*," whose worship was often
associated not only with orgies of *cruelty*, but with un-

---

[1] Deut. vi. 4, 5.   [2] Isa. xlii. 8.
[3] Jer. xii. 7.   [4] Isa. liv. 5.

speakable *obscenities* which had a very debasing effect
on the worshippers ; for men always rise or sink to the
level of the object of their adoration, and as communion with Jehovah—" the Holy One of Israel "—
has the effect of making men holy because *He* the Lord
their God is holy, so the worship of the " abominations,"
and the practice of the degrading cults of the heathen,
have the effect of making men morally filthy and
abominable.   This is God's complaint about Israel.
" *I found Israel like grapes in the wilderness* "—something very rare and precious, something in which a
man finds delight and refreshment—" *but they came to
Baal-peor, and separated* (*or* " *devoted* " *themselves*) *unto
the shameful thing, and became abominable like that
which they loved.*" [1]   The character of these " abominations " of the heathen and the underlying motive in
their worship is still further set forth in the 17th
verse :

> " *They sacrificed unto demons, which were no God,*
> *To gods that they knew not,*
> *To new gods that came up of late,*
> *Which your fathers dreaded not.*"

The Hebrew noun שֵׁדִים—*shedim*—rendered in the
Authorised Version " devils," and in the Revised
Version " demons," occurs here for the first time,
and is found in only one other place in the Hebrew
Scriptures, viz. Ps. cvi. 37.   The word is of uncertain etymology, but is traced by some scholars
to the Assyrian *sedu,* which signified " *a protecting
spirit,*" while others would trace it to an Arabic root
which signifies " *lord.*"   In the LXX it is rendered
δαιμόνιον—" demons."   These wicked spirits who are
under the leadership of the chief of demons, or the

[1] Hos. ix. 10 (R.V.).

Devil, are the real power behind all the systems of idolatry in the world. It is they who first seduced the nations into it, and it is they who are still keeping so many hundreds of millions enslaved to it. That is why the worship of idols is regarded in Scripture as in reality the worship of demons. Thus the Apostle Paul also warns Christians to " flee from idolatry " because " *the things which the Gentiles sacrifice they sacrifice to demons, and I would not that ye should have communion with demons.*" [1]

And the power by which the demons keep those they enslave chained to their idolatries, and exact their cruel tribute, is *fear*. This is brought out in the last line of the 17th verse, where the contemptible " new gods " to which Israel in his folly was turning are described as those " *which your fathers dreaded not.*" The word שְׂעָרוּם—*se'arum* (rendered " dreaded ")—is probably from a root which signifies " *to shudder* "; " *to be horrified,*" and is never used for the fear of Jehovah, the underlying idea of which is *reverence*, which leads to adoration. In its adjectival form it is used in Jer. v. 30 and xxiii. 14 : " *A wonderful (or ' astonishing ') and horrible thing—sha'rurah—is come to pass in the land* "—namely, the corruption which followed in the wake of idolatry.

And it is ever so. Those who are not possessed of the filial, reverential fear of Jehovah are enslaved by a dread of evil-spirits by which, consciously or unconsciously, they are haunted and tormented ; and those who lose faith in the one true and living God, are often given over to the grossest superstitions.

That the " demons " or evil spirits (which, as already said, were the real power behind the idols which the heathen worshipped) were regarded as male-

[1] 1 Cor. x. 20.

volent for the most part, and inimical to the welfare
even of their own votaries, was taught by pagan
writers themselves.

Socrates may speak of his benevolent demon whom
he considered his guardian spirit, but Plutarch says
" it is a very ancient opinion that there are certain
wicked and *malignant* demons, who envy good men,
and endeavour to hinder them in the pursuit of virtue,
lest they should be partakers of greater happiness than
they enjoy." The chief aim, therefore, on the part of
their votaries was to *propitiate* them, and the highest
and most acceptable offering which—as they thought—
they could bring them were human sacrifices.

And to these depths of degradation " *Jeshurun* "—
the people which God chose to show forth His glory
and His praise among the nations—descended in process
of time, so that the Psalmist, echoing the words of
Moses after their fulfilment, laments :

" *They mingled themselves with the nations,*
And learned their works,
And served their idols which became a snare unto them.
Yea, they sacrificed their sons and their daughters unto
    demons,
And shed innocent blood,
Even the blood of their sons and their daughters,
Whom they sacrificed unto the idols of Canaan ;
And the land was polluted with blood.
Thus were they defiled with their works,
And played the harlot in their doings." [1]

To emphasise once more not only Israel's great sin,
but *mad folly*, the contrast between Jehovah, the true
and living God, and the " vanities of the heathen " is
again set forth in the 18th verse.

Whom was it that they were exchanging for these

[1] Ps, cvi. 35–39.

" abominations " whom the Gentiles worshipped ? Here is the answer :

> " *Of the Rock that begat thee thou art unmindful,*
> *And hast forgotten God that gave thee birth.*"

This is the third time that Jehovah is called " the Rock " in this song, and here it is especially in contrast to the contemptible " new gods " who have " sprung up of late," [1] and in whom there is no stability nor permanence.

And He is not only the Eternal, ever-abiding and unchangeable one, but, unlike the " strange " or " foreign " gods of the nations whom the *shedim,* or evil spirits, used as their outward masks and visible representations, and who are cruel and inimical to the welfare of those whom they enslave, Jehovah, so to say, *travailed in birth* for His people, and His love and compassion for His children is as strong as that of a father, and as tender as that of a mother.

" *Yea, He loveth the people,*" exclaims Moses in the next chapter, and His own words which He spoke to them later through Isaiah and Jeremiah have been true all along : " *I have loved thee with an everlasting love ; therefore with lovingkindness have I drawn thee,*" or " therefore have I *drawn out,* or *extended* to the full length, My lovingkindness toward thee." " Can a woman forget her sucking child that she should not have compassion on the son of her womb ? Yea, these may forget, yet will I not forget thee." [2] And it was this " Rock that begat them," to whom they owed their

---

[1] מִקָּרֹב—*miqarobh*—rendered " of late," literally means " from near," but it is an adjective both of place and of time. Here it means " of near time," *i.e.* " gods only recently invented or discovered." What a contrast to the Eternal One !

[2] Jer. xxxi. 3 ; Is. xlix. 15.

very existence as a nation, whom Israel in their sin
and folly exchanged for idols ; it was such tender love
and faithfulness that they " provoked to jealousy "
with vanities and abominations ! Well may we apply
the words in Jeremiah ii. : " *Wherefore I will yet contend with you, saith Jehovah, and with your children's
children will I contend. For pass over to the isles of
Kittim and see ; and send unto Kedar, and consider
diligently ; and see if there hath been such a thing. Hath
a nation changed its gods which yet are no gods ? But
My people have changed their glory for that which doth
not profit. Be astonished, O ye heavens, at this, and be
horribly afraid, be ye very desolate, saith Jehovah. For
My people have committed two evils : they have forsaken
Me, the fountain of living waters, and hewed them out
cisterns, broken cisterns, that can hold no water.*" [1]

And gross idolatry marked only the culmination of
the first stage in Israel's national apostasy. The
climax was reached when, after a long process of disobedience and self-hardening, and because their hearts
were already alienated from God, Israel turned their
backs upon Him who is " the brightness of God's glory,
and the express image of His person."

" The Scribes and Pharisees in Christ's time, and the
majority of the Jews of the present day, would have
us believe that they rejected Jesus of Nazareth because
He sought to mislead and turn them away from God
and His holy law. Many of them in their ignorance
sincerely believed, and still believe, this to be the case.
But, alas ! this very ignorance is part of the awful
consequences of Israel's prior alienation from their
heavenly Father, and from the true spirit of Moses and
the prophets. No : Israel rejected Christ, not because
He went counter to, or sought in any way to lead them

[1] Jer. ii. 9–13.

astray from, God, or because His teaching was con-
tradictory to the law and to the testimony which was
already in their hands, but because, on the contrary,
He sought to bring them back to God, and was Himself
the very image of God, who, as the only true Israelite,
not only bore witness to the law and the prophets, but
Himself *magnified* the law and fulfilled and exemplified
it in His own life." [1]

Before passing on to the next strophe which speaks
of the punishment which was to befall Israel, I would
pause for a moment to remind you once again, dear
reader, that the history of Israel is in this respect
typical of the history of the professing Church, and that
the apostasy of the Jewish nation is paralleled and
exceeded by the apostasy of Christendom.

How beautiful was the Church in its first days—so
long as it knew itself to consist of the poor of this world,
but rich in faith, and heirs of the Kingdom—so long as
it was lowly in mind, and walked in simplicity and in
conscious dependence on her heavenly Bridegroom!
But when world power began to smile upon her, and
she became allied to ungodly kings and emperors who
in process of time endowed her with temporal power,
she too became proud and wanton in her worldly
prosperity, and " waxed fat and kicked." And the
idolatries and abominations, and the " shedding of
blood," of which Christendom stands guilty, is not less,
but more heinous in God's sight than that which is
laid to the charge of Israel, because committed in fuller
light, and in spite of the object lesson and warning
supplied by the history of the Jews.

[1] From my book, *The Shepherd of Israel and His Scattered Flock.*

6

ISRAEL'S PUNISHMENT

THE next strophe, consisting of verses 19-25,
announce in advance the fearful judgments
which would come on Israel in consequence of apostasy.

" *And Jehovah saw it, and abhorred them,*
Because of the provocation of His sons and His
daughters."

Because punishment does not immediately overtake
the wicked in their evil doings, they say, " How doth
God know ? and is there knowledge in the Most High ? " [1]
The elders of the house of Israel who carried on in the
dark—" every man in his chambers of imagery "—their
defiling idolatrous practices, flattered themselves, saying, " *Jehovah seeth us not ; Jehovah hath forsaken the*
earth." [2]   But " Jehovah saw it," and knew it all, and
in His book every step in the progressive apostasy,
and every deed of evil, was written down.   Great and
marvellous was the patience and long-suffering which
He exercised toward them : He sent messenger after
messenger to remonstrate with and to warn them ; He
even condescended to *plead* with them, " *Oh, do not this*
abominable thing that I hate . . . wherefore commit ye
*this great evil against your souls ? *" [3]   But in the end
even the long-suffering of God was exhausted, and " *He*
abhorred (or *contemned*) *them.*"

And the anger of God, when roused, at last was all
the greater because it was provoked by " *His sons and*

[1] Ps. lxxiii. 11.   [2] Ezek. viii. 12, ix. 9.   [3] Jer. xliv. 4, 7.

His daughters "—those to whom He had shown such
infinite grace by bringing them into such near relationship with Himself, and from whom He had every right
to expect filial reverence and love, instead of persistent
" provocation " and rebellion. This is the explanation
of the " double " portion of punishment which came
upon Israel, and of the fact that " under the whole
heaven " there hath not been done to any other city
" as it hath been done upon Jerusalem." [1]

It is not that they were greater sinners than the
other nations ; no, their *guilt* was greater in that *they*,
who stood so near to Him, and whom he had exalted
to the position of " His sons and His daughters,"
mingled with the Gentiles, " and learned of their ways,"
and practised the same sins and abominations. And
from this we may learn, dear Christian reader, that sin
on the part of God's professing people is more grievous
in His sight, and more provocative to the eyes of His
holiness, than the sins of those who stand in no relationship with Him.

But to proceed to the following verses, which set
forth the terrible consequences of His abhorrence of
them.

" *And He said, I will hide My face from them,*
I will see what their end shall be :
For they are a very perverse generation,
Children in whom is no faithfulness."

This is but a terse summary in poetic form of what
God had told Moses in the verses which form the introduction to this sublime Song—namely that when they
shall turn away from Jehovah after strange gods and
forsake Him and break the covenant which He made
with them : " *Then My anger shall be kindled against*

[1] Dan. ix. 12.

*them in that day, and I will forsake them and I will hide
My face from them, and they shall be devoured, and many
evils and troubles shall come upon them . . . and I will
surely hide My face in that day for all the evil which
they shall have wrought in that they are turned unto
other gods.*"

Yes, *the hiding of His face* is the greatest of all the
calamities which has befallen the Jewish nation, and
is the primary cause of all their long-continued sorrows
and troubles, for that betokened the withdrawal of His
presence from them.   In the light of His countenance
is life and joy, and peace, and His presence in their
midst constituted their protection and safety, but
when He " hideth His face " there is " trouble," [1] and
the Jewish people has experienced this to the full during
their long night of sorrow and weeping.

In the lines which follow we are again reminded—
in vindication of God's righteous dealings with them—
that it was Israel's manifold iniquities which have
separated between them and their God, and their
sins which have caused His face to be hid from
them.[2]

" *For they are a very perverse generation* "—or,
literally, *dor tahpukhoth,* " a generation of perversities,"
the word being a feminine plural substantive—that is,
they are so perverted that they have become perversity
itself : " *Children in whom there is no faithfulness* "—
i.e. who have not kept faith with God, and in whom
He could put no reliance.

The 21st verse reads literally :

" *They have moved Me to jealousy with a no-god ;
They have provoked Me to anger with their vanities :
And I will move them to jealousy with a no-people ;
I will provoke them to anger with a foolish nation.*"

---

[1] Ps. xxx. 7, civ. 29.   [2] Isa. lix. 2.

This is poetic retribution ; it is like for like. The treatment which they meted out to God, God meted out to them. They provoked His holy jealousy, and insulted His majesty by turning away from Him, the living and true God, to run after those who were " no-gods," but dumb idols, and He would give them over into the hands of those whom they looked down upon and despised as " no-people," that is, the Gentiles. They " lightly esteemed " (va-y'nabal—" treated as foolish ") the Rock of their salvation, and vexed and angered Him with " vanities " or " nothingnesses," and He would vex or anger them with a goi nabal— " a foolish nation," which also, I think, is best understood of the Gentiles in general, as not being possessed of the true knowledge of God which is the basis of all true wisdom.

Blessed be God, since the coming of Christ into the world, millions from among those who were formerly " no-people " are now, together with the remnant according to the election of grace from Israel, " the people of God," while the Jews as a nation are for the time being Lo-ammi—" not My people " ; and those who were before " foolish " and followed their own vain imaginations, are now made wise unto salvation, and possess the wisdom of God in their inward parts, while " the wisdom of their wise men and the understanding of their prudent men has perished " [1] from the leaders of the Jewish nation since their rejection of their Messiah, who is the personified wisdom of God, as well as the righteousness, sanctification, and redemption of His people. And thus also in this respect is poor Christless Israel " provoked," as it were, " to jealousy " by those whom they formerly despised as " no-people." [2]

[1] Isa. xxix. 14.   [2] See Rom. x. 19, 20.

Something of the terribleness of the wrath of Almighty God, when once provoked, is expressed in the next verse :

" For a fire is kindled in Mine anger,
And burneth unto the lowest Sheol,
And devoureth the earth (or ' land ') with its increase,
And setteth on fire the foundations of the mountains."

There is no escape from it, as sinners must sooner or later discover—not even if they were " to make their bed in Sheol," or take up their abode in the uttermost parts of the sea.[1] And it is no mere poetic hyperbole when we read that the anger of God, when kindled, devoured also " the land with its increase," for, as already explained in the notes on the preceding strophe, the barren desolate condition in which Palestine has lain for so many centuries is accounted for in the Bible by the fact that it *has* been visited by the judgment of God because of the sins of the people that dwelt therein.

Verses 23–25 speak of the " tribulation and anguish " which Israel was to experience as the expression of God's anger and fiery indignation which they provoked by their sins and apostasies. To translate literally :

" I will heap evils upon them ;
I will spend Mine arrows upon them :
(When) wasted with hunger and devoured with burning
   heat,
And bitter destruction,
I will also send the teeth of beasts upon them,
With the poison of crawling things of the dust.
Without shall the sword bereave,
And in the chambers terror ;
(It shall devour) both young man and virgin."

[1] Ps. cxxxix. 8, 9.

Famine, pestilence, consuming fevers, wild beasts, poisonous reptiles, war, and terror of calamities yet to come—these were the evils which God threatened to " heap " upon them, the " arrows " which He would let loose among them. It is not necessary to enter into a minute exposition of these verses, which only summarise in terse poetical form the fuller and more detailed catalogues of the plagues and calamities which were to come upon them in case of their apostasy from Jehovah—as contained in the 28th chapter of this Book of Deuteronomy, and in the 26th chapter of Leviticus. I would only pause to make one or two general observations.

(1) The terrible threatenings and denunciations which are pronounced against Israel in case of apostasy have proved no empty words, but have been *literally and minutely* fulfilled, as is proved by the woeful annals of the nation from the very beginning of " the times of the Gentiles " to this day. What people on earth have endured so many sorrows and calamities and *for so long*, as the Jews ? Jeremiah, who was an eye-witness of the destruction of Jerusalem and of the first Temple by the Chaldeans, which marked the close of the first stage of Israel's apostasy and the beginning of their great and many national tribulations, exclaims : *" Is it nothing to you, all ye that pass by ? Behold and see if there be any sorrow like unto my sorrow, which is done unto me ; wherewith Jehovah hath afflicted me in the day of His fierce anger."* And some five and a half centuries later, after the second stage of Israel's national sin culminated in the rejection of Christ, which brought about the destruction of the second Temple and the inauguration of the *universal* stage of their dispersion among the nations, Josephus, who was an eye-witness of the calamities which befell them

then, in commencing to write the history of *The Jewish Wars*, says in the Preface : "*Accordingly it appears to me that the misfortunes of all men from the beginning of the world, if they be compared with those of the Jews, are not so considerable as they were . . . this makes it impossible for me to contain my lamentations.*"

This is what Josephus wrote at the very beginning of our " Christian Era." What would he have said if he could have foreseen the untold woes and miseries which have been heaped upon this people in the nineteen centuries which have intervened since ? The history of the Jews since the destruction of the second Temple is one long martyrology, the record of an almost unbroken chain of unparalleled sufferings —a chronicle of massacres, oppressions, banishments, fiendish tortures, spoliations, and degradations which have been inflicted upon them for the most part by so-called Christian nations.[1]

Even within these past few years—not only *during* the great World War, but *since*—how great and terrible have been the sorrows and sufferings of the great masses of the Jews in Central and Eastern Europe. In the Ukraine alone in 1919 and 1920 about 150,000 Jews were done to death. The following is an extract from the opening address by the Chief Rabbi of Great Britain at a Conference of Jewish preachers which took place in London in July 1923, in which he reviewed the condition of the Jews since the last meeting of this kind in 1914 :

I shall confine myself to the sufferings of Israel in old Russia, in that Russia which until very recently was the home of one-half of the world's Jewish popula-

---

[1] I am quoting here words from my book, *The Shepherd of Israel and His Scattered Flock : A Solution of the Enigma of Jewish History*, where a condensed summary of Jewish history will be found.

tion. During the period under review, Anti-Semitism in that land resulted in volcanic eruptions of hatred and devastating tornadoes of human malice, rarely surpassed in history. In spite of the Beilis Trial and three centuries of Romanoff rightlessness and oppression for the Jew, no less than 400,000 Jews fought under the banner of the Czar. And yet very soon after the Great Conflict began, all the forces of Russian reaction combined in what was nothing less than a war within the war against Israel. Time will permit me to refer only to two cataclysms, both of them veritable furnaces of suffering unto our people, both of them engraved for all time in letters of blood on the pages of Jewish history.

In consequence of shameless calumnies and craziest hallucinations of suspicion, the entire Jewish population of the Russian Western War Zone was compulsorily expelled to the interior of Russia ; the *entire* population, the old men and the infants, the sick, the dying, and the insane, driven forth often at only twelve hours' notice. And this summary evacuation of a million and a half human beings, with the incalculable suffering it entailed, did not remain the worst calamity of the war.

The second cataclysm, when the 3,000,000 Jews of the Ukraine were handed over, helpless and hopeless, to murder and dishonour infinitely transcends it' in horror. Historians have for centuries dwelt on the tragedy and inhumanity of the expulsion of the 150,000 Jews of Spain. But throughout 1919 and 1920 we have had in the Ukraine not merely the expulsion of a similar number of human beings, but their extermination by the wild hordes of Denikin, Petlura, Grigorief, Makhno, and other bandits, raging like wild beasts amid the defenceless Jewries of South Russia. " The massacres of the Jews in the Ukraine can find, for thoroughness and extent, no parallel except in the massacres of the Armenians," is the deliberate verdict of Sir Horace Rumbold, H.M. Minister at Warsaw, in a Report to the Foreign Office that was widely circulated at the time.

Wholesale slaughter and burials alive, rape, and torture, became not merely commonplaces, but the order of the day.   There were pogroms that lasted a week ; and in several cases the systematic and diabolic torture and outrage and carnage were continued for a month.   In many populous Jewish communities there were no Jewish survivors left to bury the dead, and thousands of Jewish wounded and killed were eaten by dogs and pigs; in others, the synagogues were turned into charnel-houses by the pitiless butchery of those who sought refuge in them.   If we add to the figures quoted above, the number of those indirect victims who, in consequence of the robbery and destruction that accompanied these massacres, were swept away by famine, disease, exposure, and all manner of privations—the dread total will be very near half a million human beings.

This is a tale, not of the Middle Ages, when entire Jewish communities were again and again exterminated by the fanatical fury of hordes of so-called Christians, but *of the twentieth century,* and as a sequel to the war, the outcome of which they had hoped would bring amelioration and liberty to the masses of their people, especially in countries like Russia.   And those who were killed outright are almost to be envied as compared with the lot of masses of the Jews in Eastern Europe who have survived.   The following is from the report of a prominent and wealthy Jew from South Africa, Mr. Isaac Ochberg, who spent four months in Russia in 1923 as administrator of relief :

You need not go very far into Russia in order to see the tragedy.   Trouble comes to meet you all along the route on which you are travelling.   You take a glance through your carriage window, and immediately you have a cross-view of the situation.   You see all the misery, the dead towns, the hordes of hungry, sick, naked, freezing human beings.   Whenever the train stops you are besieged by hundreds of men, women, and children who beg you to give them bread. The times have been so cruel for our people over there that they have been likened to the days of the destruction of the Temple, when babes perished at their mothers' breasts. . . .

(2) At the cost of repetition, it must be emphasised that the calamities and sufferings of Israel *are due in the first instance to God's retributive anger against His people on account of their sins and apostasies, and are in fulfilment of prophetic forecasts, predictions, and warnings, some of which were uttered at the very beginning of their national history.* If it be true as their own prophets and historians pathetically complain, that " under the whole heaven hath not been done as it hath been done to Jerusalem," and that the misfortunes of all the rest of mankind from the beginning of the world do not equal those which have befallen this nation, what is this but a fulfilment of the solemn and awful words of God through Moses : " *If thou wilt not observe to do all the words of this law that are written within this book, that thou mayest fear this glorious and fearful Name, Jehovah, thy God, then Jehovah will make thy plagues wonderful, and the plagues of thy seed, even great plagues and of long continuance, and sore sickness and of long continuance.*" And again, in the same prophecy : " *Because thou servest not Jehovah thy God with joyfulness and with gladness of heart, by reason of the abundance of all things ; therefore shalt thou serve thine enemies that Jehovah shall send against thee in hunger and in thirst and in nakedness and in want of all things ; and He shall put a yoke of iron upon thy neck until He have destroyed thee.*" [1]

(3) The fact that the sufferings of the Jewish people are all foretold, and that they are due in the first

[1] Deut. xxviii. 47, 48, 58, 59.

instance to God's anger against sin—especially *the* great national sin of the rejection of their Messiah, is no excuse for the Gentile nations for their cruelties and brutalities which they have perpetrated against them.

The sufferings of Christ were also minutely foretold, and were moreover in accord with the predetermined counsel of God, yet the Jews were held responsible for it because it was " with wicked hands " that they delivered Him to the Romans to be crucified; and so also the nations who inflict sufferings on the Jews are held guilty before God, and history, as well as Scripture, bears witness that, sooner or later, the oppressors of Israel come under His judgments. It was so in ancient times, as is proved by the fate which overtook the world powers of antiquity which have oppressed and persecuted this peculiar people, and it is true also in modern times, for the God of Abraham still lives, and has never rescinded His solemn word : " *I will bless them that bless thee, and him that curseth thee will I curse.*"

(4) Judgment is not the *last* word which God has spoken concerning this nation. This very sublime Song which (as we have seen) is a condensed prophecy of the whole of Israel's history, from the very beginning to the end—foretells not only Israel's apostasy and the terrible judgments which would come upon them in consequence, but goes on to speak (as we shall see) of their final deliverance by the interposition of God, when not only they themselves shall be blessed, but when the nations shall be blessed and " rejoice " with them.

" God's judgment of Israel," says another Hebrew Christian brother, " is the most terrible thing in history —yet they have been preserved to this very day through the power of that very God who punished them so terribly. Here they are, a monument of the truth of God's word—a monument also of God's faithfulness,

None of the persecutions which they have endured have availed to destroy them, neither have they broken their energy, nor subdued their indomitable will, nor crushed their power of mind ; and no sooner was the great pressure which the nations—so-called Christian nations —put upon them removed than we see them prosper in every country, and take leading positions in every sphere of life—in commerce and politics, as well as in literature and art, showing that the Lord God has made them to be a peculiar people, a nation to be perpetuated ; and that it was He who gave them nerve to endure, in order that in the future, when His grace shall melt their hearts, they may be a mighty instrument to show forth His praise.   There is still visible among scattered Israel something of blessing and influence, the effect of God's training through so many centuries.   Their history since the rejection of Christ is unspeakably sad ; yet we cannot help noticing that in the midst of Christ- less Israel some traces of the grandeur and beauty of their Father's house still linger.

" Behold their zeal for God, their zeal for the Scrip- tures, their zeal for the Sabbath Day ; behold the sacrifices they make in order to carry out the injunctions of the Law !   Yes, there are many features in the Jewish character which we cannot explain in any other way than this—that there is still a blessing resting on them ; that the voice of God, which was heard upon Sinai, has still its echo in their hearts and consciences ; and that the prayers which have been offered up on their behalf by patriarchs, kings, prophets, and saints, are still held in remembrance before the throne of God." [1]

[1] From an address by C. A. Schönberger.

7

JEHOVAH'S YEARNING OVER HIS NATIONAL PRODIGAL

THE fifth strophe of this sublime prophetic Song (verses 26–33) sings both of mercy and of judgment. It reveals also something of the yearning of God's heart for His national prodigal. Not utterly would He cast off His people ; not for evermore would His anger burn against them.

The punishment which has come upon Israel is great and terrible, but it is much less than their great guilt deserved. If Jehovah had dealt with them strictly according to their sin and given them the *full* reward of their iniquity, they would long ago have been utterly destroyed as a people, and their very remembrance would have ceased among the nations. But for His own holy Name's sake He refrained from making " a full end " of them, and tempered His holy wrath with mercy.

" *I said I would scatter them afar,*
I would make the remembrance of them to cease from
among men ;
Were it not that I feared the provocation of the enemy,
Lest their adversaries should judge amiss,
Lest they should say, Our hand is exalted,
And Jehovah hath not done all this."

The word אַפְאֵיהֶם *aph'ey-hem* (rendered " I will scatter them ") is found only in this one place in the Hebrew Bible, and has been variously rendered by lexicographers and interpreters. Gesenius derives it

from the verb פָּאָה *pa-ah* "to which," he says, "I do
not hesitate to assign the significance of *breathing*, or
blowing," in which case *aph'eyhem* would mean "*I will
blow them away*," *i.e.*, "scatter them like the wind ";
while the new "Oxford Lexicon" gives another signi-
fication to the verb, viz. "to cleave" or "to split,"
and would render the first two words in our text "I
said I would cleave them in pieces." ¹

Jewish interpreters derive it from פֵּאָה *pe-ah*,
"corner," and render the phrase "I said I would scatter
them into corners," which rendering is followed in the
Authorised Version.² But I think the rendering given
by Gesenius (which is accepted by most of the more
modern scholars) to be the correct one. Jehovah said,
"I would scatter them like the wind," "I would blow
them away," *i.e.*, I would make an utter end of them ;
"I would cause their very remembrance to cease among
men, were it not that I feared the wrath (or more
literally ' *the provocation* ') of the enemy."

This is the strongest and boldest of the anthropomorphisms in this sublime Song—so bold indeed that,
as one scholarly writer observes : "No man would
dare to put such an argument into the mouth of the
Most High," if the words had not been actually spoken
by Himself through the mouth of Moses. But these
bold figures—these fervent or even vehement expressions, and the application to Himself of attributes and
qualities which belong to man, are but another mark of
God's condescension in stooping down to the level of
our comprehension in His endeavour to communicate to
us His infinite thoughts, and the feelings of His heart.

¹ Kautzsch's critical translation of *Die Heilige Schrift des Alten
Testaments* renders : "Ich spräche : Wegblassen will ich sie."
² The LXX seems to have read : אֲפִיצֵם *aphitsem* instead of אַפְאֵיהֶם,
and renders simply, "I will scatter them."

That Jehovah, the Everlasting God " who sitteth above the circle of the earth," before whom " the inhabitants of the world are as grasshoppers," [1] had in His infinite condescension a care as to what effect His dealings with Israel—whether in mercy or in judgment —would have upon the Gentile nations, and as to what they would think and speak of Him in consequence, we see also from other Scriptures. Thus at critical points at the very beginning of their history, when, in consequence of outstanding acts of sin and rebellion, His anger was kindled against them, and He threatened utterly to destroy them, and to make of Moses a new nation " greater and mightier than they," the great law-giver was bold to remind Him in his intercession how closely the honour of His own Name was at stake in the matter. " *The Egyptians will hear it . . . and they will tell it to the people. . . . Now if Thou shalt kill this people as one man, then the nations which have heard the fame of Thee will speak, saying, Because Jehovah was not able to bring this people into the land which He sware unto them, therefore He hath slain them in the wilderness.*" [2] And the same argument, namely, that " the Egyptians will hear of it," and in their ignorance speak evil of His name, formed also part of his prevailing intercession on an earlier occasion, when Israel sinned so grievously in the matter of the golden calf, and God had said, " Let me alone that my wrath may wax hot against them, and that I may consume them." [3]

This is " the provocation of the enemy " which Jehovah " feared," and which caused Him to refrain from utterly destroying His rebellious people—namely the misinterpretation the Gentile nations would put

[1] Isa. xl. 22.   [2] Num. xiv. 13–20.
[3] Ex. xxxii. 7–14. See also Deut. ix. 25–29.

upon it, who instead of beholding in it the deserved punishment of Israel's great and many sins, and laying this object-lesson to their own hearts, would blasphemously speak of Jehovah as a God who either lacked the power to deliver His people, or as unfaithful in fulfilling the word of promise which He had made to them—whereas one great purpose in the election of the Jewish nation, and in all His dealings with them, was that through them the glorious perfections of His character, not only His almighty power and wisdom, but His grace and faithfulness, *and marvellous long-suffering*, might become known among the nations. Therefore, He says, " I wrought *for My Name's sake*, that it should not be profaned in the sight of the nations," and did not make " *a full end* " of them, as they so well deserved." [1]

That Israel's adversaries—who are regarded also as the adversaries of God—wilfully ignoring the fact that it was He who was using them *as a scourge* for the infliction of punishment upon His people—were only too prone to say " *our* hand is exalted," and take glory to themselves as if it were in their own strength, or perchance by the help of their idols that they prevailed over the land and people of Israel, we know only too well.

A typical instance of such boastfulness we have in the King of Assyria, who was commissioned of God to overthrow the ten tribed Kingdom, when Jehovah's long-suffering with them as a people was at last exhausted.

" Ho (or ' woe to the ') Assyrian," the Lord says, " *the rod of Mine anger, the staff in whose hand is Mine indignation!* I will send him against a profane nation, and against the people of My wrath will I give him a

[1] Ezek. xx. 14–17.

charge, to take the spoil, and to take the prey, and to tread them down as the mire of the streets. *Howbeit he meaneth not so, neither doth his heart think so "*—he does not see or consider that he is but a rod in God's hand, and that he must not and cannot go beyond what God has appointed—" but it is in his heart to destroy and to cut off nations not a few. For he saith, are not *my* princes all of them kings ? is not Calno as Carchemish ? is not Hamath as Arpad ? is not Samaria as Damascus ? *As my hand hath found* the kingdom of the Idols, whose graven images did excel them of Jerusalem and of Samaria ; *shall I not, as a have done unto Samaria and her idols, so do to Jerusalem and her idols ?* Wherefore it shall come to pass, that when the Lord hath performed His whole work upon Mount Zion and on Jerusalem, I will punish the fruit of the stout heart of the King of Assyria, and the glory of his high looks. *For he hath said, By the strength of my hand I have done it, and by my wisdom ;* for I have understanding : and I have removed the bounds of the peoples, and have robbed their treasures, and like a valiant man I have brought down them that sit on thrones. . . . Shall the axe boast itself against him that heweth therewith ? Shall the saw magnify itself against him that wieldeth it ? . . . Therefore will the Lord, Jehovah of Hosts, send among his fat ones leanness : and under His glory there shall be kindled a burning like the burning of fire." [1]

This then—*the honour of His Name,* which would have been still more blasphemed among the Gentiles,[2] and to prevent the adversaries of Israel, who are viewed

---

[1] Isa. x. 5–16.

[2] " The idolatry and rebellions of Israel deserved, and the justice of God seemed to demand, that they should be ' scattered into the corners ' of the earth, or even *extirpated.* But God knew that His enemies would attribute this to a wrong cause ; they would be emboldened to blaspheme, and have their hearts hardened in infidelity, and to deny scripture records. He therefore spared Israel, and continues them still to be *living witnesses* of the truth of the Bible, and

as being also the enemies of God, from boasting themselves against Him—was one great reason why He restrained His anger against His people, and did not execute the *full* punishment of their sins which justice demanded.

That they well deserved to be utterly *exterminated* is again emphasised in the verses which follow.

The 27th verse may in a sense be viewed as parenthetical, and the 28th as in direct continuity of thought to the 26th, thus :

> " *I said I would blow them away (scatter them to the winds)* "
> *I would make the remembrance of them to cease from among men. . . .*
> *For they are a nation void of counsel,*
> *And there is no understanding in them.*"

In the next verse there is revealed to us something of the yearning of God's heart over His national prodigal.

How different would their whole history have been if they had not been so foolish and stubborn ! How gladly would He who " doth not willingly afflict, nor grieve the children of men," but delights in mercy, have spared them their bitter sorrows, and their many and great sufferings which their unbelief and disobedience have brought them :

" *Oh that they were wise, that they understood this,*"

confutations of infidelity. By their existence as a people at this day, they confront such daring blasphemies ; and he who knows the spirit of modern infidels and deists, will perceive that they would have been more insolent and abundant in blasphemies, had there been no traces of such a people as the Jews upon the earth. They are preserved for wise and holy purposes, and the prophecies give us some idea what those purposes are."—MATTHEW HENRY.

viz., what it was all leading up to ; the terrible consequences of their departure from God :

" *That they would consider their latter end.*"

This reminds us of many other laments of God over
Israel's folly which was hastening their national down-
fall.

" *Oh that there were such a heart in them that they
would fear Me and keep My commandments always that
it might be well with them and their children for ever !* " [1]

" *Oh that My people would hearken unto Me,*
That Israel would walk in My ways !
I would soon subdue their enemies
And turn My hand against their adversaries.
The haters of Jehovah should submit themselves **unto**
 *   Him :*
But their time should endure for ever.
But My people hearkened not to My voice,
And Israel would none of Me."

So He *had to* " let them go " or " to give them over " to
the stubbornness of their heart, that they might walk
in their own counsels,[2] and it is due only to His infinite
sovereign mercy that they are not altogether consumed
as a people.

And to these laments of Jehovah in the Old Testament, we must add also the pathetic farewells of Christ
to His nation, in which the yearning heart of God
over His people expresses itself even more fully—" *O,
Jerusalem, Jerusalem, that killest the prophets and stonest
them which are sent unto thee, how often would I have
gathered thy children together, even as a hen gathereth her
chickens under her wings, and ye would not !* " And
again, in the so-called triumphal entry into Jerusalem, on the way from the Mount of Olives, " *when He*

[1] Deut. v. 29.   [2] Ps. lxxxi. 8–16.

beheld the city He wept over it, saying, If thou hadst known, even thou in this thy day things which belong unto thy peace, but now they are hid from thine eyes! For the days shall come upon thee that thine enemies shall cast a trench about thee, and compass thee round and keep thee in on every side, and shall lay thee even with the ground and thy children within thee ; and they shall not leave in thee one stone upon another ; because thou knewest not the time of thy visitation." [1]

Oh that they had been wise, and had considered their latter end, and had understood and laid to heart the things which belonged to their peace—how different would it have been with them !

And that the calamities and humiliations which have come upon them are due to the withdrawal of God's presence and protection ought to be manifest to all for :

" *How should one (of their enemies) chase a thousand (of them)*
And two put ten thousand to flight,
Except their Rock had sold them,
And Jehovah had delivered them up ? "

The very contrary was promised them if they had hearkened to God's voice : " *Jehovah will cause thine enemies that rise up against thee to be smitten before thee : they shall come out against thee one way, and shall flee before thee seven ways.*" And again : " *Ye shall chase your enemies, and they shall fall before you by the sword. And five of you shall chase a hundred, and a hundred of you shall chase ten thousand.*" [2] And this was the case so long as " *their Rock* "—the Almighty God of Israel, was their defence. All the powers of the world com-

[1] Matt. xxiii. 37–39 ; Luke xix. 41–44.
[2] Deut. xxviii. 7 ; Lev. xxvi. 7, 8.

bined could not have prevailed against them. But when His long-suffering was exhausted, and He withdrew His presence, He " sold them," *i.e.*, " gave them over " in His anger into the power of their enemies ; or, to use the language of the parable of the Vine or Vineyard which He had planted with such care—when at last in His righteous anger against the husbandmen he broke down " the hedges thereof," *i.e.*, withdrew His protection—then " they that passed by " began to " pluck " at it ; " the boar out of the wood doth waste it, the wild beast of the field (*i.e.* the Gentile world powers) doth devour it." [1]

That there is *no other* possible cause for their sorrows and miseries than their iniquities, which have separated them from their God, and their sins, which have caused His face to be hid from them,[2] is also manifest. For it cannot be that Jehovah's hand is too short to save, or that He, the Everlasting God, the Creator of the ends of the earth, has grown faint or weary ; or that perchance the idols of their Gentile oppressors to whom they ascribed the credit of their victories, were too strong for Him to deal with—Oh, no :

> " *For their rock is not as our Rock*
> *Even our enemies themselves being judges.*"

The nations who were brought into contact with Israel, and whom God used as scourges for the punishment of His people, had their false gods in whom they trusted, but they themselves never claimed for their idols the glorious attributes which belong only to Jehovah, the one true and living God. Some might falsely *think* that their gods were mighty to do good or evil, or that it was through their assistance that they gained victories, but they never claimed that

[1] Ps. lxxx. 8–15.   [2] Isa. lix. 1, 2.

they were *al*mighty. The fact that they had to *share* their glories with other supposed gods, is a confession on the part of their votaries that their power was but limited. But Jehovah is the Almighty God—" *He hath made the earth by His power, He hath established the world by His wisdom, and by His understanding hath He stretched out the heavens.*" [1]

The idols of the nations were, according to their own claims, but *local* deities, whose power extended at the most only over a particular district or land, but Jehovah alone is the Infinite One who fills the whole universe with His presence. " *Can any one hide himself in secret places that I shall not see him, saith Jehovah? Do I not fill heaven and earth, saith Jehovah?*" [2] " *Thus saith Jehovah, Heaven is My throne, and the earth is My footstool: what manner of house will ye build unto Me, and what place shall be My rest? For all these things hath My hand made, and so all these things come to be.*" And so in many other ways, as one may go on to show, the God of Israel is infinitely exalted above all that the Gentile nations claimed for their false gods.

Well might Moses exclaim :

" *Who is like unto Thee, O Jehovah, among the gods? Who is like Thee, glorious in holiness, Fearful in praises, doing wonders?*" [3]

Truly, " their rock is not as our Rock, even our enemies themselves being judges."

The 31st verse is *parenthetical*—a side explanation, so to say, of the fact that Israel's defeat at the hands of their enemies cannot be attributed to any other cause than their sins, certainly not to the power of the false gods of their adversaries. The 32nd verse is linked on to the 30th verse thus : One of their enemies

[1] Jer. x. 12.   [2] Jer. xxiii. 24.   [3] Ex. xv. 11.

would chase a thousand of them, and two would put
ten thousand to flight, because

> " *Their Rock had sold them,*
> *And Jehovah had delivered them up—*
> *For their vine is the vine of Sodom,*
> *And of the fields of Gomorrah ;*
> *Their grapes are grapes of gall,*
> *Their clusters are bitter ;*
> *Their wine is the poison of serpents*
> *And the cruel venom of asps.*"

The language is highly poetical and figurative, but it
sets forth the extent to which Israel corrupted himself
by his sins and apostasies. Well might God lament
over them, saying : " *Yet I had planted thee a noble
vine, wholly a right seed : how art thou turned into the
degenerate branches of a foreign vine unto Me?* " [1]   Or,
in the language of Isaiah v. : " *What could have been
done to My vineyard, that I have not done in it?   Wherefore, when I looked that it should bring forth grapes,
brought it forth wild grapes ?—for the vineyard of Jehovah
of Hosts is the house of Israel and of the men of Judah
His pleasant plant* (or literally, ' *the plant of His delight* ') *: and He looked for justice but behold oppression*
(or ' *the shedding of blood* ' [2]) ; *for righteousness and
behold a cry.*" These are the " wild grapes," the wine
of which was " as the poison of serpents, and the cruel
venom of asps " which degenerate Israel—the vine on
which God had bestowed so much care—brought forth,
and this is the cause of the hiding of His face from
them, and of His " delivering them up " for a time
into the hands of their enemies.

Before proceeding with the exposition of the last
strophe, I may be permitted again to make one or two
observations.

---

[1] Jer. ii. 21.   [2] מִשְׂפָּח mis'pach, from שָׂפַח saphach, " to pour out."

(1) First let us admire the marvellous grace of God and *His perseverance* with His sinful, rebellious people. And remember that in His dealings with Israel, we have not only a display of the glorious attributes of His character through which we may learn to know Him more fully, but also a revelation of the principles of His dealings with us. As we read, therefore, such scriptures as we have been considering, and the confessions of the godly remnant, that though Israel *deserved* that He should make an utter end of them, that "nevertheless, *for His great mercies' sake He did not utterly consume them, nor forsake them, because He is a great and merciful God,*" [1] we must humbly confess that the same is true of us also, and that if God had dealt *with us* after our sins, and rewarded us according to our iniquities, He would have cast us away from His presence, and given us over altogether to walk after the imaginations of our own hearts.

We may learn from His dealings with froward Israel that the path of disobedience brings nothing but sorrows and calamities, and that God will "in no wise leave the sins of His people unpunished," [2] but, "though He cause grief, yet will He have compassion according to the multitude of His lovingkindnesses.[3] "*For Jehovah will not forsake His people, for His great Name's sake, because it hath pleased Jehovah to make you His people.*" [4]

(2) As we read here of Israel's folly and God's yearning lament, "*Oh that they were wise; that they would consider their latter end!*" should we not ask: How is it with us? How do *we* live and act? Do *we* sufficiently consider "our latter end," and apply

[1] Neh. ix. 31. [2] Jer. xxx. 11.
[3] Lam. iii. 32. [4] 1 Sam. xii. 22.

our hearts unto wisdom ?   Do we judge of the present
in the light of the future : of time in the light of
eternity ; and is it our aim above all things to walk in
the path of well-pleasingness unto God ?   And how
much fruit, and of *what kind*, do we bear unto Him
for whom He has done even more than He did for
Israel as a nation ?

8

JEHOVAH'S INTERPOSITION ON BEHALF OF HIS PEOPLE: THE FINAL EVENTS OF THIS AGE

THE last strophe—as stated in the brief analysis at the beginning of the exposition—speaks of the judgments which will be poured out on the enemies of God and of His people, and will reach their climax in the last solemn events of this age.

As Jehovah " saw " (verse 19) and took note of the sins and rebellion of Israel, and in due time, when His long-suffering was exhausted, sent the terrible judgments which have overtaken them, and which are to culminate in the final great tribulation through which as a nation they have yet to pass, so also is He by no means indifferent to the conduct of the nations in relation to His people. He has " seen " and noted all the oppressions, the pitiless cruelties and brutalities of which the Gentile world-powers have been guilty in their dealings with the people which—in spite of all their many sins and long-continued apostasy—is still " beloved for the fathers' sake."

" Is not this laid up in store with Me,
Sealed up among My treasures" (or *"in My treasuries")?*

i.e., kept safely and ready to be brought forth at the appointed time when—Israel's day of mercy having come—He shall " put all these curses upon their enemies, and on them that hate him and persecute him " [1] and " pour out His fury upon the nations that know Him not, and upon the families that call not on His Name ; because they have devoured Jacob, yea, they have devoured him and consumed him, and have laid waste his habitation."

The wicked actions of the nations together with the wrath of God which is sure to follow, are spoken of as " laid up," and " sealed " in God's treasuries, in the same way as the transgression and iniquity of the individual are said to be " sealed up in a bag," [2] *i.e.*, kept safe to be produced in the day of judgment when they shall all be " set in order " again before the eyes of the sinner,[3] so that the opened book of his own conscience may attest the faithful accuracy of the terrible record which has been preserved by God ; for although (to use another figure) " sin does not purpose to remember or be remembered, it registers itself with perfect and unfailing regularity in two books—the book of God which shall be opened on that day, and on our own character, mind and imagination. Only the blood of Christ can blot out sin from the one book, only the Spirit of God from the other." [4]

But to return more closely to our context : the day when the " seals " shall be broken so that the iniquity which the nations have committed may be laid bare, and the successive judgments which have also been " laid up " in God's treasuries be let loose, is " the day of vengeance of our God " [5] which synchronises with the commencement of " the year of His redeemed " [6] when Israel's Redeemer shall be manifested a second time, not as the meek and lowly one to be led as a lamb to the slaughter, but in His power and glory to execute the judgments committed to Him by the Father, to

---

[1] Deut. xxx. 7. [2] Job xiv. 17. [3] Ps. l. 21.
[4] Adolph Saphir. [5] Isa. lxi. 2. [6] Isa. lxiii. 4.

" tread down the peoples in His anger, and to trample them in His wrath." And this long-delayed work of vengeance He has reserved entirely for Himself. This is brought out with emphasis in the order in which the words are placed in the original :

" *Mine is vengeance and recompense.*"

To no one else can the execution of it be entrusted, and least of all to frail, passionate man. Only in the hands of the Judge of all the earth is there an absolute guarantee that its infliction will be in the fullest accord with perfect righteousness without excess, or a spirit of vindictiveness on the one hand, or a stopping short of the strictest requirements of justice on the other hand.

Twice is this verse from the national song of Israel quoted with slight variations in the New Testament. Once as an exhortation to Christians not to avenge themselves, but to endure patiently and to give place to the wrath of God which—except they repent—is sure to overtake their enemies and oppressors in due time ; [1] and once as a solemn warning to those who stood in danger of apostasy from the faith, after they had once received the knowledge of the truth, and for whom—should they yield to the temptation and fall away—there would be nothing left " but a certain fearful expectation of judgment and a fierceness of fire which shall devour " God's adversaries. " *For we know Him that said vengeance belongeth unto Me, and I will recompense. . . . It is a fearful thing to fall into the hands of the living God.*" [2]

I ought, however, to state that some scholars regard the little Hebrew word ‫לִי‬—*li* (" to me ") with which the 35th verse begins as an abbreviation of ‫לְיוֹם‬—*l'yom*——" for the day," and that this is the reading in the

[1] Rom. xii. 19.   [2] Heb. x. 26–31.

Septuagint version, and the Samaritan Pentateuch, as well as of the Targum of Onkelos.   This also is more in accord with the context.   Verses 35 and 36 together would then read thus :

> " *Is not this laid up in store with Me,*
> *Sealed up in My treasuries ?*
> *For the day of vengeance and recompense,*
> *For the time when their foot shall slip ?* "

The figure of the " slipping " or tottering foot is often used in the Scriptures for sudden calamity or " reverse of fortune."   In the case of the righteous it is an occasion for the Lord to intervene with His sustaining grace and power.   This the Psalmist could sing :

> " When I said, My foot slippeth
> Thy mercy, O Jehovah, held me up." [1]

But in the case of the wicked it is the beginning of a whole series of judgments, and the occasion for God to hasten their complete destruction.   For when their cup of iniquity is quite filled up, and the appointed " day of vengeance " has at last come, there will no longer be delay in the execution of the wrath of God which has for long been " laid up in store " with Him, ready to be poured out on His adversaries :

> " *For the day of their calamity is at hand,*
> *And the things that are to come upon them shall make*
> *haste.*"

And it is *the extremity of Israel's need* which provokes God's final interposition on their behalf :

> " *For Jehovah will judge His people,*
> *And repent Himself for His servants.*"

These two lines are repeated *verbatim* in Ps. cxxxv. 14.

[1] Ps. xciv. 18.

" Judge " means here to " vindicate " ; to assert
Himself on their behalf as the God who pleadeth the
cause of His people.[1] In this sense the term יָדִין—
yadin—from דִין—*din*—is often used in the Scriptures.
Thus, for instance, Rachel said, when her handmaid
Bilhah had born her a son : " *God hath judged me, and
hath also heard my voice ; therefore she called his name
Dan* " (*i.e.* " He judgeth ") ;[2] and David prays :
" *Save me, O God, by Thy Name, and judge me* (i.e.
" *strive for me*," " *vindicate my cause* ") *by Thy might.*" [3]
Thus He will " judge His people " by identifying Himself with their cause, and by pouring out His wrath
upon their enemies.

And He will do this when they are brought quite to
an end of themselves :

" *When He seeth that their power is gone
And there is none remaining shut up or left at large.*"

Just as in the past, when they were under premonitory
judgments, " *Jehovah saw the affliction of Israel that it
was very bitter ; and that there was none shut up nor left
at large,*" [4] *i.e.* none remaining safe from the power of
their oppressors, He was moved with compassion for
them, and sent them temporary deliverance ; so also
in their final trouble, at the time of the end, when the
cry of the confederated hosts will be : " *Come and let
us cut them off from being a nation ; that the name of
Israel be no more in remembrance,*" their extreme
wretchedness, and the danger of their being totally
annihilated, will stir up His heart of compassion for
them and cause Him to appear as their deliverer.

And in that day of the extremity of their need God
will speak to their hearts and consciences, and bring

---

[1] Isa. li. 22.   [2] Gen. xxx. 8.
[3] Ps. liv. 1.   [4] 2 Kings xiv. 26.

home to them the conviction that the false gods in
which they trusted were but refuges of lies, and thus,
by creating a spirit of repentance in their hearts, make
it possible for Him to interpose on their behalf.

> " *And He will say, Where are their gods,*
> *The rock in which they took refuge ;*
> *Which did eat the fat of their sacrifices,*
> *And drink the wine of their drink-offerings ?*
> *Let them rise up and help you,*
> *Let them be your protection."*

The term " rock " is in this passage (as also in verse
31) ironically applied to the false gods on whom they
had built their hopes, but which in time of need proved
only *sand.* Some regard these verses as addressed to
the Gentile oppressors of Israel as a warning that in
the day when Jehovah rises up in judgment against
them, their idols in whom they trusted and to whom
they offered their sacrifices and drink-offerings, will not
be able to deliver them from His wrath. But similar
language is addressed by God *to Israel* in Judg. x. 14–16,
and Jer. ii. 28, and it is best to understand the words
here too as spoken to them. In Judg. x., we read,
that after God had said : " *Go and cry unto the gods
which ye have chosen ; let them save you in the time of
your distress,*" that they turned unto Him with the
cry, " *We have sinned . . . do Thou unto us whatsoever
seemeth good unto Thee . . . and they put away the
foreign gods from among them and served Jehovah ; and
His soul was grieved for the misery of Israel,*" and He
wrought deliverance for them.

So also will it be in their final trouble, when the
folly as well as the sin of their having forsaken Him,
the fountain of Living Waters, to hew out for themselves
cisterns, broken cisterns that can hold no water, will
be brought home to them by the Spirit of God. A

bitter cry of repentance will rise from among them, and
" *a voice shall be heard upon the high places, even the
weeping and supplications of the children of Israel,
because they have perverted their way, they have forgotten
Jehovah their God.*" And when the voice of Jehovah
breaks in upon them with the gracious words : " *Return,
ye backsliding children, I will heal your backslidings,*"
the ready response of the godly remnant will be, " *Behold
we come unto Thee, for Thou art Jehovah our God. Truly
in vain is help (or ' Salvation ') looked for from the hills,
and from the multitude (or ' the tumult ') of the mountains :
truly in Jehovah our God (and in Him alone) is the
salvation of Israel.*" [1]

But, it may be asked, the Jews are not now idolaters,
and no longer worship the vanities of the heathen as
they so frequently did before the Babylonian captivity.
How, then, can these Scriptures be applied to the time
of the end ? The answer is that the present condition
of unbelief and the rejection of the Messiah by the
Jewish nation " is the continuation of their ancient
idolatry, apostasy, and rebellion." Idolatry was the
climax of the first stage in the progressive apostasy of
Israel which brought about the Babylonian captivity
with which commences " *the times of the Gentiles,*" which
only close with the end of this age, when the Kingdom
shall once again be restored to Israel.

It was because of the alienation of their hearts from
God, which is the very essence of idolatry, that—when
in the fulness of time He appeared who is the very
image of the invisible God—the Jews recognised Him
not, and turned their backs upon Him. Besides, there
are other idols than those made of silver, or gold, or
wood, or stone, and to these " idols of the heart " (or
of the intellect)—the worship of which is no less

[1] Jer. iii. 21–23.

idolatry, and not less symptomatic of apostasy from the true and living God—Jews and Gentiles are still offering their devotions, and presenting their sacrifices and their drink-offerings. And in the day of God's wrath these modern idols will avail men as little as the false gods of the heathen.

But to return to our context : How glorious is Jehovah our God, when contrasted with the " vanities of the nations," as the prophets characterise their false gods ! [1]

" *See now* (He says) *that I, even I, am He,*
And there is no god with Me :
I kill, and I make alive ;
I wound, and I heal ;
And there is none that can deliver out of My hand."

The sublime reiteration—אֲנִי אֲנִי הוּא—*ani, ani-hu*—" I, I, am He," occurs here for the first time, and is frequently echoed in later Scriptures, and particularly in the *second* part of Isaiah.

" *I (even) I, am Jehovah* "— to quote only one brief passage out of many similar ones in that sublime prophecy—" *and besides Me there is no Saviour . . . since the day was, I am He ; and there is none that can deliver out of My hand. I will work and who can hinder it ?* " [2]

See then, now, " *that I, even I, am He,*" i.e. " God exclusively, and God for ever " : the Great " *I Am* "; the everlasting, unchangeable *living* God—the unseen, yet omnipresent and self-consistent Ruler of the universe. This is the Bible's answer to the polytheistic systems of the heathen on the one hand, which start with the lie that there be gods many, and lords many, and to the pantheistic philosophies of the

[1] Jer. xiv. 22.   [2] Isa. xliii. 11–13.

modern world on the other hand, which deny a personal creator, and *confound God with His creation.* And He is the absolute and sovereign Lord : " There is no god with Me," He says. " Before Me there was no god formed, neither shall there be after Me." There is none to withstand His power or to resist His authority :

> " *I kill and I make alive ;*
> *I wound and I heal* "—

sublime words which are echoed by Hannah in her prophetic song,[1] and other inspired souls, and denote not only " His incontestable authority to dispose of all His creatures and the being He has given them, so as to suit His own purposes by them," but describe His process with those whom He chooses, and calls, and fits for communion with Him now, and for still more intimate friendship with Him through eternity. Note, it is not life before death, but *death before life.* The end He has in view in His dealings with His people is always beneficent, and if He kills, it is in order to make them truly alive ; and if He wounds, it is with a view to their healing. Some Jewish Rabbis see here a reference to the life after death, which may be true ; but this life does not begin in " the world to come," as they express it, but is the new life in God which follows the being " killed " (or death) to self, and begins already in time, but *goes on* through eternity.

And His power, when once exerted—whether in the deliverance of His people or in the punishment of His enemies—is *irresistible.* " *There is none that can deliver out of My hand,*" He says, for " as there can be no appeal from the sentence of God's justice, so is there no escape from the execution of His power."

---

[1] 1 Sam. ii. 6–8 ; Lam. iii. 31–33 ; Hos. vi. 1, 2.

In the last four verses, the sublimity and solemnity
of this inspired Song attain their climax.

It is the day of Jehovah's manifested glory, and He
stands forth in His terrible majesty as the avenger of
His people. He announces beforehand the judgments
He is about to inflict on the nations, to warn them and
to give them still the chance to avert His wrath by
true repentance. We think of the solemn warning in
the 2nd Psalm, which refers to the same time :

" Now therefore be wise, O ye kings :
    Be instructed, ye judges of the earth . . ."
" Kiss the Son, lest He be angry and ye perish in the
    way,
    For His wrath will soon be kindled." [1]

For when He at last rises up in judgment there will
be no more delay nor escape.

" *For I lift up My hand to heaven*
And say, as I live for ever
If I whet My glittering sword (literally, ' *the lightning*
    of My sword ')
And My hand take hold on judgment ;
I will render vengeance to Mine adversaries,
And will recompense them that hate Me.
I will make Mine arrows drunk with blood,
And My sword shall devour flesh ;
With the blood of the slain and the captives
From the head of the leaders of the enemy (*or* ' *of the*
    chief leader of the enemy ')."

The lifting up of the hand as a gesture on the part
of one taking an oath, is frequently used in Scripture,[2]
and is intended to imply that He appeals to God as a

---

[1] Or " Lest ye perish in the way if His wrath be kindled but a
little."

[2] Ex. vi. 8 ; Num. xiv. 30 ; Ezek. xx. 5, 6, 15, 23 ; Dan. xii. 7 ;
Rev. x. 5, 6.

witness to the truth of His affirmation, and that He is willing to incur the vengeance of Heaven should He prove false to His pledged word. This Jehovah in His condescension applies to Himself, and since He can swear by no greater, He swears by Himself. Not that His bare word is not sufficient, or needs confirmation, but to impress the minds of doubting men with the *double* certainty (of His word and His oath) that what He promises or threatens He will assuredly fulfil. " I lift up My hands to Heaven, the habitation of My holiness," He says, and " swear by Myself who lives for ever, if I whet My lightning sword," etc.

Jehovah is depicted here as a mighty warrior arming Himself for the conflict. He lays hold on judgment as though it were a weapon lying at His side in readiness to be hurled at His foes. It reminds us of the description in Isaiah lix., which refers to the same time, and also describes His final interposition on Israel's behalf : " *And He saw that there was no man, and wondered that there was no intercessor : therefore His own arm brought salvation unto Him, and His righteousness it upheld Him. And He put on righteousness as a breastplate, and an helmet of salvation upon His head ; and He put on garments of vengeance for clothing, and was clad with zeal as a cloak. According to their deeds, accordingly He will repay, fury to His adversaries, recompense to His enemies ; to the islands He will repay recompense.*"

And the lightning sword of Jehovah's judgments will fall first on the " head of the leaders of the enemy," or the " *head of the chief leader of the enemy,*" [1] as the

---

[1] The last clause of the 42nd verse is somewhat difficult, and has been variously rendered and interpreted. The three Hebrew words are מֵרֹאשׁ פַּרְעוֹת אוֹיֵב—*merosh par'oth oyebh.* The first and the last words are simple enough, and mean " from the head " (of the) " enemy,"

last clause of the 42nd verse may be rendered—in which there is a probable prophetic reference to the Antichrist, " the chief leader " in the final confederacy of the Gentile hosts, in their attempt to exterminate the Jewish nation.[1] Anyhow, this apocalyptic vision of Moses, of the final overthrow of the enemies of God and of His people with which the " National Song of Israel " closes, will receive its full historical fulfilment at the manifestation in Divine glory of our Lord Jesus, the executor of God's vengeance on the antichristian nations, as well as on individuals who know not God and obey not His Gospel ; and who shall first of all " slay with the breath of His mouth " that " wicked " or " lawless one," who will not only martyr the saints of God, but be " the chief leader " in the final desperate effort to destroy the nation with which the Name of Jehovah as " the God of Israel " is specially bound up.

" And I saw the heaven opened ; and behold, a white horse, and He that sat thereon, called Faithful and True ; and in righteousness He doth judge and

---

but the second or middle word is not only uncertain as to its derivation, but has the peculiarity of being a masculine noun with a plural feminine termination. The Authorised Version has translated the clause " from the beginning of revenges upon the enemy " ; the Revised Version " From the head of the leaders of the enemy," with an alternative marginal reading, " From the hairy head of the enemy " ; while Keil, Knobel, Driver, and others translate " from the long-haired heads of the foe." Luther's translation is " über dem entblössten Haupt des Feindes " (" over the exposed head of the enemy "), but the critical translation of " Die Heilige Schrift " by Kautzsch and others renders " Vom Haupte der Führer des Feindes " (" From the head of the leader of the enemy "). The Septuagint makes a paraphrase of the sentence, thus : " From the captivity of the heads of their enemies that rule over them." The word pira'oth is found in the Song of Deborah (Judg. v. 2), where the phrase בִּפְרֹעַ פְּרָעוֹת בְּיִשְׂרָאֵל—biph'ro'a pira'oth b'ysrael is rendered in the Authorised Version " for the avenging of Israel," but more correctly in the Revised Version, " For that the leaders took the lead in Israel."

[1] Zech. xii.

make war. And His eyes are a flame of fire, and upon
His head are many diadems; and He hath a name
written, which no one knoweth but He Himself. And
He is arrayed in a garment sprinkled with blood : and
His name is called The Word of God. And the armies
which are in heaven followed Him upon white horses,
clothed in fine linen, white and pure. And out of His
mouth proceedeth a sharp sword, that with it He should
smite the nations; and He shall rule them with a rod
of iron : and He treadeth the winepress of the fierceness
of the wrath of Almighty God. And He hath on His
garment and on His thigh a name written, KING OF
KINGS AND LORD OF LORDS.

" And I saw an angel standing in the sun ; and he
cried with a loud voice, saying to all the birds that fly
in mid-heaven, Come and be gathered together unto
the great supper of God ; that ye may eat the flesh of
kings, and the flesh of captains, and the flesh of mighty
men, and the flesh of horses and of them that sit thereon,
and the flesh of all men, both free and bond, and small
and great " (Rev. xix. 11–18).

In the last verse we reach the climax and goal, not
only of this sublime Song, but of all prophecy. It
contemplates the time when the purpose of God in the
call and election of Abraham and his seed—that in and
through them all the families of the earth should be
blessed—will be fully realised. When not only shall
Israel be pardoned and cleansed and reconciled, and the
land itself be purged from its defilements, and become
indeed the " Holy Land," but when all nations shall walk
in the light of Jehovah, and rejoice *together with saved
Israel* in the blessings of Messiah's reign, which shall
extend from Mount Zion even unto the ends of the earth.

" *Rejoice (or ' shout for joy '), O ye nations, with His
    people :* [1]

[1] The verb *har'ninu* is in *hiphil* form, and is capable of being rendered, " O ye nations, make His people to rejoice." Another possible

For He will avenge the blood of His servants,
And will render vengeance to His adversaries,
And will make expiation for His land and for His
    people."

The first line of this verse is quoted by the Apostle
Paul in Romans xv. as part of his argument that
Gentiles too may now glorify God for His mercy in
sending our Lord Jesus Christ into the world. But
the fulfilment of this Scripture (like some of the other
great prophecies about the future which are quoted in
the New Testament) is only a *partial one* so far. Many
millions of individuals from among the Gentiles have
indeed " rejoiced " with " the remnant according to
the election of grace from among Israel "—" His
people "—since Christ came into the world, and have
glorified His Name for His great mercy to them in
making them who were before " far off," *i.e.* " outside
the commonwealth of Israel and strangers from the
covenants of the promise," " nigh in the blood of
Christ."

But it is only after " the receiving again " of Israel
as a nation that *the full tide of universal blessing* will
come to the world, and that the call will go forth,
" *Rejoice, O ye nations, with His people.*" Then the
knowledge of the glory of Jehovah shall cover this
earth as the waters cover the sea.

The saved nations, together with Israel, are to
rejoice also because God at last avenges the " blood
of His servants," and " renders vengeance to His
adversaries."

translation is, " O ye nations, shout for joy at His people." The Vulgate
has, " Ye nations praise His people," and still other renderings have
been suggested, but the translation in the English versions, which is
also that of the Septuagint, is doubtless the correct one, and has the
sanction of the Apostle Paul, who quotes it in this form from the Greek.

The occasion of this joy is not that terrible sufferings are inflicted on their persecutors and tormentors,
but the fact that God's justice and righteousness are
manifested and vindicated in the judgments which are
poured out on their enemies and " His."

In like manner we read in the 18th and 19th chapters
of Revelation, in connection with the pouring out of
God's judgment on Babylon the great—the rival of
Zion, the city of God at the time of the end : " *Rejoice
over her, thou heaven and ye apostles and ye prophets ;
for God hath judged your judgment on her.*" And again :
" *After these things I heard as it were a great voice in
heaven, saying, Hallelujah, salvation and glory and power
belong to our God ; for true and righteous are His judgments,
for He hath judged the great harlot, her that had corrupted
the earth with her fornication, and He hath avenged the
blood of His servants at her hand.*" [1]

The last line of this truly wonderful prophetic Song
is rendered in the Authorised Version : " *And will be
merciful unto His land and to His people,*" but the three
Hebrew words, עַמּוֹ אַדְמָתוֹ וְכִפֶּר—*v'khiper ad'matho amo*
literally mean : " *And He will atone,*" or " *make
expiation,*" for His land and for His people," and reveal
the ground of God's merciful dealings with Israel. At the
typical redemption—on the night when the avenging
angel executed judgment on Egypt—Israel was saved on
the ground of the sprinkled blood of the paschal lamb.
So also in the future final greater national and spiritual
redemption, the Jewish people will be saved by blood
—the much more precious blood of the Lamb of God,
" who died for the nation," and " not for the nation
only, but that He might gather together into one the
children of God that are scattered abroad " ; [2] for what
is meant here by " making atonement " is the *applica-*

[1] Rev. xviii. 20, xix. 112.   [2] John xi. 51, 52.

tion to their own hearts and consciences as a people of
the atoning work of their Messiah, accomplished once
and for all on Calvary's Cross.

And this will take place when the Spirit of grace
and of supplications is poured out on them as a nation,
and they look upon Him whom they have pierced,
and mourn. That—as I have shown elsewhere [1]—will
be Israel's great national Day of Atonement, when
Jehovah of Hosts " will remove the iniquity of that
land in one day," [2] for not only will the people be
pardoned, cleansed, and reconciled, but—as already
stated above—*the land itself* shall be purged from
defilement so that it shall be " the Holy Land " as
never before.

Note *the last words* of this great Scripture, which
might be said to sum up all prophecy in relation to
the Jews and Palestine : " *His* land, and *His* people."
Of no other land, and of no other people *as a people*,
does He speak in the same way. For the land is
in a very special sense " Immanuel's Land," [3] and
" Jehovah's portion is His people ; Jacob is the lot of
His inheritance."

This, then, is how Jewish history ends : not in
unbelief and apostasy, but in a glorious restoration, to
be followed by a national conversion which will be as
" life from the dead " to the whole world. Well might
the Apostle Paul conclude his unfolding of the
" mystery " of God with Israel in chapters ix., x., and
xi. of the Epistle to the Romans with the adoring
exclamation :

" *O the depth of the riches both of the wisdom and
the knowledge of God ! how unsearchable are His judg-*

[1] See the exposition of Zechariah iii. in *Visions and Prophecies of
Zechariah.* Reprinted 1972 by Kregel Publications
[2] Zech. iii. 9.   [3] Isa. viii. 8.

*ments, and His ways past tracing out!   For who hath
known the mind of the Lord?   or who hath been His
counsellor?   or who hath first given to Him, and it shall
be recompensed unto Him again?   For of Him, and
through Him, and unto Him, are all things.   To Him be
the glory for ever.   Amen* " (Rom. xi. 33–36).

Part 2

JEHOVAH'S MARVELLOUS WORKS FOR HIS PEOPLE

Psalm 105

Psalm 105

Oh give thanks unto Jehovah, call upon His name
Make known among the peoples His doings.
Sing unto Him, sing praises unto Him ;
Talk ye of all His marvellous works.
Glory ye in His holy name :
Let the heart of them rejoice that seek Jehovah.
Seek ye Jehovah and His strength ;
Seek His face evermore.
Remember His marvellous works that He hath done :
His wonders, and the judgments of His mouth,
O ye seed of Abraham His servant,
Ye children of Jacob, His chosen ones.
He is Jehovah our God :
His judgments are in all the earth.
He hath remembered His covenant for ever,
The word which He commanded to a thousand generations,
The covenant which He made with Abraham,
And His oath unto Isaac,
And confirmed the same unto Jacob for a statute,
To Israel for an everlasting covenant,
Saying, Unto thee will I give the land of Canaan,
The lot of your inheritance ;
When they were but a few men in number,
Yea, very few, and sojourners in it.
And they went about from nation to nation,
From one kingdom to another people.
He suffered no man to do them wrong ;
Yea, He reproved kings for their sakes,
Saying, Touch not Mine anointed ones,
And do My prophets no harm.
And He called for a famine upon the land ;
He brake the whole staff of bread.
He sent a man before them ;
Joseph was sold for a servant ;
His feet they hurt with fetters :
He was laid in chains of iron,
Until the time that His word came to pass,
The word of Jehovah tried him.

The king sent and loosed him ;
Even the ruler of peoples, and let him go free.
He made him lord of his house,
And ruler of all his substance ;
To bind his princes at his pleasure,
And teach his elders wisdom.
Israel also came into Egypt ;
And Jacob sojourned in the land of Ham.
And He increased His people greatly,
And made them stronger than their adversaries.
He turned their heart to hate His people,
To deal subtly with His servants.
He sent Moses His servant,
And Aaron whom He had chosen.
They set among them His signs,
And wonders in the land of Ham.
He sent darkness, and made it dark ;
And they rebelled not against His words.
He turned their waters into blood,
And slew their fish.
Their land swarmed with frogs
In the chambers of their kings.
He spake, and there came swarms of flies,
And lice in all their borders.
He gave them hail for rain,
And flaming fire in their land.
He smote their vines also and their fig-trees,
And brake the trees of their borders.
He spake, and the locust came,
And the grasshopper, and that without number,
And did eat up every herb in their land,
And did eat up the fruit of their ground.
He smote also all the first-born in their land,
The chief of all their strength.
And He brought them forth with silver and gold ;
And there was not one feeble person among His tribes.
Egypt was glad when they departed ;
For the fear of them had fallen upon them.

He spread a cloud for a covering,
And fire to give light in the night.
They asked, and He brought quails,
And satisfied them with the bread of heaven.
He opened the rock, and waters gushed out ;
They ran in the dry places like a river.
For He remembered His holy word,
And Abraham His servant.
And He brought forth His people with joy,
And His chosen with singing.
And He gave them the lands of the nations ;
And they took the labour of the peoples in possession :
That they might keep His statutes,
And observe His laws.
Praise ye, Jehovah.

9

" REMEMBER HIS MARVELLOUS WORKS THAT HE HATH DONE "

AN EXPOSITION OF PSALM CV

THIS Psalm is a recital of the earliest part of Israel's history, viz. from the call of Abraham to the entrance into Canaan.

The object of the inspired singer is not only to stir up the hearts of the people with praise and worship to their all-glorious and faithful God, but to strengthen their faith and awaken new hope in relation to the future, by a consideration of His wondrous works of power and of grace which He wrought for them in the past.

Let us first take a brief glance at the Psalm as a whole.

There is, perhaps, some probability in the suggestion that the " Hallelujah," which stands at the end of Psalm civ., does not belong there, but really forms the first word of Psalm cv.

It would then begin in the same way as the 106th, which is clearly intended as a companion Psalm, for it takes up and continues the narrative where it is left in the 105th. Both are retrospective and didactic ; but Psalm cv. deals entirely with God's unfailing faithfulness to Israel, while Psalm cvi. sets forth the sad contrast presented by Israel's continued faithlessness to God.

" Each theme is made more impressive by being pursued separately, and then set over against the other. The long series of God's mercies massed together here confronts the dark uniformity of Israel's unworthy requital of them there. Half of the sky is pure blue and radiant sunshine ; half is piled up with unbroken clouds. Nothing drives home the consciousness of sin so surely as contemplation of God's loving-kindness."

The whole of Psalm cv. may be divided into six strophes of unequal length.

The first six verses form the *call*, or *exhortation*, addressed to the people to make joyful confession unto Jehovah, and to praise His Name, in view of His marvellous dealings with them, as attested by their history which the Psalm is about to narrate.

The narrative itself properly falls into five parts :

I. God's dealings with them in the earliest part of their history, viz. the Patriarchal period.

This section lays special and joyful emphasis on the everlasting covenant which the faithful God, out of His free grace, made with the fathers, which covenant is the basis of all His subsequent dealings with them as a nation (verses 7–15).

II. An inspired poetic summary of God's overruling providences which brought Israel into the land of Egypt—a link in the chain which led to the fulfilment of the promise in reference to the land (verses 16–22).

III. Israel's experiences in Egypt (verses 23–27).

IV. The story of the signs and wonders which God wrought on Israel's behalf in Egypt—the series of plagues which paralysed the power of Egypt and made the Egyptians willing to let Israel go (verses 28–38).

V. Then, finally, the story of God's wonderful works on their behalf in the wilderness, until He brought them safely into the Promised Land (verses 39–45).

From this bare outline let us now turn to the actual contents and seek to enter into the spirit of the Psalm.

THE CALL TO PRAISE AND TESTIMONY

Not to enter more fully into the discussion as to the proper place of the word Hallelujah, with which Psalm civ. ends, the 105th, as it now stands in all MSS. and versions, begins with the word הודו—*Hodu* (" give thanks "), as is the case also with three other Psalms.[1]

The etymological significance of this word, which is frequently used for praise in the Hebrew Scriptures, is that of *praiseful acknowledgment,* or *thankful confession,* and the phrase *Hodu la-Yehovah* means not only " *give thanks,*" but " *joyfully confess* unto Jehovah " —that is, confess His goodness, confess His faithfulness, seek in a spirit of worship and adoration to set forth in His presence and in the presence of His people what you have actually learned and known of the praiseworthiness of His character, and what you have yourself experienced of His grace and loving kindness.

This is one great difference between the praise which men render to their fellow-men and that which we seek to render to God. In our ascriptions of praise to men, however relatively worthy, we are frequently in danger of stepping over the bounds of truth and of falling into flattery and adulation, but never so in our offerings of praise to the all-glorious Jehovah, " Who is exalted above all blessing and praise " which human lips can render to Him. The very utmost, therefore, to which we can rise in our worship and thanksgiving to Him are but feeble and inadequate *confessions,* which fall short by ten thousand degrees of the actual

[1] *i.e.* cvii., cxviii., and cxxxvi.

glories of His character, and the Divine perfection of all His ways.

The phrase which follows, קִרְאוּ בִשְׁמוֹ—*qir'u bhish'mo*, is not adequately rendered in our English versions by the words, " *Call upon His Name.*" The expression is used in the Hebrew Scriptures not only of solemn attestation of God in praise and prayer, but in discourse.[1] It is brought over from Genesis. Of Abraham, God's first great missionary, we read that wherever he was in his wanderings, after each fresh revelation of the God of Glory, that he " builded an altar "—*va'y-qra, beshem Yehovah*—and called not only *on*, but *in* and *with* ; that is, he openly *published,* or proclaimed, the Name Jehovah (*i.e.* the Being, the character of the true and living God), as a solemn confession and testimony against the idolatries all around.

This is a call, or invitation, then, to Israel—in view of God's wonderful works on their behalf, which the Psalm is about to narrate—not only to " *call upon* His Name " in solemn praise and thanksgiving, but to *publish abroad* the ever-blessed Name, the significance of which has already been explained in a previous chapter.

A confirmation of what has just been said is found in the last sentence of the first verse, which in the Hebrew is an exact repetition of words already found in Psalm ix. 11.

" *Make known,*" not among the *people,* as in the Authorised Version, but " *among the peoples His doings.*"

---

[1] Thus we have the idiom—*qir'u tsom,* " ' call upon ' (or ' *proclaim* ') a fast " (1 Kings xxi. 9). *Qir'u a'tsarah,* " ' call ' (*i.e.* ' *proclaim* ') a solemn assembly " (Joel i. 14, ii. 15). *Qir'u baggoyim,* " ' call ' (or ' *proclaim* ') among the nations " (Joel iii. 9). *Qir'u ele-ah,* " ' call ' (or ' *proclaim* ') unto her " (Isa. xl. 2). All of which show that *qir'u* means, not only to call, but to publish, or proclaim.

Now עַם—*am*, in the singular, generally stands for
the people, *i.e.* Israel, but the plural עַמִּים—*amim*, for
the other " peoples," *i.e.* the Gentile nations. It is
a call, therefore, to Israel " to declare the glory of
Jehovah *among the nations*,"[1] and a reminder of the
original purpose which God had in the election and
call of this peculiar people.

Men sometimes ignorantly talk of the God of the
Hebrews, especially as He is said to be represented
in the earlier part of their history, as the tribal, or
national God of the Jews. But this is altogether
contrary to fact. From the very beginning, when God
called Abraham, His word of promise to him was
" In thee " (which was a little later more fully defined
as " in thy seed ") " shall all the families of the
earth be blessed." It is true—to repeat words of
my own from elsewhere—that for centuries God
limited the knowledge of Himself to one land and one
people, but the very limitation was designed with a
view to the better accomplishment of its ultimate
diffusion.

Israel's inspired historians, psalmists, and prophets
do often speak of Jehovah as their very *own* God, but
only in the sense in which the New Testament speaks
of God as " the Saviour of all men, *but especially of
them that believe*."

For ages He *was* their God only, and in the words
of the Hallel, " Judah was His sanctuary, Israel was
His dominion," when the gods of the other nations
were vile abominations, " the works of men's hands."
With right, therefore, could they cry unto Him, " We
are Thine ! As for our adversaries, Thou never barest
rule over them, they were not called by Thy Name,"
but, at the same time, they rejoiced in the expectation,

[1] Ps. xcvi. 3.

and greeted from afar the promises of a time when, from Israel and Jerusalem as the centre, the knowledge of Jehovah would cover the earth and all the nations would walk in His light.

Apart from 1 Chron. xvi. 8–22, where the first fifteen verses of our Psalm are found embodied, the whole of the first verse is found also in the beautiful little millennial song which forms the conclusion and climax of the " Book of Immanuel." [1] There we are, so to say, prophetically transplanted into the time when Israel, as a nation, shall at last respond to this call and fulfil the original purpose which God had in choosing them from among the other nations, viz. that they may be His witnesses and show forth His praise throughout the earth.

"And in that day," we read—the " day," viz. not only of their national restoration but of *their conversion,* when " with joy they shall draw waters from the wells of salvation," and when the " Holy One of Israel," in the person of the long-rejected, but now exalted, Messiah, shall be visibly manifested in the very " midst " of them—" *shall ye say, ' Hodu la-Yehovah,' ' give thanks '* (or, ' *make joyful confession ')* *unto Jehovah, publish abroad His Name, declare His doings among the peoples, make mention "* (or, " *cause it to be remembered ")* " *that His Name is exalted."* Thus shall they encourage and stir up one another in this holy task of spreading abroad the knowledge of their glorious Redeemer and King, until in a short time the earth shall be filled with the knowledge of His glory, as the waters cover the sea.

It is significant also that, as in Psalm cv., so also in

[1] Isa. xii., chaps. vii.–xii. have been thus designated, because the hope and promise contained in the name Immanuel are prominent throughout this section of Isaiah's prophecies.

Isa. xii. 4, the " making known of His doings " is the parallelism to the " publishing abroad of His Name," for it is in these deeds of power and grace that His character is revealed. " What God has done," to quote from another writer, " is the best revelation of what *God is*. His messengers are not to speak their own thoughts about Him, but to tell the story of His acts and let these speak for Him. Revelation is not a set of propositions, but a history of divine facts." But to proceed to the second verse :

> " *Sing unto Him, sing praises unto Him ;*
> *Talk ye of all His marvellous works.*"

The verb שִׂיחוּ—*sichu* (from שִׂיחַ—*si'ach*), rendered in the English versions " talk ye," primarily means " to *muse*," " to *meditate*," " to *consider*," and is used also *occasionally* for " talking " or " speaking." Both ideas are meant to be expressed here, viz. " meditate " on God's wonderful works for yourselves, and " talk " of them to others ; and, as a matter of fact and experience, the more we are given to meditation, the more ready also are we to talk of God's wonderful character and ways to others. " *While I was musing*," says the inspired poet in Psalm xxxix., " *the fire kindled, then spake I with my tongue.*" [1]

This has ever been the experience of God's redeemed people ; and the reason why our hearts are so often cold, and that there is such unreadiness on our part to speak for God with our tongues, is that we do not sufficiently " muse " or " meditate " on " all His marvellous works," nor consider the greater things which God has done for us in Christ, as compared even with that which He did for Israel, as a nation, when He brought them out of Egypt.

[1] Ps. xxxix. 3.

The Holy Name

The first line of the third verse reminds us of Israel's unique calling and mission—

"*Glory ye in His holy Name.*"

" The Name " (as we have already seen in the exposition of Deut. xxxii. 3) is *the embodiment of God's revealed character*, as He has progressively made Himself known to His people, not only as their Creator, but as *their Saviour and Friend*—in short, as " Jehovah," the God of covenant and promise, " the God of Abraham, of Isaac, and of Jacob," of which He says, " *This is My Name for ever, and this is My Memorial unto all generations.*"

And it is of importance to note that the outstanding characteristic—the chief glory which attaches to the self-revealed name of Jehovah—is *holiness.* " *Holy and terrible is His Name,*" [1] is the unanimous testimony of those who stood nearest to Him and knew Him best. Or, as another inspired Psalmist expresses it, " *Let them praise Thy great and terrible Name, for it is holy.*" [2]

It is this glorious fact, above all others, that distinguishes the religion of Israel from all other religions, and lifts the Bible above the so-called sacred books of the heathen, as high as the heavens are above the earth. The false gods of the pagan nations were vile, and their worship was often accompanied by unspeakable abominations, which had a most debasing effect on their

---

[1] Ps. cxi. 9.   The English version translates rather weakly, "Holy and reverend is His name." But *nora* means " terrible," " dreadful," " fearful," and is so translated in every other instance that I am aware of.

[2] Ps. xcix. 3, xxxiii. 1, ciii. 1, cvi. 47, cxiv. 21.

votaries. " *They that made them became like unto them, so did every one that trusted in them.*"

Holiness as an attribute of the gods never even entered into the heart of the heathen nations. Even amongst the most civilised of the Gentile nations religion was something absolutely apart from morality, not to speak of holiness. " The priest and augurs of ancient Greece and Rome never for one moment regarded it as any part of their duty to exhort or help men to a purer life. Alike public life and private were steeped in a heartlessness of cruelty and an abandonment of vice, such as we can hardly realise ; but pagan religion made no protest—for, on the contrary, its mysteries often screened, and its ministers sanctioned, the grossest iniquities." [1]

But Jehovah is " *the Holy One of Israel* "—" the Father of lights," in whom " is no darkness at all " ; " dwelling in light, which no man can approach unto." At the sight of His glory even an Isaiah falls down, crying, " Woe is me, for I am undone, for I am a man of unclean lips " ; while Seraphim veil their faces and cry, " Holy, holy, holy, is Jehovah of hosts ; the whole earth is full of His glory." And not only is He holy in Himself, but He says to His people : " Be ye holy, for I, Jehovah your God, am holy," and requires of them that would worship Him to worship Him not only in spirit and truth, but " *in the beauty of holiness.*" [2]

Well, therefore, might the Psalmist exhort Israel to " glory in His holy Name " ; for this, as already stated, is his unique calling and mission. Let the other nations glory in what they may—the Greek, for instance, in his wisdom and sense of beauty ; the Roman in his invincible might and power of organisation ; but when

[1] *The Fact of Christ,* by P. Carnegie Simpson, D.D.
[2] Ps. xcvi. 9.

the Jew, instead of glorying in Jehovah and in the fact of his being the witness to, and the appointed disseminator of, the knowledge of " His Holy Name," boasts of his mastery of the Gentile arts and philosophies, or of his power in the spheres of commerce and politics, he misses the special aim of his existence and of his high calling of God ; for this is the word of Jehovah to Israel : " Let not the wise man glory in his wisdom, neither let the mighty man glory in his might, let not the rich man glory in his riches ; but let him that glorieth glory in this, *that He hath understanding and knoweth Me, that I am Jehovah* who exerciseth lovingkindness, justice, and righteousness in the earth : for in these things I delight, saith Jehovah " (Jer. ix. 23, 24).

And assuredly a day is coming when, like the Apostle Paul (who is in many respects the type and representative of the Jewish nation) Israel—counting these things which they had formerly considered " gain," but " loss " for the excellency of the knowledge of their Messiah Jesus—shall glory in Him only.

It is the day, viz. when, in and through Him, who is Himself the highest and fullest revelation of God, and in whom all the glorious attributes of His character and the divine perfection of His being met and were manifested, they shall fully learn to know the holy and blessed " Name." [1] Then " in Jehovah shall all the seed of Israel be justified and shall glory." [2] Then, like David, the sweet Psalmist of Israel, their soul " shall make her boast in Jehovah," and " the meek " among all the nations " shall hear thereof and be glad." [3]

In the second line of the third verse the inspired

---

[1] See John xvii. 6–26.   [2] Isa. xlv. 25.

[3] Ps. xxxiv. 2. The original word for " boast " is the same as rendered " glory " in all the other passages quoted.

singer proceeds with his exhortation : " *Let the heart of them rejoice that seek Jehovah* " ; or, as it *may* also be rendered, " *the heart of them that seek Jehovah shall rejoice* " ; for it is in itself a gladsome work to seek Jehovah, the fountain of life, and light, and blessedness ; and they " rejoice," because if they truly " seek " they assuredly find Him, and, finding Him, they find in His own blessed presence the very " fulness of joy," and at His right hand the " pleasures which are for evermore." [1] Therefore the Psalmist proceeds in the 4th verse : " *Seek ye Jehovah and His strength ; seek His face evermore.*"

Two different verbs are used for " seeking " in the original in this 4th verse—the verb in the first line דִּרְשׁוּ—*dir'shu,* expressing the idea of diligently " inquiring," or " searching " ; and the second בַּקְּשׁוּ—*baq'shu,* of earnestly desiring, or of a " seeking to find." Thus, *whole-heartedly,* we are to " seek " Jehovah, and " His strength " and " His face "—" His strength " for our weakness, and " His face," which stands not only for " His favour," but for His own blessed presence—for the light of His blessed countenance, that it may dispel all our darkness, whether it be within us or around us. And we are to seek Him " for evermore," or " *continually,*" or ceaselessly, as the Hebrew word *tamid* means, for never is there a time when we can stand in our own strength, or be happy when the light of His blessed " face " does not shine upon us.

The 5th verse may be regarded as the key to the Psalm :

" *Remember His marvellous works that He hath done, His wonders and the judgments of His mouth.*"

What these marvellous works are, he will proceed

[1] Ps. xvi. 11.

to narrate from the 7th verse to the end of the Psalm. They are, viz., the "marvels" of His power and grace which are displayed in their past history.

By the "judgments of His mouth" the Jewish commentators understand "the laws and statutes given at Sinai"; but more probably the word *mishpat* has the same meaning here as in verse 7, viz., His judicial utterances, "His righteous decisions," the execution of which no power on earth can hinder—such, for instance, as those which spelt destruction to Egypt.

These they are to remember and ponder over, so that their souls may be stirred up within them with adoring gratitude, and their hearts be strengthened in the present and for the future by a contemplation of God's gracious and wonderful dealings with them in the past.

Alas! in spite of this oft-repeated exhortation to "remember," "they soon forgot His works"; "they remembered not the multitude of His lovingkindnesses" which He showed them as a nation, as the same inspired writer sorrowfully confesses in the very next Psalm, which is the continuation of the narrative, as we have already observed at the very beginning of this exposition.

And are we any better in this respect, dear Christian reader? Has not God done even greater things for us in and through Christ than He did for Israel? Has He not accomplished a greater redemption for us than the redemption from Egypt, and brought us into a more glorious inheritance than Canaan? And do *we* sufficiently "remember His marvellous works" on our behalf, and the great and manifold benefits which He hath bestowed upon us, so as to be stirred up to ever greater thankfulness and a more perfect consecration of our life to Him who has done so much for us?

The exhortation in the first strophe concludes with a reminder of Israel's special privilege and responsibility to respond to the call, or invitation, which is addressed to them in these verses, to show forth God's praise, and to publish abroad the glory of " His holy Name " and " His marvellous works " among the peoples.

> " *O ye seed of Abraham, His servant ;*
> *Ye children of Jacob, His chosen ones.*"

In these very names are contained the reasons why *ye*, above all others, should devote yourselves to the worship and service of Jehovah. For remember the special relationship in which ye stand to Him. Ye are " *the seed of Abraham*," to whom, when darkness covered the earth and gross darkness the peoples, the God of glory appeared, calling him, and his seed after him, into special fellowship with Himself, to be His witnesses on the earth ; who, when the voice of God came to him, readily obeyed and went out, not knowing whither he went ; and whom, because of his faithfulness and ready obedience to God's word, even to the point of offering up his son, his only one, whom he loved, God delights to call, not only " His servant," but His " friend." [1]

And ye are " *the children of Jacob*," whom of His free sovereign grace He " chose " and " loved " rather than Esau,[2] and whom, in spite of his own natural perversity and crookedness, he turned into " Israel." And ye, his children, too, are " His chosen ones," even as we read in Deut. vii. 6, " *Thou art a holy people unto Jehovah thy God. Jehovah thy God hath chosen thee to be a people for His own possession above all peoples that are upon the face of the earth.*" Who, then, should show

[1] Isa. xli. 8 ; 2 Chron. xx. 7.   [2] Mal. i. 2.

forth His praise and spread abroad the knowledge of His name, if not ye ?

But you, too, dear Christian reader, are neither excluded nor exempted from uttering God's praise, or from offering Him acceptable service ; for, though you may not be bodily descendants of Abraham, ye are, through the grace of Christ, children of Abraham by faith, and are now included in the " Israel of God." Indeed, during the period of Israel's national apostasy and unbelief, it is the true Church of Christ which is called upon to take Israel's place as God's witness to the nations, and to fill up Israel's lack of worship and service. Only remember that your *inclusion* into the sphere of promise and of blessing does not imply the exclusion of Abraham's natural descendants. Still, they are " His people," " His chosen," " His inherit-ance," and His original purpose in and through them as a nation shall yet be fulfilled : " *This people have I formed for Myself ; they shall show forth My praise.*"

10

JEHOVAH'S EVERLASTING COVENANT

WITH the 7th verse begins the historical narrative
—the actual recital of " His marvellous works "
in their past history, which the Psalmist calls upon
them in the introductory verses to " remember," and
" muse " on, and " talk " about, so that their hope in
God may be strengthened in reference to the present
and the future. But, at the head of all His works,
and better than all He has ever done for them, is
Himself. Therefore the narrative begins with the
words, *Hu Yehovah eloheinu*—" He, Jehovah," the
everlasting self-existent, great " I AM," who has made
himself particularly known by this name in the history
of redemption, the God of covenant and of promise—
" *is our God.*" What depths of blessedness for His
people is contained in this assurance !

Truly, as one has remarked, " This short sentence
contains a greater wealth of meaning than all the
eloquence of orators can compass, and there is more joy
in it than in all the sonnets of them that make merry."
Well might the Psalmist exclaim, " Blessed is the
nation *whose God is Jehovah ; the people whom He hath
chosen for His own inheritance.*"

But while Israel, His own redeemed people, can
claim Him in a very special sense as " their own God,"
and Palestine is the centre of His self-manifestations
and righteous rule, " His judgments "—*i.e.*, His judicial
decisions, the display of His attribute of justice as the

righteous Judge and Ruler of men—" *are in all the earth.*"

This is true now, for Jehovah the God of Israel is " the God of the whole earth," and whether men know it or not, it is *His* kingdom which " ruleth over all." But it shall become manifestly and universally true by and by, after Israel as a nation shall, in and through Christ, enter experimentally into the relationship expressed in the first line of this verse, and say with a depth of meaning as never before, " *He, Jehovah, is our God.*" Then indeed shall Jehovah be King over all the earth [1] and His righteous rule be visibly displayed in the sight of all nations.

The sign and pledge—the embodiment, so to say— of God's grace and faithfulness to Israel, and the basis of all His dealings with His redeemed people, is the covenant ; and of this the next four verses of the Psalm proceed to speak.

" *He remembers* " [2] (not " remembered ") " *His covenant for ever,*" *i.e.* He *always does* so ; and this cannot be otherwise so long as He is the everlasting, unchangeable God. Note the word " *His* covenant." God made a covenant with Israel on Mount Sinai— the covenant of the law—but in that covenant there is no hope either for the nation or for any individual, because it was in the nature of a contract between God and the people, in which blessing and prosperity were promised them on *certain conditions.* But these conditions Israel did not, and could not, so long as they were under the law, fulfil. The prophets and psalmists only speak of *that* covenant when they want to remind Israel of their unfaithfulness and apostasy with a view

[1] Zech. xiv. 9.

[2] זָכַר—*za-khar*, is the perfect, as Delitzsch observes, " of practically pledged certainty."

to awaken in their hearts a sense of sin. But long
before that covenant on Sinai, God had made a covenant
with Abraham. This was altogether *His* covenant.
It originated in His own heart of love without any
promptings from without. It was altogether unconditional, God alone being pledged to its fulfilment.
This is brought out very clearly and beautifully in the
inspired record of the process of the ratification of
the covenant, when contrasted with that which took
place at the foot of Mount Sinai.

At the ratification of the covenant of the law, after
Moses had " written all the words of Jehovah," which
set forth the conditions of the covenant, he " builded
an altar under the mount, and twelve pillars, according
to the twelve tribes of Israel "—the altar thus repre-
senting God, and the twelve pillars around it the
people. Then sacrifices were slain, " *and Moses took
half of the blood and put it in basins ; and half of the
blood he sprinkled on the altar. And he took the book
of the covenant and read in the audience of the people ;
and they said, All that Jehovah hath spoken will we
do and be obedient. And Moses took the blood, and
sprinkled it on the people, and said, Behold the blood of
the covenant which Jehovah hath made with you concerning all these words.*" [1] Thus, in this solemn manner,
both parties, God and the people, were pledged to the
fulfilment of the articles of the covenant which were
written in the book of the law.

It is the failure on the part of Israel to fulfil the
conditions of this covenant which brought upon him
all the curses which are written in that book. But in
the original covenant which God made with Abraham,
in which is included the great promise that in his seed
all families of the earth should be blessed, the manner

[1] Ex. xxiv. 4–8.

of it was altogether different. It was wholly of the nature of promise on God's part, without any conditions whatever being attached. " God," as the apostle expresses it in his Letter to the Galatians, " was one " (or " alone " [1]), the fulfilment of this covenant being dependent on *Him only*. And in keeping with its character was the way it was ratified.

God's word by itself is sure and certain, and needs no further confirmation, but " being minded " in His infinite grace " to shew more abundantly unto the heirs of the promise *the immutability of His counsel*," that they might have strong consolation (or " encouragement ") who have fled for refuge to lay hold of the hope set before us, He condescended to embody His word in the concrete form of a covenant, and to confirm it with an oath.

But when everything had been arranged according to the ancient custom for the ratification of a covenant, and Abraham had slain the animals according to God's command, " and divided them in the midst, and laid each half over against the other," leaving a path between, through which he probably expected that he as well as the Lord would have to pass, according to the recognised custom [2]—the parties to the covenant thus pledging their lives to its fulfilment, and calling down upon themselves the fate of the slain animals in case of unfaithfulness—God mercifully interposed and put Abraham into " a deep sleep," thus preventing him from passing through the slain sacrifices. " *And it came to pass, when the sun went down and it was dark, behold a smoking furnace and a flaming torch that passed between these pieces.*" [3]

The smoking furnace and flaming torch were the symbols of God's presence, and are very significant

[1] Gal. iii. 17–21.   [2] Jer. xxxiv. 18   [3] Gen. xv. 9–11.

as setting forth His dealings with the people of the covenant. By very reason of their special relationship to Him they are always in the furnace of affliction and suffering until all the dross shall be consumed, and they are purified and made a holy people unto the Lord. But however hot the furnace of affliction may be, there is ever alongside of it " a flaming torch " of promise, that He would ever be with them—that no waters of affliction, however deep, would drown them ; and no fires of tribulation, however hot, would consume them.

But this is partly a digression. The point I desire to emphasise, even at the risk of repetition, is that " *God was alone* " in that covenant—He only being pledged to its fulfilment—and that therefore it is called " *His* covenant."

And this original covenant which He made with Abraham, which " the law which came 430 years later could not disannul to make the promise of none effect," is in its essence the same as the " New Covenant," which God promised through the prophets to make " with the house of Israel and the house of Judah," only enlarged and amplified, as containing many additional promises which God made to David and his house.

It is the *covenant of grace*, into the spiritual blessings of which believers from among all nations are brought because of their union by faith with Christ, who is the true seed of Abraham and Son of David, in whom all the promises of God become " Yea and Amen."

It is called the " *Everlasting Covenant*," because God, who is pledged to its fulfilment, can never fail. It is also spoken of as " *the covenant of peace*," as, for instance, in Isa. liv. 10 : " *The mountains may depart, and the hills be removed, but My loving kindness*

*shall not depart from thee, neither shall the covenant of
My peace be removed, saith Jehovah, that hath mercy on
thee* " ; while in another passage the same prophet
speaks of it as " the sure mercies of David," [1] because
what God had originally spoken to Abraham, especially
concerning the promised seed, in whom all the nations
should be blessed, was confirmed and made, so to say,
doubly " sure " to David, out of whose family He was
to spring.

This—to return more closely to the exposition of
our Psalm—is " His covenant," which " he remembers
for ever," and on the ground of which He acts in grace
and blessing at every juncture of failure and faithlessness on the part of His people.[2]

And because of its character as a covenant of grace,
it is further defined in our Psalm as :

" *The word* (*i.e.* of promise) *which He commanded to a
thousand generations,
The covenant which He made with Abraham,
And His oath unto Isaac,
And confirmed the same unto Jacob for a statute,
To Israel for an everlasting covenant.*"

In all which, to quote from another writer, " The
general idea of explicit declaration of Divine purpose, *which henceforth becomes binding on God by reason
of His faithfulness*, is contained." And " The various
designations are heaped together in order to heighten
the thought of the *firmness* of His promise.   It stands

[1] Isa. lv. 3.
[2] See, *e.g.* Ezek. xvi., after depicting Israel's spiritual adultery and
lewdness, and the terrible punishment which would come on her for
her unfaithfulness, God says (verses 60–63), " Nevertheless, I will
remember My covenant with thee. . . . I will establish unto thee an
everlasting covenant, . . . but not by thy covenant.   And I will
establish My covenant with thee, and thou shalt know that I am
Jehovah."

' for ever,' ' to a thousand generations ' ; it is ' an everlasting covenant.' The Psalmist triumphs, as it were, in the manifold repetition of it," and glories in the fact that what God had thus " commanded " to be established as an *inviolable law to last for ever*, can never be frustrated or forfeited, even by Israel's sin.

And each of the fathers of the nation had it confirmed to himself. To Abraham the great foundation promises of this covenant was repeated several times, and finally confirmed by oath, on the solemn occasion when, after his obedience had been tested to the utmost, God said, " *By Myself have I sworn, saith Jehovah,* . . . *that in blessing I will bless thee, and in multiplying I will multiply thy seed as the stars of the heavens, and the sand which is upon the seashore,* . . . *and in thy seed shall all the nations of the earth be blessed.*" [1]

And this same promise and oath " which Isaac had first heard as he stood trembling, but unharmed, by the rude altar where the ram lay in his stead," he had renewed to himself when the Lord appeared unto him in Gerar, and said, " *Go not down into Egypt ; dwell in the land which I shall tell thee of,* . . . *and I will be with thee, and will bless thee, for unto thee and unto thy seed will I give all these lands, and I will establish the oath which I sware unto Abraham thy father.*" [2]

And this was afterwards transferred and " established " to Jacob, not only " as he lay beneath the stars at Bethel," [3] but on his return to the same spot after many years to renew the consecration of himself and his house.[4]

[1] Gen. xxii. 16–18.   [2] Gen. xxvii. 2, 3.
[3] Gen. xxviii. 13, 14.   [4] Gen. xxxv. 9–15.

11

THE UNCONDITIONAL PROMISE OF THE LAND

IN this unconditional covenant of free grace which God made with the fathers are included, as already stated, many exceeding great and precious promises ; it includes the greatest of all promises, viz. Christ and the Gospel, for, as the apostle reminds us, " the Scripture foreseeing that God would justify the Gentiles by faith, preached the Gospel beforehand unto Abraham, saying, In thee shall all the nations be blessed." [1]

But to Israel, nationally, there was *one outstanding promise* confirmed by oath, which our Psalm proceeds in the 11th verse more particularly to emphasise :

" *Saying, Unto thee will I give the land of Canaan,
The lot of your inheritance.*"

The suffix " your " to the word in the original for " inheritance " is in the *plural*, because the promise, though spoken in the first instance in turn to individuals —whether to Abraham or to Isaac—was intended for the nation that should spring out of their loins.

Now this may be said to form the central thought in the Psalm. " Out of the whole storehouse of the promises of God vouchsafed to the patriarchs," observes another writer, " only one is brought prominently forward, viz. that concerning the possession of Canaan. *Everything revolves round this.* The wonders and the judgments of which the Psalmist proceeds to

---
[1] Gal. iii. 8.

speak have all, for their ultimate design, the fulfilment of this purpose."

As sure, then, as God is true, this land of Canaan is the inalienable possession of the Jewish nation, whatever the Gentile world-powers may plan about it.[1] That is the reason why God has never permitted any other nation to get permanent hold of it. Both in ancient and in modern times almost all the Great Powers of the world have striven and fought for it. To quote words of mine from elsewhere, " It has been conquered in turn by the Egyptians, Assyrians, Babylonians, and Persians. When Alexander the Great set out to conquer Asia, one of the first things he did was to conquer Palestine. Then it became the bone of contention between the Ptolemies and the Seleucids. Since the new phase in the dispersion brought about by the rejection of Christ, many Gentile nations have sought to establish their dominion over it.

" It has been occupied in turn by Romans, Persians, Saracens, Crusaders, Mamelukes, Tartars, and Turks ; *but none of them have been permitted to possess it for long.* The Turk has been permitted of God in more recent times to tread it down and desolate it, but he cannot be said to have possessed it. Rather has he served, in God's good providence, as the custodian to prevent others from taking possession of it, and as the unconscious guardian of the land until the lawful possessors of it should return."

And what a wonderful demonstration of God's faithfulness to His promises we have before our very eyes at this present day in the truly marvellous de-

---

[1] To the believer in God's Word this is a sufficient answer to those who, out of prejudice against the Jews, are asserting that the Moslem and so-called Christian Arabs and not the Jews are the true claimants to Palestine.

velopments which the great World-War has brought about in relation to the Jews and Palestine !

" In that day," we read in Gen. xv. 15–18—that is, some four thousand years ago, and when Abraham was himself but a stranger and sojourner in the land— " *Jehovah made a covenant with Abraham, saying, Unto thy seed have I given this land, from the river of Egypt, unto the great river, the river Euphrates.*" Centuries intervened between the promise and its first fulfilment, for the promised seed was not yet even born at that time ; and when the descendants of Abraham, through Isaac, had grown into a company of families and tribes, they had first to be sent into the furnace of Egypt, there to be melted and welded together into a people, and patiently to wait under oppression and suffering until God's purposes should ripen, " for the iniquity of the Amorites," the original occupants of the land now promised to Abraham's seed, " was not yet full."

It seemed altogether improbable, from a human point of view, during these centuries of bondage in Egypt, that the Jews would possess the land of Canaan ; but God never forgot His word to Abraham, and at the appointed time, in spite of apparent natural impossibilities and human improbabilities, the promise, as far as the original possession of the land is concerned, was fulfilled. " It came to pass at the end of 430 years, even the self-same day, it came to pass that all the hosts of Jehovah went out of the land of Egypt." [1]

" *For He remembered His holy word,*
And Abraham His servant,
And He brought forth His people with joy,
And His chosen with singing,
And He gave them the lands of the nations ;
And they took possession of the labour of the peoples." [2]

[1] Ex. xii. 41.   [2] Ps. cv. 42–45.

After a few centuries of chequered history in
Palestine, both the Israelitish kingdoms—the northern
and the southern—were finally broken up by Assyria
and Babylon, and the people carried into captivity
by the great Gentile world-powers, who said among
themselves, " Aha ! the ancient high places (*i.e.* the
mountains of Israel) are ours in possession." ¹ It
seemed to all appearances very unlikely that there
would ever again be a Jewish nation in the land of
Palestine. But after the " seventy years' " captivity
in Babylon, in fulfilment of His original promise to the
fathers, and " and that the word of Jehovah, by the
mouth of Jeremiah, might be accomplished," ² a large
representative remnant of all Israel returned and took
possession of the land.

This new period of about five hundred years of
chequered history—during which only a part of the
nation was in the land, while the greater number remained a diaspora—culminated in the great national
catastrophe, viz. the destruction of the city and sanctuary by the Romans, and the inauguration of the second
or *universal* stage of the scattering of the Jewish people
among all the nations of the earth.

These past nineteen centuries Israel has been a
wanderer on the face of the earth—" scattered and
peeled," tossed about among the nations, " even as
corn is tossed about in a sieve." At times it seemed as
if they would be altogether rooted out of existence,
there being only one million of them left at the beginning
of the sixteenth century, after the most terrible fiery
ordeal of persecution and suffering, through which they
passed in the dark Middle Ages. Was there any human
likelihood that they would ever again be restored as a
nation in their own land ? They themselves were

¹ Ezek. xxxvi. 1–8.   ² Ezra i. 1.

ready to renounce all hope of a national restoration, and said : " *Our bones are dried up, and our hope is lost ; we are clean cut off* " ; [1] while the whole world laughed at the very possibility of a Jewish nation being re-established in Palestine.

But God " remembers His covenant *for ever*—the word which He had spoken to *a thousand generations*," and therefore it has come to pass, in God's wonderful overruling providence, that, as one result of a great world catastrophe, the Jews are once more acknowledged as a nation, and the governments of the greatest of the Gentile nations are publicly pledged to facilitate the re-establishment of their " national home " in Palestine. Truly our God is faithful, and His word can never fail !

But while writing thus, it is, perhaps, not unnecessary to utter a word of warning lest it should be thought that we regard the return of a large number of Jews to Palestine in a condition of unbelief, which is taking place under our very eyes, as the final and exhaustive fulfilment of the great promises in reference to Israel's future. The return in unbelief is, we believe, *the necessary precursor to the resumption of God's dealings with them as a nation* ; but of this we are certain, on the ground of prophetic Scripture, that the Jews will never possess the land *in blessing* until God's long-standing controversy with them is ended. And this will not be until Israel's national repentance and conversion, when they shall broken-heartedly confess their great national sin, and look upon Him Whom they have pierced, and mourn.

The promises of God, which are of a national character, remain for ever true *to the nation*, which God takes care to preserve—but generations of Jews may exclude themselves from the enjoyment of the blessings promised them through unbelief and disobedience. It was so

[1] Ezek. xxxvi. 11.

with the whole generation nearly, of those who came out of Egypt, concerning whom " God sware in His wrath that they should not enter into His rest " ; and it has been so with the generations of Jews these past nineteen centuries, who, as a nation could not " enter into His rest," or into the enjoyment of God's promises of either temporal or spiritual blessing because of unbelief.[1]   No, the Jewish nation will yet learn, after bitter experience, the truth of the words of Joseph Rabinowitch, one of the noblest Jewish patriots and pioneers, that " the key to Palestine (as well as into the Kingdom of God) lies in the hands of Jesus our Brother."

[1] Heb. iii. 16–19.

12

GOD'S PROVIDENTIAL CARE—THE PATRIARCHAL PERIOD

BUT to return to the more immediate context of our Psalm.

In order to the ultimate fulfilment of the oath and covenant in reference to *the land*, it was necessary that *the people*—the heirs of the promised " inheritance "— should be preserved. This—the marvellous preservation of Abraham and his seed, more particularly in the earliest part of their history—is the theme of the Psalmist's song in the next four verses. Just consider how vulnerable and helpless they were.

I. " *When they were but a few men in number* " : literally, מְתֵי מִסְפָּר—*m'thei mispar*, " men of number," *i.e.* so few that they could easily be counted.[1]

II. " *Yea, very few* " (כִּמְעַט—*kim'at*) : literally, " *like a little*," *i.e.* a *very* small number—so small as to be altogether *insignificant*.[2]

III. And not only were they very few and insignificant in their own strength, but they were " sojourners," גֵּרִים—*gerim*, " new-comers," without any

---

[1] The phrase is used by Jacob in Gen. xxxiv. 30, when, on departing from Shechem, full of fear, he exclaimed, " I, being few in number (*m'thei mispar*) they (*i.e.*, the Canaanites and the Perizzites) will gather themselves together and smite me ; and I shall be destroyed, I and my house." Which might easily have been the case but for the " terror of God which came upon the cities which were round about them, so that they did not pursue after the sons of Jacob " (Gen. xxxv. 5).

[2] The word is used also of littleness of *worth*, and is found in Prov. x. 20, " The heart of the wicked is little worth " (*kim'at*).

hereditary rights or claims in the land where they sojourned.

IV. And their circumstances were such that they had to be, as it were, continually on the move. " *They went about from nation to nation, from one kingdom to another people.*" And these " nations " and " peoples " were by no means *naturally* disposed to be friendly to these strangers who came amongst them. What power was it that watched over the patriarchs and preserved them from extermination as they moved from one danger zone into another—now in Egypt, now in Syria, now in Canaan, again amongst the Philistines ?

Here is the answer :—

" *He suffered no man to do them wrong* " : literally, " to oppress them," *i.e.* with impunity.

" *Yea, He reproved kings for their sakes (saying), Touch not Mine anointed ones, and do My prophets no harm.*"

The primary allusions are to the " reproof " which God administered to Pharaoh of Egypt, for Abraham's sake,[1] and to Abimelech of Gerar, for Isaac's sake,[2] and perhaps also to the restraint which He put upon Esau from falling on his brother Jacob, when he went out to meet him with 400 armed men on his return from Padan Aram ; and of the Canaanites and Perizzites after the slaughter of the Shechemites.

Under the special care and protection of the Almighty, who claimed and acknowledged them as His " anointed " or " consecrated " ones (מְשִׁיחָי— *meshichay*) and His prophets, they were invulnerable and inviolable, however great the dangers by which they were surrounded. And if we ask *in what sense* were the patriarchs " God's anointed ones " and " prophets," the answer is, that the outward " anoint-

---

[1] Gen. xii. 17.　　　　　　[2] Gen. xx. 3, etc.

ing " is in the Scriptures—both of the Old and New
Testaments—the standing symbol and type of the
communication of the gifts of the Holy Spirit. Now
these men were called and chosen to be God's witnesses
on the earth, " the consecrated bearers of God's revelation "—men "in whom the Spirit of God is," as Pharaoh,
for instance, witnessed of Joseph.[1]

" Prior to prophetic utterance," as one observes,
" is prophetic inspiration ; and these men received
Divine communications, and were in a special degree
possessed of the counsels of Heaven." [2] Prophets " in
the narrower sense " they may not have been, yet it
was in and by the spirit of prophecy that they dreamt
dreams, and saw visions, and published abroad the
Name of the one true and living God who had revealed
Himself to them, and spoke with prophetic certainty
of the future. Well, therefore, may God Himself say
of Abraham to Abimelech, " He is a prophet." [3]

But, secondly, the patriarchs, I believe, are called
God's " anointed ones " and " prophets," not merely
in their own personal individual capacity, but as the
representatives and embodiment, so to say, of the
nation which was to spring out of their loins, *in whom
is vested the spirit of prophecy*, and who were to be gifted
with the Spirit, and consecrated as God's special
witnesses on the earth, and the medium of His self-
revelation to the whole of mankind.

It is true that hitherto God's purpose in and through
the chosen seed—that they should be a kingdom of
priests and His prophets among the nations—has only
been fulfilled through the few specially chosen and
anointed ones, such as a David, an Isaiah, a Daniel, a

[1] Gen. xli. 28.
[2] Gen. xv. 15, xxvii. 27, xxviii. 10–19, xliv. 1–27, xlviii. 8–20.
[3] Gen. xx. 7.

Paul, a John, and—not to stop short of the climax—
Christ Himself, who is pre-eminently God's "Anointed
One" and "Prophet," and who, though "God over all
blessed for ever," is also the true seed of Abraham
according to the flesh, and who in His human nature
was, so to say, in the loins of the patriarchs when God
designated them His "anointed ones" and "prophets."

But what has been the case hitherto of only the
very few out of this chosen nation, shall in and through
Christ yet become true of *all* the seed of Abraham:
"*For they shall* ALL *know Jehovah, from the least of
them unto the greatest of them, saith Jehovah.*" [1] "*And
it shall come to pass afterward that I will pour out My
Spirit upon all flesh; and your sons and your daughters
shall prophesy, your old men shall dream dreams, your
young men shall see visions; and also upon the servants
and handmaidens in those days will I pour out My
Spirit.*" [2]

"*And their seed shall be known among the nations
and their offspring among the peoples; and ye shall be
named the priests of Jehovah; men shall call you the
ministers of our God.*" [3]

Before passing on to the exposition of the next paragraph of our Psalm, I have yet one or two observations
to make on the last four verses which we have been
considering.

I. What we read here of the very beginning of
Israel's history, and of God's watchful care over the
patriarchs, is typical also of the whole subsequent
history of the nation. Even during the centuries of
dispersion, on account of sin and apostasy, His eye has
still been upon them. He has narrowly watched also
the conduct of the nations toward them, and no nation
or individual has lifted up his hand against His peculiar

---

[1] Jer. xxxi. 34.   [2] Joel ii. 28, 29.   [3] Isa. lxi. 6, 7.

people and prospered. As compared with the great world-powers, among whom they have been scattered, they have always been, comparatively speaking, " very few in number," and, at the best, mere strangers and sojourners in the lands of their dispersion. But even when driven " from nation to nation, and from one kingdom to another people," God did not suffer any nation or people to oppress or persecute them with impunity ; and modern as well as ancient history can testify to the fact that He often " reproved " (or, as the word may also be rendered, " *punished* ") kings for their sakes ; for His word to Abraham has verified itself not only in his own life, but in all the centuries which have intervened since. " *I will bless them that bless thee, and him that curseth thee I will curse.*"

II. These verses of our Psalm, though speaking primarily of " God's marvellous works " on behalf of Israel, contain also a very precious message of hope and encouragement to Christians of whatever nation. The God of Israel is the God and Father of our Lord and Saviour Jesus Christ, whose faithfulness to Israel nationally is the pledge of His faithfulness to the Church and to the individual believer. We, too, though not bodily descendants, are " the seed of Abraham " by faith, and share in the blessings of the covenant which is now more sure than ever since it has been ratified in the precious blood of Christ. We have no portion in the land which God has given to *Israel as a nation* for " an everlasting possession," and can never, as we have seen, be alienated from them. But Israel's earthly inheritance in Canaan is the type of our much more glorious possession—the " inheritance which is incorruptible and undefiled, and that fadeth not away," and which, as sure as God is true, can never be forfeited

160 Israel in the Plan of God

by those whom He has of His own free grace constituted heirs and joint-heirs with Christ Jesus.

And, like Israel and Canaan, so it is with us. While our inheritance is safely " reserved " by God Himself " in heaven " for us, and can never be taken from us, we, His poor weak children, even while still in the great moral desert of this world, and often, " if need be," " put to grief in manifold trials," [1] are by His power " guarded through faith unto a salvation ready to be revealed in the last time."

And finally, to complete the parallel, we too are His " anointed ones " and His " prophets " in the New Testament sense of the words, to whom is entrusted the Word of Life, that we may be witnesses for Him in the world. " God's people," to quote from an old writer, " have ever been but ' men of number ' (a little minority), often accounted as vile, but they are precious in His sight. They are not distinguished by external dignity, numbers, and power, as Rome sets forth the marks of her communion : they are in the midst of kingdoms, but not of them. They form usually the humblest portions of most communities, and yet they receive honour from God. Despised by the world, but unto God, kings and priests, ordained and anointed to reign with Christ for ever."

[1] 1 Pet. i. 3–6 (R.V.).

13

THE STORY OF JOSEPH

THE second brief strophe of the narrative proper
(verses 16–22) sings of God's wonderful overruling providences which led to Israel's coming into the
land of Egypt. This may seem a roundabout way to
the fulfilment of the covenant, and particularly of the
promise in the 11th verse : " *Unto thee will I give the
land of Canaan, the lot of your inheritance* "—upon which
the preceding section lays such emphasis. But it was
God's way, and, as we have already seen in the course of
our consideration of the earlier verses of this Psalm,
it was the wisest and best way ; for the chosen people
had to undergo a preparatory course of training for
their promised inheritance, and certain subsidiary
purposes of God, both in relation to Egypt and to the
" Amorite," had to ripen and unfold themselves before
Israel could enter Canaan—even as God Himself had
fore-announced to Abraham at the time when the
promise in relation to the land was first made.[1]

From Abraham, Isaac, and Jacob, who are the outstanding figures in the first fifteen verses of the Psalm,
the narrative moves on to Joseph, and these seven
verses epitomise the last fourteen chapters of Genesis,
in which he is the most prominent personality and
central link in the further development of Israel's
marvellous history.

> "*And He called for a famine upon the land;
> He brake the whole staff of bread.*"

[1] Gen. xv. 12–21.

Both the thought and the words in which it is expressed are sublime : " *He called for a famine* "[1]—as a master calls for his servant ready to do his bidding.

It reminds us of what we read of Jehovah's omnipotent creative voice in Ps. xxxiii. 9 : " *For He spake, and it was done : He commanded, and it stood fast* "—or more literally, " *He said, and it was : He commanded, and it stood forth* "—the idea being, as Delitzsch well expresses it, that " He need only speak the word, and that which He wills comes into being out of nothing." He need only utter His creative " Let there be," and that which He commands " *stands forth*," like an obedient servant who appears in all haste at the call of his lord.

And this is not only true in creation, as, for instance, when He said " Let there be light, and there was light," but in *providence*. It was He who called for the seven years of famine upon the land, because, though not recognised at the time—and whatever other subsidiary purposes of His it had to accomplish—it was God's appointed means of bringing Joseph and his brethren together once more. The exact opposite to this, as Fausset points out, is Ezek. xxxvi. 29, where God says, " *I will call for the corn and will increase it, and lay no famine upon you.*"

The figure מַטֵּה לֶחֶם—*matteh lechem*, " the staff of bread," is found already in Lev. xxvi. 26, and reminds us of the weakness and dependence of human life. Feeble man is dependent on " bread," even as the lame or cripple upon his " staff," and it is *God* who provides this means of support for him, and who also can " break " it.

The second step in the chain of His overruling providences is set forth in the 17th verse : " *He sent*

[1] The expression is found also in 2 Kings iii. 1.

a man before them : Joseph was sold for a servant" (or
"*slave*"). It was his brethren who, out of malice and
" with wicked hands," sold him to the Midianite
merchants for twenty pieces of silver, but all the time
it was God's invisible hand which was overruling it
to the accomplishment of His purpose, and causing
even the wrath of man to praise Him. This in the end
was seen and acknowledged by Joseph himself. "*God,*"
he said, " *sent me before you to preserve you a remnant in
the earth, and to save you by a great deliverance. So now
it was not you who sent me hither, but God.*"[1] And
again : " *As for you, ye meant evil against me ; but God
meant it for good, to bring to pass as it is this day, to save
much people alive.*"[2]

But before Joseph could become the saviour of
" much people " and fulfil his God-appointed mission,
he had first to descend into the deepest depths of
humiliation and suffering, and his faith had to be put
to the severest test. Of these sufferings, which were
the appointed way to glory, the Psalmist proceeds
pathetically to speak. Joseph, he says, the beloved
and tenderly cherished son of his father, for whom
Jacob had made " a coat of many colours," which,
among other privileges, carried with it exemption
from hard toil,[3] *was sold for a slave,* whom his pur-

---

[1] Gen. xlv. 7, 8.   [2] Gen. l. 20.

[3] כְּתֹנֶת פַּסִּים—*kh'thoneth passim,* rather vaguely rendered "a coat of
many colours," may more properly be described as " a long dress with
sleeves extending to the wrists and ankles," פַּסִּים—*passim,* being the
plural of פַּס—*pas,* signifying " extremity."

The gift of this " tunic with sleeves," as Dr. Griffith Thomas well
observes in his *Devotional Commentary* on Genesis, " was about the
most significant act that Jacob could have shown to Joseph. It was
a mark of distinction that carried its own meaning, for it implied
that exemption from labour which was the peculiar privilege of the
heir, or prince, of the Eastern clan.

" Instead of the ordinary work-a-day vestment which had no

chaser could use as he pleased, and put to the most degrading tasks. And not only so, but, though perfectly innocent, and the purest and noblest of the sons of Jacob, he was treated as a criminal, and had to endure cruel sufferings of body and soul. " *His feet they hurt* " (or " *afflicted* ") *with fetters ;* " *he was laid in chains of iron.*" [1] This, we may be sure, is not poetic hyperbole, but was literally the case. That Joseph was " bound " or " fettered " (אָסוּר—*asur*) in prison we are expressly told in Gen. xl. 3, though his fetters were doubtless much lightened after he obtained the favour of the keeper of the prison. A little glimpse into the intense suffering of mind as well as of body, which he endured through the cruel treatment of his brethren when they handed him over as a slave to the Midianite merchants, we get in the remorseful soliloquy of Jacob's sons when their conscience began to awaken in the unexpected trouble in which they found themselves on their first visit to Egypt—" *We are verily guilty concerning our brother, in that we saw the distress* " (or " *agony* ")

sleeves, and which, by coming down to the knees only, enabled men to set about their work, this tunic with sleeves clearly marked out its wearer as a person of special distinction, who was not required to do ordinary work."

It is of interest to note that the only other place in the Hebrew Bible where *kh'thoneth passim* is used, is in 2 Sam. xiii. 18, 19, where it describes the garment which poor Tamar, Absolom's sister, wore, and where it is added that " with such robes were the king's daughters that were virgins apparelled."

[1] בַּרְזֶל בָּאָה נַפְשׁוֹ—*barzel ba-ah naph'sho*, lit., " *his soul came into iron*," an idiom intended, I believe, to express the intensity of his sufferings. It was not only his feet which were hurt by the fetters, or his body which was bruised by the chains, his *soul*, i.e. his *whole being*, his mind and spirit, as well as his body, was in the " iron." To a sensitive nature like Joseph's the false charge and the *injustice* of his treatment must have occasioned torture of mind. The old English Prayer Book version has, " the iron entered into his soul." But the word for *iron* is masculine, and the verb is feminine, which agrees with the feminine noun *soul*.

" *of his soul when he besought us, and we would not hear.*"[1]
And this " distress," or agony of soul, was not less
when, on the false charge of a wanton woman, he was
bound with fetters and cast into prison, without any
apparent chance of ever being delivered.

There is some ambiguity in the text as to whose
word is intended in the first line of the 19th verse—
whether God's or Joseph's ; but I agree with the
observation of another writer that it is Joseph's word
which is intended, as there seems to be an intentional
contrast between " his word " in the first line, and
" the promise of Jehovah " in the second line of this
verse.   But a further question may be asked, Which
of Joseph's words is it that the Psalmist has in his
mind ?   Is it Joseph's word of interpretation of the
dreams of his fellow-prisoners, the verification of which
led, " after two full years," to his liberation and exaltation, as   Hengstenberg   and   others   interpret ?   or
was it " his word " in which he recounted his own
dreams to his brethren ?

It is the latter which I believe is intended, for these
dreams on account of which his brethren " hated him
yet more," and concerning which Jacob himself was
puzzled, though " he kept the saying in his mind," were
Divine premonitions—yea, revelations—of his future
exaltation which became literally true, however unlikely that seemed when he first open-heartedly related
them to his father and brethren.[2]

But between that " word " concerning his future
glorious destiny when first uttered, and its eventual
fulfilment, lay a valley of humiliation and suffering
some thirteen years long—the imprisonment in Egypt
alone lasting over ten years.   And all this time " *The
word of Jehovah tried him.*"

[1] Gen. xlii. 21.   [2] Gen. xxxvii. 5–11 ; xlii. 6–9.

The אִמְרַת יְהֹוָה—*imrath Yehovah*, in the second line, which is a different word in the original from that used for the word of Joseph in the first line, is the gracious " saying," or, as Delitzsch expresses it, " the revelation of God conveying His promises concerning his future exaltation, which came to him in those dreams." But this very revelation, or promise, " tried," tested, and " purified " him, [1] inasmuch as he was not to be raised to honour without having, in a state of deep abasement, proved a faithfulness that wavered not, and a confidence that knew no despair.[2]

" Consider for a moment his position," observes another writer, " and you will see the purpose of that trial. A youth educated amidst all the quiet simplicity of the early patriarchal life, he was haunted by dream-visions of a mighty destiny. Those visions were mysteriously foretelling his government in Egypt, and the blessings which his wise and just rule would cause on the land ; but while unable to comprehend them, he yet believed that they were voices of the future, and promises of God. But the quietude of that shepherd-life was not the proper preparation for the fulfilment of his promised destiny. The education that would form the ruler whose clear eye should judge between the good and the evil, and discern the course of safety in the hour of a nation's peril—all this was not to be gained under the shadow of his father's tent ; it must come through trial, and through trial arising from the very promise of God in which he believed. Hence a great and startling change crossed his life, that seemed to forbid the fulfilment of that dream-promise, and tempted him to doubt its truth. Sold into Egypt as a slave, cast into prison through his

---

[1] The word וַצְרָפַתְהוּ—*ts'rapha-thehu*, from צָרַף *tsaraph*, the primary meaning of which is " to *refine* " (as metals are refined), " to purify " —hence, also, to " try," or " prove."

[2] Delitzsch.

fidelity to God, the word of the Lord most powerfully
tried his soul.

" In the gloom of that imprisonment it was most
hard to believe in God's faithfulness when his affliction
had risen from his obedience, and most hard to keep
the promise clearly before him when his mighty trouble
would perpetually tempt him to regard it as an idle
dream. But through the temptation he gained the
strong trust which the pomp and glory of the Egyptian
Court would have no power to destroy ; and when
the word of deliverance came, the man came forth,
strong through trial, to fulfil his glorious destiny of
ruling Egypt in the name of God. Thus his trial by
the word of the Lord—his temptation to doubt its
truth—was a divine discipline preparing him for the
fulfilment of the promise."

But immediately the " need be " for the long and
painful trial was over, a rapid and wonderful transformation in his circumstances was brought about by
the providence of God, whose eye had been upon him
all the time, even while His word tried and tested him :

> " *The king sent and loosed him :*
> *The ruler of the peoples let him go free.*
> *He made him lord of his house,*
> *And ruler of all his possessions ;*
> *To bind his princes at his pleasure,*[1]
> *And to teach his elders wisdom.*"

" There is a ring of triumph," as one has truly
observed, " in the singer's voice, as he tells of the
honour and power heaped on the captive, and how
the king of many nations sent—as the mightier King

---

[1] The word is בְּנַפְשׁוֹ—*b'naph'sho*—lit., " with his soul," which some
have explained, is a bold metaphor describing Joseph's mind, or soul,
as the cord, or chain, with which he bound the Egyptians, *i.e.*, forced
them to perform his will. But the idiom *b'naph'sho*, " with his soul,"
is here simply the equivalent of בִּרְצוֹנוֹ—*birtsono*, " by," or " at his
will."

in heaven had done (verses 17–27), and not only liberated him, but exalted him—giving him, whose " soul " had been bound in " fetters," power to bind princes " according to his ' soul,' and to instruct and command the elders of Egypt."

The scripture on which these verses in our Psalm are based, is Gen. xli. 14–46 :

" *Then Pharaoh sent and called Joseph, and they brought him hastily out of the dungeon.* . . .

" *And Pharaoh said unto Joseph, ' Forasmuch as God has showed thee all this, there is none so discreet and wise as thou : thou shalt be over my house, and according unto thy word shall all my people be ruled.* . . . *See, I have set thee over all the land of Egypt. And Pharaoh took off his signet ring from his hand and put it upon Joseph's hand, and arrayed him in vestures of fine linen, and put a gold chain about his neck, and he made him ride in the second chariot which he had, and they cried before him, ' Abrech ' (' Bow the knee,' or ' kneel down,' i.e., in token of allegiance). And Pharaoh said unto Joseph, ' I am Pharaoh, and without thee shall no man lift his hand or foot in all the land of Egypt ' ; and Pharaoh called Joseph's name Zaph'nath-paneah,*[1] *and he gave him to wife, Asenath, the daughter of Poti-phera, priest of On.*"

And all this, as the Psalmist would remind us, God wrought in His wonderful providence with a view to the ultimate fulfilment of His covenant, and more particularly of the promise :

" *Unto thee will I give the land of Canaan,*
    The lot of your inheritance."

[1] *Zaph'nath-paneah.* There is disagreement among scholars as to the actual meaning of this Egyptian name which Pharaoh bestowed upon Joseph ; but whether it means " the support of life," or " the deliverer of the world," or " the revealer of secrets," as have been variously suggested, its significance is equally manifest.

Truly wonderful are the ways of God, and His thoughts unfathomable as the " great deep " !

But before proceeding to the next short paragraph, which sings of Israel's actual experiences in Egypt, I am constrained to add one or two observations on the seven verses we have been considering.

I. Who can fail to recognise in the touching and beautiful story of Joseph a foreshadowing of the experiences of Him of whom all the prominent personalities in Bible history are—in a greater or lesser degree of distinctness—types and shadows, and for whose coming into the world in the fulness of time the whole previous history of the chosen nation was, so to say, a prophetic preparation ?

Out of the very many striking points of resemblance between Joseph and Christ I would mention only the following :

(1) Joseph was the specially-beloved son of his father, reminding us of Him of whom we read, " This is my beloved Son, in whom I am well pleased."

(2) Joseph, because he was beloved of Jacob, was hated of his brethren, who were more or less estranged from their father by evil conduct [1] which he condemned.

---

[1] In the Midrashim and Rabbinic Commentaries Joseph is greatly blamed for bringing " the evil report " of his brothers to his father, as if it were a case of malicious tale-bearing. The chief accusations which he is supposed to have brought against them to Jacob are also mentioned, viz., that they ate limbs cut from living animals without first killing them properly, and that they treated the sons of the handmaidens (the sons of Bilhah and Zilpah) harshly and with contempt, calling them " slaves," instead of brothers. But the whole history of Joseph is against this Rabbinic conception of the case, and there is nothing in the Bible narrative to lead us to think that his conduct in the matter was blameworthy. Rather do we think that it was with a pure conscience and with pain in his heart that he brought to his father the " evil report " of their misconduct, which, as we may gather from the Hebrew idiom, was well known and notorious in the district—being zealous for the honour of his father's name and house.

And it was the unique and peculiar relation of our
Lord Jesus also to His heavenly Father, and the fact
that He loved righteousness and hated iniquity, which
were the chief and primary reasons why He was hated
of those who were " His own " brethren, but who, as
the result of a long process of self-hardening, were
estranged in their hearts from God, whom they also
claimed as their Father.

If, like the false prophets, He had come to them
with flatteries and cried, " Peace, peace ! " they would
have received Him with favour, but the keynote of
His preaching and testimony was " Repent ye, for
the Kingdom of Heaven is at hand," and that they
could not stand.

(3) Of Joseph we read that " they hated him yet
the more for his dreams and for his words." [1] But
these dreams were, as we have already seen, Divine
premonitions, prophetic revelations of his future
exaltation, which, after his testing time was over,
were abundantly fulfilled. And one chief cause of the
ever-growing opposition and hatred on the part of the
Scribes and Pharisees to our Lord Jesus was His clear,
full, conscious testimony concerning Himself—His
Divine claims as the Son of God, whom all men
should honour, even as they honour the Father, and
of the glory which belonged to Him in virtue of His
being not only the Son of God, but as the Son of
Man.

" For this cause, therefore," to quote only one
passage, " the Jews sought the more to kill Him,
because He not only (according to their perverted
ideas) brake the Sabbath, but also called God His own
Father, making Himself equal with God." [2]

(4) Not only was Joseph *hated* by his own brethren,

[1] Gen. xxvii. 8.   [2] John v. 18 (R.V.).

but they abused and ill-treated him, and in the end
sold him into Gentile hands for twenty pieces of silver.
In Egypt, where he was taken and resold by the
Midianite merchants, he was, though pure and innocent,
treated with the greatest indignity as a vile criminal,
and for over ten long years kept in a " dungeon,"
where his very " soul entered into the iron."

And does not this remind us of the still greater
humiliations of the " Man of Sorrows and acquainted
with grief," Who, though Himself " holy and undefiled
and separate from sinners," was " reckoned with transgressors," and had all sorts of sufferings heaped upon
Him ? He also was sold—not for twenty, but thirty
pieces of silver—and handed over by His own brethren
into the hands of the Gentiles.

And Jesus our Lord was not only thrown into a pit
and dungeon, but, after suffering the most ignominious
death on the cross, had His grave appointed " with
the wicked " and was buried in the pit of death.

(5) For many long years, after they handed him
over into the hands of the Midianites, Joseph's brethren
—indeed, Jacob's whole family—thought and spoke
of him as *dead*. In their account of themselves in
his own presence in Egypt before he made himself
known to them,[1] they said (referring to himself), " One
is not " (*i.e.*, is no longer in existence), and again as
actually " dead." [2]

And even so do the Jews think of Jesus. According to them He is dead.

" Christianity," tauntingly writes one of the Zionist
leaders in a recently published book, " centres round
a sepulchre," and he compares his false representation
of Christian belief with Judaism, which, according to
him, is a religion of life and hope.

---

[1] Gen. xlii. 13.   [2] Gen. xliv. 20.

(6) But while his brethren thought and spoke of Joseph as no more, he was not only alive, but greatly exalted among the Gentiles, as the " Support of Life," or " Deliverer of the World," before whom all had to " bow the knee " in humble allegiance.

Even so is it with our Lord Jesus. Despised and rejected and accounted as dead among " His own " people, He is not only alive for evermore, but exalted and extolled, having a Name which is above every name—before whom hundreds of millions in the Gentile world " bow the knee " in humble worship, because He is indeed the true " Support of Life," being Himself the " Living Bread " which came down from heaven, of which if any man eat he shall live for ever.

(7) The separation and estrangement between Joseph and his brethren did not last for ever. In the extremity of their need they were again brought face to face with him, and though at first, while yet unknown to them, he spake and dealt " roughly " with them, so as to awaken their conscience and bring home to them the sense of guilt, his heart was all the time full of yearning love and compassion for them, and the account of Joseph's making himself known to his brethren is one of the most touching and thrilling stories in the Bible.

And this, too, as I do verily believe, foreshadows what will yet take place between Christ and Israel. In the extremity of their need, in " the time of Jacob's trouble," the Jewish people will yet be brought face to face with their long-rejected Messiah, and broken-heartedly confess " We are verily guilty concerning our brother "—Jesus—whom we handed over to the Romans to be crucified, and " denied before the face of Pilate, when he had determined to release Him, . . . and asked for a murderer to be granted unto us, and killed the Prince of Life," [1] calling down His blood upon us and our children. And then Jesus will make *Himself* known to His brethren, and comfort them in their great sorrow, saying, " I am Jesus, your Brother, whom you handed over to be crucified, and for so long thought to be dead ; and now be not grieved, nor angry with yourselves, . . . for God sent Me before you to preserve life."

This will be a great and glorious event in the world's history, and the effect of it as " life from the dead " [2] for all peoples. Then not only the Church, but angels, will join in the adoring exclamation, " Oh, the depth of the riches, both of the wisdom and knowledge of God ! How unsearchable are His judgments and His ways past finding out ! "

II. In the story of Joseph there is reflected also the spiritual experience of every one of God's children. There is no other way to glory for the saints of God than through suffering. It is " through much tribulation " that we finally enter into the kingdom. Like Joseph, we receive at the very beginning of our Christian career the revelation and pledge of our future greatness, but between the promise and its final realisation there is often a long and dark valley of humiliation and suffering to pass, when we are tempted to forget our high calling and to doubt our ever attaining the glorious destiny pictured for us in the scripture of truth.

And, as was the case with Joseph, all those years until the time that his dreams at last came to pass, " the word of Jehovah tries " us. But with us, also, it is only with a view to " purify " and perfect, and make us meet for the position of " authority " and glory which He has purposed for us from eternity.

And even in the severest trial God never leaves,

[1] Acts iii. 13–15.   [2] Rom. xi. 15.

nor forsakes, nor forgets, the soul that trusts Him
and holds fast to His word and promise, however
remote and improbable the fulfilment may appear.
Let us, then, not grow weary under trial, but " let
patience have her perfect work, that we may be perfect
and entire, wanting nothing," and " that the proof of
our faith being more precious than gold that perisheth,
may be found unto praise and glory and honour at the
revelation of Jesus Christ." It is a true saying that,
if God's people are " proved," it is in order that they
may be *approved* and " tested," in order that they
may be *attested* as sure heirs of the kingdom which
God has prepared for them from before the foundation
of the world.

14

ISRAEL'S EXPERIENCE IN EGYPT AND THE EXODUS

THE next short strophe (verses 23–27) carries us a stage farther in the development of God's purpose in reference to Israel. It sings of Israel's actual experience in Egypt:

> " Israel also came into Egypt,
>   And Jacob sojourned in the land of Ham."

This is the middle verse of the Psalm, and emphasises a prominent fact. It is connected with all that goes before it, as well as with the verses which follow.

When God first made the covenant with Abraham, saying:

> " Unto thee will I give the land of Canaan,
>   The lot of your inheritance,"

on which verses 8 to 11 lay such stress, He told him in advance that before his seed would enter into their promised possessions they " shall be sojourners in a land that is not theirs, and shall serve them ; and they shall afflict them four hundred years . . . and afterward shall they come out with great substance.[1]

This land where Israel, by God's appointment, was to sojourn so long, and to suffer much affliction precursory to their being established as a nation in Palestine, was Egypt ; and in the short strophe immediately preceding the verses we are now considering

[1] Gen. xv. 13, 14.

we were reminded of the links in the wonderful chain of God's providence which prepared the way for Jacob and his family being brought there : " *He* called for a famine upon the land ; *He* sent a man before them, namely, Joseph, who was sold for a slave," and endured much affliction until the time came that His word came to pass, then " the king sent and loosed him, the ruler of peoples let him go free." And not only so, but he made him lord of his house, and ruler of his substance, to bind his princes at his pleasure and teach his elders wisdom. *And thus*—as the final link in the chain of providential events—" *Israel came into Egypt and Jacob sojourned (the word being the same as in Gen. xv.* 13) *in the land of Ham.*"

This marks off one stage of God's providential leadings of His people with a view to the accomplishment of His purpose, which was not only the fulfilment of His promise that they should possess Palestine but that they should be the centre of His kingdom on earth, and that in and through them all the families of the earth should be blessed.

Between verses 23 and 24 there is a gap of time as long as there is between Genesis and Exodus, viz., about four hundred years, but all the time God's eye was upon them, and He never forgot His promise to Abraham.

In the furnace of Egypt the family of Jacob developed and was welded together into a people, and as His purposes in reference, not only to Israel, but to Egypt and " the Amorite," ripened, and the time was come for the seed of Abraham to take possession of the promised land, God began more manifestly to work again.

Firstly, " *He increased His people greatly, and made them stronger than their adversaries.*"

This is an echo of Ex. i. 7-9, " *And the Children of*

Israel were fruitful and increased abundantly and multi-plied, and waxed exceeding mighty, and the land was filled with them," so that Pharaoh became alarmed at the growing power of the Jews, and in his fear, even exagg-erated the danger : " Behold," he said, " the people of the children of Israel are more and mightier than we : "

Secondly, " *He turned their heart to hate His people, to deal subtilly with His servants.*"

Some have stumbled at the apparent moral diffi-culty that God should have " turned " the hearts of Pharaoh and the Egyptians to hate His people.   But as has been well said by the great English preacher, " It was His goodness to Israel which called forth the illwill of Pharaoh and his Court.   Thus far, but no farther, did the Lord turn the hearts of the Egyptians. God cannot in any sense be the author of sin so far as to be morally responsible for its existence, but it often happens through the evil which is inherent in human nature that the acts of the Lord arouse the ill feelings of ungodly men.   Is the sun to be blamed because while it softens wax it hardens clay ?   Is the orb of day to be accused of creating the foul exhalations which are drawn by its warmth from the pestilential marsh ?   The evil is in men, and the honour of turning it to good and useful purposes is with the Lord." [1]

God " turned " their hearts to hate His people in the same manner as He is said in Exodus to have " hardened " Pharaoh's heart so that he refused to let Israel go.   In either case, what God did, or permitted to come on Pharaoh and the Egyptians as a punishment was in direct consequence of a process of rebellion and *self-hardening.*

To translate from an old German writer : " Man first hardens his own heart against God's gracious

[1] C. H. Spurgeon.

remonstrances and invitations ; *this is his sin.* Afterwards (if persisted in) he *becomes* hardened so that he is
no longer able to turn from the evil ; *this is his punishment.* Deliberate and persistent rejection of God's
great salvation ultimately leads to the exclusion from
the possibility of salvation." Or, in the words of
Augustine, " God hardens not by implanting evil, but
by a withdrawing of His grace. He hardens it so far
as He does not soften ; and blinds in so far as He does
not enlighten." In the words of yet another old
writer : " Just as the going down of the sun makes
night, so God blinds men by being no longer present
to them as the light : and He is no longer present to
them because of the wickedness that is in them."

But to return to the more direct context of our
Psalm. The expression of their hatred to God's people
was shown in the first instance by their dealing
" subtilly " with them. " *Come now,*" said Pharaoh,
" *let us deal wisely with them, lest they multiply and fight
against us, and get them out of the land.*" So they set
task-masters over them to afflict them with their
burdens, with a view to repress them, and when that
did not answer their purpose they concerted measures
for their destruction and eventually issued that cruel
decree that all the Hebrew newly-born male children
should be put to death. But God taketh the wise in
their own craftiness, and proved His over-ruling power
and wisdom even " in the thing wherein they dealt
proudly against them." [1] For " the more they afflicted
them the more they multiplied and the more they
spread abroad." And not only so, but while letting
Pharaoh and the Egyptians freely express in deed all
that was in their evil hearts in relation to the oppressed
people, so as to make it manifest how deserving they

[1] Ex. xviii. 11.

were of the righteous judgments which were about to
fall upon them, God controlled their actions with a view
to loosen Israel's attachment to Egypt and to make
them willing to leave the land where they had been
settled so long.

Thirdly, when the time for the fulfilment of His
original promise to Abraham was now come, and their
nest had, so to say, been shaken up by the persecutions
and cruel bondage which they had to endure, *He sent
Moses His servant (and) Aaron whom He had chosen.*"
He had " sent a man " before them—even Joseph,
which prepared the way for their coming into Egypt,
and now when the appointed time for their sojourn in
the land of Ham was come to an end, " He sent " His
chosen servant, Moses, who, with the assistance of
his brother Aaron, was to lead them out of it.   And this
is ever the case.   In all crises in the history of His
redeemed people God has the appointed human instrumentality ready at hand to accomplish His purpose.

And the very perversity of Pharaoh and the
Egyptians, who refused to let Israel go, gave the oppor-
tunity for God to display His glorious power on behalf of
His people :

" *They set among them His signs* [1]
And wonders in the land of Ham."

The reference is to the miraculous judgments of the
ten plagues.   These were " *His signs* "—displays of
His mighty power, and expressions of His righteous
anger at the ill-treatment of His people.   But they

[1] The Hebrew words are דִּבְרֵי אֹתוֹתָיו—*dibh'rei othothav*—literally, the
" words," or " matters " of His signs, *i.e.*, that which pertained to the
whole series of signs and wonders displayed in Egypt.   Delitzsch
renders the phrase " They performed upon them facts of His signs."
A more suggestive rendering is that of Dr. Kay : " They planted among
them His long record of signs."

were called down and inflicted through the instrumentality of Moses and Aaron.

The story of the signs and wonders which God
wrought in Egypt on Israel's behalf, which paralysed
the power of Egypt and made the Egyptians willing
ultimately to let Israel go, is the substance of the
Psalmist's song in the next strophe (verses 28–38).

We dare not, for lack of space, enter minutely into
an examination of this section, but we may notice in
passing that in the rehearsal of the plagues (as is the
case also in Psalm lxxviii.), the inspired poet does not
follow the historical order of the book of Exodus, and
omits altogether the fifth and sixth.

He begins with the ninth, viz., the thick darkness
which rested on Egypt for three days, " darkness which
might be felt," during which as we read in Exodus,
" they saw not one another, neither rose any one from
his place "—probably because " it was the most distinct
self-representation of Divine wrath." [1]   We have to
remember, also, God's word to Moses that He would
inflict His judgments not only on Pharaoh and his
people, but also " against all the gods of Egypt I will
execute judgments : I am Jehovah."   The execution
of His judgments on Egypt's idols, by showing up their
helplessness to defend their worshippers from the wrath
of Jehovah, the true and living God of the Hebrews,
was one object accomplished, not only in the slaying of
the first-born, but more or less in all the plagues.

" *He sent darkness*," the Psalmist says—it was
Jehovah's messenger of judgment to Egypt—" *and
made it dark.*"

" Such a preternatural continuance of absolutely
impenetrable ' blackness of darkness ' would cause to
any man a feeling of intense alarm and horror.   To the

[1] Delitzsch.

Egyptians it would be peculiarly painful and terrible. Ra, the sun god, was among the principal objects of their worship, especially in the Delta, where Heliopolis and Pithom were cities dedicated to him. Darkness, accordingly, to Egyptian mythology, was a creation of Seth—the evil Principle, the destroyer of Osiris—and of Apophis the great serpent, the impeder of souls in the lower world.

"It would have seemed to the Egyptians that Ra was dead, that Set had triumphed over his brother, that Apophis had encircled the world with his dark folds and plunged it in eternal night." [1]

Thus, to quote yet another writer, " all the forms of Egyptian will-worship were covered with shame and confusion by the plagues."

The second line of the 28th verse has occasioned much discussion among commentators : " *And they rebelled not against His word.*" Of the Egyptians it is not true, for although—as several times before—Pharaoh and his Court were cowed by this plague and offered to let Israel go, it was still with the reservation that their flocks and their herds should be left behind. And when Moses insisted, " Our cattle also shall go with us : there shall not a hoof be left behind," Pharaoh, in the full pride of his heart exclaimed, " Get thee from me, take heed to thyself ; for in the day thou seest my face thou shalt die." [2]

Hengstenberg, to get over the difficulty, regards the words in the first line, " *He sent darkness and made it dark,*" as referring, not to the ninth plague, but as used in a figurative sense of " the impending displeasure and misery—the darkness with which the Egyptians were, so to say, covered during the whole period of the judgments which were poured upon them."

[1] Professor George Rawlinson.   [2] Ex. x. 24–29.

And thus " as *comprehending all the ten* plagues including the destruction of the first-born," it may be said that *in the end* they no longer rebelled against the word of Jehovah, but suffered Israel to depart. But this does not seem to me satisfactory, for the impression naturally left on the reader's mind is that the Psalmist speaks of the literal plague of darkness ; though it may be conceded that he viewed it also as in a special sense symbolic of the Divine wrath which manifested itself in all the plagues, and therefore mentions it first. The true explanation, is, I believe, that given by Delitzsch and others, viz. that the second line of the 28th verse goes back for its subject to the 27th verse, and that the words refer to Moses and Aaron. The context is as follows :

" *He sent Moses, his servant ;*
Aaron whom He had chosen.
They set (or planted) among them (i.e. the Egyptians)
    His signs
And wonders in the land of Ham. . . .
And they rebelled not against His words,"

i.e. " they shrank not from their perilous embassage, but executed the terrible commands accurately and willingly," in contrast to their behaviour at *Meribah*, when these divinely chosen messengers did rebel against His word.[1]

---

[1] The Septuagint and Syriac versions get over the difficulty by omitting the negative אֹל, which makes it to read, " And they rebelled against His word." This is copied in the Prayer Book Version, which has, " And they were not obedient unto His word." Another suggestion is that the verb should be taken as " imperfect subjunction," in which case it would read, " He sent darkness and made it dark, that they might not rebel against His words." But none of these renderings and explanations are satisfactory, and they are all based on the supposition that the words refer to the Egyptians.

From the ninth plague, the Psalmist comes back to the first :

" *He turned their water into blood, and slew their fish.*"

This also was a judgment, and adapted to strike the Egyptians with peculiar horror, and in which God's *retributive* justice was particularly manifested. " It struck the Egyptians," says Professor Rawlinson, " two several blows :

" (1) It involves an insult to their religion, and brings it into discredit, since the Nile-god, Hapi, was a main object of worship, closely connected with Osiris, and even with Ammon, celebrated in hymns with the most extravagant titles of honour.

" (2) It is a great physical affliction. They are accustomed to use the Nile water for drinking, for ablutions, for the washing of their clothes, and for culinary purposes ; they have great difficulty in procuring any other ; they delight in the Nile water, regard it as the best in the world, are in the habit of drinking deep draughts of it continually. This is all put a stop to. They suffer from thirst, from enforced uncleanliness, from the horror of blood all about them, even in their cisterns. Again, their fish are killed.

" Fish was one of their principal foods, perhaps the main food of the common people ; and the river was the chief source whence the fish supply was obtained, for even the Lake Moeris was an off-shoot from the river. Their fish supply is stopped. *The punishment is retaliatory :* for as they had made the Nile the means of destroying Hebrew infants (Ex. i. 22), so that Hebrew parents had loathed to drink of it, as though stained with the blood of their children, so it is now made by means of blood undrinkable for themselves. The plague lasts seven days—a longer time than any other ; and if not so destructive as the later ones, was perhaps of all the most nauseous and disgusting."

After the first plague the Psalmist follows in the main the historical sequence of the plagues, as given in Exodus, except that he inverts the order of the third and fourth, and omits, as already stated, the fifth and sixth.

We must not linger on the remaining verses of this section, except to notice the emphasis which the inspired singer puts upon the fact that it was *He*—Jehovah Himself—who inflicted all these judgments on Egypt, though it was by the hands of Moses and Aaron. " *He* sent darkness," " *He* turned their rivers into blood," and made their land swarm with frogs. " *He* smote their vines also, and their fig-trees, and broke the trees of their borders." Especially sublime and expressive of the Divine power and majesty is the phrase, twice repeated (verses 31, 34) — אָמַר וַיָּבֹא—*amar v'yabho*— " He spake (or " said ") and it came—for all the forces of nature are at His command, and even the " swarms of flies," and the locusts and grasshoppers obey His voice, and fulfil His errands. Thus, to quote from Psalm lxxviii. :

" *He cast upon them the fierceness of His anger, wrath, and*
indignation, and trouble; a band of angels of evil." [1]
" *He made a path for His anger ; He spared not their*
souls from death."

The tenth plague, which finally broke Pharaoh's [2] stubborn will and Egypt's power of resistance, is briefly narrated in two lines :

" *And He smote all the first-born in their land,*
The chief of all their strength,"

and we come to the triumphant climax of the Exodus,
" *And He brought them forth with silver and gold* "—in

---

[1] *i.e.* The ten plagues came like a company of evil " Messengers," or " Angels " of destruction, which God sent into the midst of Egypt.
[2] Ps. lxxviii. 79, 80.

accord with His original promise to Abraham, that when their long servitude in Egypt shall be ended they shall come out with great substance." [1]

" *And there was not one feeble one among His tribes.*" [2]

This is a beautiful and significant touch on the part of the Psalmist. To the Egyptians and unsympathetic onlookers they may have appeared a mere rabble, an unorganised and untrained multitude of slaves, but Jehovah of Hosts was now manifestly identified with them, and these were *His* tribes, which He was leading forth in triumph and strengthened with His might, there was not one " feeble one " (or, literally, " one ready to stumble," כּוֹשֵׁל—*Koshel*) in the whole of that vast company of men, women, and children.

" *Egypt was glad when they departed, for the fear of them had fallen upon them.*"

Yea, Pharaoh and the Egyptians were urgent upon the people to send them out of the land in haste ; for they said, " We are all dead men."

This ends the story of the Exodus, which marks off another important stage of the development of God's purpose, and brings us much nearer the fulfilment of the original promise, which He made to Abraham :

" *Unto thee will I give the land of Canaan, the lot of your inheritance.*"

---

[1] Gen. xv. 14.

The rendering in the A.V. of Ex. xii. 35, 36, is misleading. The children of Israel did not " borrow," but (as it is properly translated in the R.V.), " they *asked* of the Egyptians jewels of silver and jewels of gold, and raiment ; and Jehovah gave the people favour in the sight of the Egyptians, so that they let them have what they asked "—for they were well entitled to it all after the long years of servitude and hard labour which had been exacted from them.

[2] Not " their " tribes, as in the A.V.

15

A PARALLELISM BETWEEN THE PAST AND THE PRESENT PHASE OF THE JEWISH QUESTION

BEFORE expounding briefly the concluding short section of our Psalm, consisting of the last seven verses, let me point out that in the story of Israel's experience in Egypt, and in the Exodus, we have a forecast also of the present condition of things. If we substitute the word " nations " for Egypt we have an epitome in these verses which we have been considering, of the origin, development, and issues not only of the ancient, but also of the modern phase of the Jewish question.

The origin of the Jewish Question [1] in Egypt is summed up in the words : " He increased His people greatly ; and made them stronger than their enemies." This is brought out still more clearly in the original account in Exodus, where we read : " And the children of Israel were fruitful, and increased abundantly, and multiplied, and waxed exceedingly mighty ; and the land was filled with them." It was on that account that the new Pharaoh, who knew not Joseph, became alarmed and took counsel with his people, saying, " Come on, let us deal wisely with them," the result of which were measures of repression, and when these did not answer, the promulgation of an edict for their extermination.

---

[1] This subject is dealt with more fully in the chapter on anti-Semitism in my book, *The Ancient Scriptures and the Modern Jew.*

Now the modern phase of the Jewish Question originated and becomes from year to year intensified from the same cause.

The rapid increase of the Jews since the middle of the nineteenth century is one of the most striking and significant signs of the times.

At the beginning of the eighteenth century there were, according to high authorities, only about one million Jews left in the world after the continual dispersions, terrible sufferings, and almost wholesale massacres which they had to endure in the dark and middle ages.

With the Reformation there was a certain lessening of the oppression and persecution from which they had so long suffered, and in consequence they experienced a slight national revival.

But even at the beginning of the eighteenth century, when Basnage published his *History of the Jews from Jesus Christ to the Present Time* (1708)—the first orderly and scientific account of the Jewish people which appeared in Europe—he estimated that there were not more than three millions of Jews in the world.

At the commencement of the nineteenth century there were said to be five millions ; at the end of another century—in 1896—the greatest living authority on Jewish statistics gave their number as eleven millions ; less than two decades later the fresh census taken in Russia (where nearly half the Jewish nation was located) and other countries revealed the fact that there were no less than thirteen million Jews in the world.   And the surprising feature in connection with these figures is the officially authenticated fact that in the country where they were most persecuted (Russia) just there they increased most rapidly.

Within the past thirty-five years some three million Jews have been driven by persecution to emigrate from Russia, Galicia, etc., chiefly to the United States and Canada, yet the number of Jews in those countries has not become diminished, but has rather increased. The Slavic peoples are the most prolific among the

European races, but the Jews increase four or five times as rapidly as the Slavs.

Within two years (in 1919 and 1920), 150,000 Jews were massacred in the Ukraine alone, and many scores of thousands perished during the war, and since by the sword, famine, and pestilence, and yet, according to the *Jewish Year-book* for 1923, the total number of Jews has increased to over 15,000,000 or, according to Davis Trietsch (a great authority on Jewish statistics), to over 19,000,000.

Truly, the old story of Israel in Egypt renews itself to-day : " The more they afflicted them, the more they multiplied, and the more they spread abroad."

And not only is it in point of numbers that God is again causing His people to " increase greatly," but by their superior wits and energy, and by their habits of frugality and thriftiness, He makes them " stronger than their enemies," so that in those regions where the bulk of the nation is to be found, wherever the Jew has a fair chance, he naturally places his Gentile neighbours in a less favourable position in the struggle for existence. The superior ability of the Jew is openly acknowledged by anti-Semites, and often appealed to as a ground for the restrictive and repressive laws, which until recently were in vogue against them in most countries.

The following is taken from a chapter in a work which summarizes " The Case for Russian anti-Semitism " before the war. " But there is still another element which the rulers of Russia are constrained to take into their consideration. The intellect of the Jew is masterful. His assiduity, his deadly resolve to get on, his self-denial and ambition surmount all natural obstacles. If all careers in the Russian Empire were thrown open to the Russian Jew, not a decade would go by before the whole Russian Administration from Port Arthur to Eytkuhnen, and from Archangel to Yalta, must pass into Hebraic hands. This is a sober statement of facts."

The same is true of other continental countries. The following is a passage from an apology for anti-

Semitism in Austria, which, though somewhat exaggerated, is largely true :

" The Jews are all-powerfully represented in every walk of life that leads to influence and fortune. In the professions of law, medicine, and literature, their numbers are out of all proportion to their quota of the population. Finance and commerce are practically in their hands. The great business houses, the banks, the railways that do not belong to the State, are all controlled by them. The Produce Exchange, and, of course, the Bourse at Vienna, Prague, or Budapest are deserted on Jewish holidays. The Press, with the exception of the Czech organs, is almost exclusively in the hands of the Jews."

The proportion of Jews in the universities of Austria has been far in excess of what might be expected from their actual number in the country. In the particular year to which the writer of the above refers, the Vienna University was attended by 6530 students, and of these 2500, or 40 per cent., were Jews. Most of the great specialists, and the best known professors in Vienna, were Jews, or of Jewish origin. The faculty of law may almost be said to be a monopoly of the Jews in Austria, and also in Germany, where they form not only a large percentage of the attorneys, but also of the judges of the highest courts, and have, as in England and France, supplied from their ranks ministers of justice and judges of appeal.[1]

The next step in the old Jewish Question in Egypt was that " He turned their hearts (that is, of Egyptians) to hate His people, to deal subtilly with His servants." This is how the Great God causes the wrath of man to praise Him, and when His purpose is accomplished, " restrains the remainder." Pharaoh and his counsellors said, " Come on, let us deal wisely with them,"

[1] Let it be noted that the statistics and what is here stated about Jewish influence in Russia, Germany, Austria, etc., refer to the condition of things as they existed before the War. A great change in their condition has taken place since, and for the time being their position in Austria, and particularly in Hungary, is a very precarious one.

and attempted to solve the Jewish Question in their own way, by persecution and extermination ; but God turned the wisdom of the Egyptians into foolishness. " The more they afflicted them, the more they multiplied and grew." Instead of succeeding in drowning them in the Nile, Pharaoh and his host were in the end drowned in the Red Sea.

But what is the meaning of God's " turning their heart to hate His people " ? It had a double significance.

In relation to Israel it was (as we have seen) the means which God employed to stir up their nests and to make them willing to leave the land in which, until the persecutions broke out, they had been content to live for centuries. And this is true also to-day. The present condition of the Jews among the nations, and the mysterious antipathy which they encounter in practically all lands of their dispersion, cannot be accounted for merely by social, economical, or political reasons. The primary cause is to be found in their special relationship to God and His overruling providence, directed with a view to preserving them a separate nation.

Israel is God's national prodigal son, who, if he found things quite comfortable in the " far country " where he is now squandering his gifts and talents, and degrading himself with occupations for which he was never intended, would gladly settle down and become assimilated among the nations and forget his sin against his Father, and his home from which he has wandered. His nest must therefore be continually stirred up, that he may be reminded that the lands of the Gentiles are not his permanent resting-place.

The millions of the poor and less-cultured orthodox Talmudic Jews in Russia, Poland, Roumania, etc., have long ago been convinced that these lands cannot much longer remain their resting-places, and that it is about time for them " to arise and depart " toward that land for which they have never ceased to cherish a yearning desire ; hence the many colonising schemes and the

more than thirty Jewish colonies which existed in
Palestine already before the War, consisting almost
entirely of Russian and Roumanian Jews.

The remarkable thing is that, as the result of the
newest phases of the anti-Jewish movement on the
Continent, the more cultured, wealthy, and rationalistic
Jews are at last digesting the truth that it is not by
the so-called " reform " movement, which aims at
assimilation with the nations, that the Jewish Question
will be solved ; for, after all their efforts in this direction
for more than half a century, and their desperate eager-
ness to strip themselves of all that is true and false in
orthodox Judaism, as a kind of peace-offering to the
mysterious, deep-seated antipathy of the Gentiles,
they find that it is just against themselves, more even
than against the less cultured of their brethren in
Russia and Eastern Europe, that the bitterest ani-
mosity is manifested, and that Christendom, though
it is itself for the most part apostate from the faith of
Christ, is even less reconciled to the rationalism and
neology of the modern cultivated " Israelite," than it
is to the Talmudism of the more consistent, orthodox
" Jew," who still wears his kaftan and peyoth.

What is this but a repetition of the warning words
which God in His providence has so often spoken to
Israel : " *And that which cometh into your mind shall
not be at all ; in that ye say, We will be as the nations,
as the families of the countries.*"

There was no other solution for the Jewish Question
in Egypt than the exodus, and so also will there be no
proper and *final* solution of the modern phase of this
ancient question than in the restoration of the Jewish
people to their own land, to be followed by their more
glorious restoration to the favour of God, and their
spiritual renewal in and through the grace of their
Messiah, our Lord Jesus Christ.

Of this national restoration we may now see the
very beginnings in the Zionist Movement, and the
wonderful developments in relation to Palestine, and
in the recognition on the part of the great Powers of

their right to a " national home " in their ancient fatherland.

And in relation to Egypt, their very hatred of the Jews was an evident token of perdition, and precursory of the plagues which came upon them. The judicial hardening of the heart of Pharaoh and the Egyptians was in itself part of the punishment of a righteous God upon a cruel nation, sinking lower and lower to the most contemptible depths of idolatry. God often chastises His own people " with the rod of man and with stripes of the children of man," but He has no pleasure in the scourge which He employs, and, as a rule, uses for the chastisement of His people, men or nations whom He designs to give up to destruction for their wickedness.

And this also is true in relation to the nations of Christendom. Anti-Semitism, which will culminate in the final confederacy of the nations against Jerusalem with the cry, " Come, let us destroy them from being a nation : that the name of Israel be no more in remembrance," is one of the manifest symptoms of the growing apostasy, and a sure omen of the approaching judgment, with which, according to the testimony of all the prophets, the present dispensation is to close— for the ten plagues which were poured out on Egypt foreshadowed, and find their counterpart in the fearful plagues set forth in the Revelation—to be poured out on an anti-Christian apostate Christendom.

God's word still holds true, " I will bless them that bless thee, and him that curseth thee will I curse." [1] " *Therefore all they that devour thee shall be devoured ; and all thine adversaries, every one of them, shall go into captivity ; and they that despoil thee shall be a spoil, and all that prey upon thee will I give for a prey.*" [2]

[1] Gen. xii. 3.   [2] Jer. xxx. 16.

16

JEHOVAH'S SHEPHERD CARE OVER HIS PEOPLE

WE now come to the last section of our Psalm, which follows up the story of the exodus with the rehearsal of God's wonderful works on Israel's behalf in the wilderness, until He brought them safely into the promised land.

In these last seven verses the inspired singer brings into light only the leading instances of God's protection and care without one disturbing reference to the sins and failures which darkened the forty years. " These are spread out at length without flattery or minimising in the next Psalm, but here the theme is God's wonders " and His grace and faithfulness to them as a people.[1]

" *He spread a cloud for a covering and fire to give light in the night.*"

He not only brought forth " His tribes " triumphantly from Egypt, but He it was who led them and cared for them all through those forty years in the wilderness, " *And Jehovah went before them by day in a pillar of cloud,*" we read, " *to lead them by the way, and by night in a pillar of fire to give them light . . . the pillar of cloud by day, and the pillar of fire by night departed not from before the people.*" [2] This " Cloud of Glory " was their protection from their many foes ; it was the visible symbol also by which Jehovah Himself guided them through " the great and terrible wilderness "—

[1] Maclaren.   [2] Ex. xiii. 21, 22.

ever going before them " to seek out a resting-place for
them.¹ " *So it was alway*," we read, " *the cloud covered
it by day and the appearance of fire by night.*" When the
cloud tarried, as it did sometimes, " many days," the
children of Israel remained encamped, but when it was
taken up and moved, they journeyed.²

But here in our Psalm the " Cloud of Glory "
is viewed in the light of a canopy which was
spread over them to shield them from the scorching
rays of the sun as they moved through the fiery
desert.³

And the same cloud which effectually shielded them
by day illuminated them at night, so that He was both
" their sun and their shield." And not only did He
shield and protect them all through their wilderness
wanderings, but He miraculously supplied all their
needs :

" *They asked, and He brought quails.*"

Their wickedness in tempting God in their heart by
asking that which should satisfy their lust, and saying,
" *Can God prepare a table in the wilderness ? . . . Will
He provide flesh for His people ?* " ⁴ is, as already said,
passed over here, and the " emphasis is laid on the
omnipotence of the Divine goodness which responded
to their request."

The flesh, however, which they coveted proved
rather a curse than a blessing ; a means of death rather
than a support of life ; because of their greed and lust.
Infinitely better than what they would choose for
themselves was what God in His wisdom and goodness

---

¹ Num. x. 33–36.   ² Num. ix. 15–20.
³ This is expressed in the word פָּרַשׂ—*parash*—" He spread it," *i.e.*,
like a canopy. See Isa. iv. 6.
⁴ Ps. lxxviii. 18–20.

provided for them ; of this the Psalmist sings in the next line :

" *And satisfied them with bread from heaven.*"

This was the manna which did sustain and " satisfy " them. It is called " bread from heaven," for, in the language of Ps. lxxviii. :

" *He commanded the skies above, and opened the doors*
    of heaven ;
And He rained down manna upon them to eat, and
    gave them food from heaven." [1]

And not only did He supernaturally supply them with bread, but in that great desert " where no water is," where they were in danger of perishing from thirst :—

" *He opened the rock, and waters gushed out,*
They (the streams) ran in dry places like a river."

This is what Israel's God did ; *this is what He still can do*—blessed be His holy name ! And all this He did in faithfulness to His Covenant :

" *For He remembered His holy word, and Abraham, His*
    servant."

This was the twofold motive which actuated Him in all the marvellous works which He did on their behalf—His holy word of promise, which can never fail, and which must stand even " to a thousand generations," [2] and " Abraham His servant," to whom the promise was first made, whom, also, in His grace, He called " His *friend.*"

And this twofold motive, as the Psalmist would remind us, still holds true, and is the chief ground of the hope which He desires to awaken in our hearts for Israel's future by the rehearsal of the wonders which

----

[1] Ps. lxxviii. 23-25.   [2] Ps. cv. 8.

God has wrought for them in the past. "*Theirs still
are the promises* "; and the people, in spite of all their
sins and wanderings, are still "*beloved for the fathers'
sake.*" [1] However dark, therefore, the present may be,
we may look up with certainty that " He will again
have compassion upon us," and that " He will perform
the truth to Jacob, and the mercy (or " lovingkindness ") to Abraham, which He hath sworn unto
our fathers from the days of old." [2]

The 43rd verse goes back to the joy and triumph of
the tribes of Israel at the exodus and at the Red Sea :

" *He brought forth His people with joy, His chosen ones
with singing* "—

language which reminds us of Isa. xxxv., and other
prophetic passages, because the redemption from
Egypt foreshadows, in many respects, the future,
greater, national redemption, when " *the ransomed of
Jehovah shall return, and come with singing unto Zion :
and everlasting joy shall be upon their heads : they shall
obtain gladness and joy, and sorrow and sighing shall flee
away.*"

The rehearsal of " His marvellous works that He
had done " for them in the past, which Israel is exhorted to " remember," draws to a close. He had
sung of God's grace and faithfulness to the patriarchs
to whom the promises—especially the one in reference
to the possession of Canaan—were first made ; of the
chain of God's providences, which brought Israel into
Egypt and Jacob to sojourn in the land of Ham ; of
His interposition on behalf of His oppressed people
when the time had come for Him to lead them out of
the land of bondage ; of the series of miraculous
judgments of the ten plagues which finally broke

[1] Rom. ix. 4–xi.   [2] Mic. vii. 18–20.

Egypt's resisting power and made them willing to let Israel go; then of the actual exodus, and of the wonders which He wrought for them in the wilderness. Now, in the 44th verse, he speaks of their taking possession of the land :

> " *And He gave them the land of the nations* (i.e., *of Canaan*), *and they took* (lit., '*inherited*') *the labour of the peoples,*"

i.e., not only the land as a whole, but "the cultivated ground, the habitable cities, and accumulated treasures" of those doomed peoples—as the word עָמָל —'*amal*—(translated, " labour ") implies.

Thus God established His faithfulness in the first fulfilment of the promise, " *Unto thee will I give the land of Canaan, the lot of your inheritance.*"

But what was God's purpose in it all ? And why did He put them in this conspicuous and advantageous position ? The last verse tells us :

> " *That they might keep His statutes, and observe His laws.*"

Not only as a redeemed and independent people in a land chosen for them by God and bestowed upon them as an everlasting possession, but as possessors and custodians of His divinely revealed law, Israel was called of God " to exhibit the pattern of a holy nation moulded after the Divine will." [1] Yea, more, as the first verses of the Psalm remind them, they were to proclaim God's Name and make known His marvellous doings among the nations, so that they also might be brought to a knowledge of Jehovah, who has thus revealed Himself in their history as the God of Redemption.

In this high calling Israel in the past has grievously

[1] Delitzsch.

failed, and were therefore driven out of their land, and
have become wanderers among the nations. Have,
therefore, the promises of God failed ? Is there to be
no restoration to the land and to the favour of God ?
The next Psalm deals with this problem, and answers
the question. There we see that where sin abounds
grace doth *super*abound, and that great as Israel's sins
and transgressions have been, the grace and faithfulness
of Jehovah are greater. But we will not anticipate.
The Psalmist began by calling upon Israel to " Give
thanks unto Jehovah," and ends with " Hallelujah ! "

To this call a saved and renewed Israel, in and
through the grace of their Messiah, will yet respond,
and the earth will yet resound with the praises of
Jehovah's glorious " Name," and with the story of
" the marvellous works which He hath done," which
shall be published abroad by Jewish lips among all the
nations.

Meanwhile, dear Christian reader, *we* will take up
this " Hallelujah ! " on our lips and give thanks unto
Jehovah with all *our* hearts, for all, and more than He
did for Israel as a nation, He has done for us. Has He
not redeemed us out of a greater bondage than that of
Egypt ? And in Christ have we not the substance of
that of which Israel in the wilderness and in Canaan had
but the symbol and shadow. We, too, are being safely
led through a great and terrible wilderness to our
promised land, and all through the dreary way He
sustains our souls with the true manna which came
down from heaven, and gives us to drink the living
waters from the once-smitten Rock.

> When Israel, by Divine command,
>   The pathless desert trod,
> They found through all that barren land
>   A sure resource in God.

A cloudy pillar marked the road,
And screened them from the heat ;
From the hard rock the water flowed,
And manna was their meat.

Like them, we have a rest in view,
Secure from adverse powers ;
Like them we pass a desert, too,
But Israel's God is ours.

His Word a light before us sheds,
By which our path we see ;
His love, a banner o'er our heads,
From harm preserves us free.

Jesus, the Bread of Life is given,
To be our daily food ;
And from the rock that once was riven
We drink the streams of God.

Part 3

ISRAEL'S GREAT SIN AND JEHOVAH'S SUPERABUNDANT GRACE

Psalm 106

Psalm 106

PRAISE ye Jehovah.
O give thanks unto Jehovah ; for He is good ;
For His lovingkindness endureth for ever.
Who can utter the mighty acts of Jehovah,
Or show forth all His praise ?
Blessed are they that keep justice,
And he that doeth righteousness at all times.
Remember me, O Jehovah, with the favour that Thou bearest
    unto Thy people ;
O visit me with Thy salvation,
That I may see the prosperity of Thy chosen,
That I may rejoice in the gladness of Thy nation,
That I may glory with Thine inheritance.

We have sinned with our fathers,
We have committed iniquity, we have done wickedly.
Our fathers understood not Thy wonders in Egypt ;
They remembered not the multitude of Thy lovingkindnesses,
But were rebellious at the sea, even at the Red Sea.
Nevertheless He saved them for His name's sake,
That He might make his mighty power to be known.
He rebuked the Red Sea also, and it was dried up :
So He led them through the depths, as through a wilderness.
And He saved them from the hand of him that hated them,
And redeemed them from the hand of the enemy.
And the waters covered their adversaries ;
There was not one of them left.
Then believed they His words ;
They sang His praise.
They soon forgat His works ;
They waited not for His counsel,
They lusted exceedingly in the wilderness,
And tempted God in the desert.
And He gave them their request,
But sent leanness into their soul.
They envied Moses also in the camp,
And Aaron the saint of Jehovah.
The earth opened and swallowed up Dathan,

And covered the company of Abiram.
And a fire was kindled in their company ;
The flame burned up the wicked.
They made a calf in Horeb,
And worshipped a molten image.
Thus they changed their glory
For the likeness of an ox that eateth grass.
They forgat God their Saviour,
Who had done great things in Egypt,
Wondrous works in the land of Ham,
And terrible things by the Red Sea.
Therefore He said that He would destroy them,
Had not Moses His chosen stood before Him in the breach,
To turn away His wrath, lest He should destroy them.
Yea, they despised the pleasant land,
They believed not His word,
But murmured in their tents,
And hearkened not unto the voice of Jehovah.
Therefore He sware unto them,
That He would overthrow them in the wilderness,
And that He would overthrow their seed among the nations,
And scatter them in the lands.
They joined themselves also unto Baal-peor,
And ate the sacrifices of the dead.
Thus they provoked Him to anger with their doings ;
And the plague brake in upon them.
Then stood up Phinehas, and executed judgment ;
And so the plague was stayed.
And that was reckoned unto Him for righteousness,
Unto all generations for evermore.
They angered Him also at the waters of Meribah,
So that it went ill with Moses for their sakes ;
Because they were rebellious against his Spirit,
And he spake unadvisedly with his lips.
They did not destroy the peoples,
As Jehovah commanded them,
But mingled themselves with the nations,
And learned their works,

And served their idols,
Which became a snare unto them.
Yea, they sacrificed their sons and their daughters unto
demons,
And shed innocent blood,
Even the blood of their sons and of their daughters,
Whom they sacrificed unto the idols of Canaan ;
And the land was polluted with blood.
Thus were they defiled with their works,
And played the harlot in their doings.
Therefore was the wrath of Jehovah kindled against His people,
And He abhorred His inheritance.
And He gave them into the hand of the nations ;
And they that hated them ruled over them.
Their enemies also oppressed them,
And they were brought into subjection under their hand.
Many times did He deliver them ;
But they were rebellious in their counsel,
And were brought low in their iniquity.
Nevertheless He regarded their distress,
When He heard their cry :

And He remembered for them His covenant,
And repented according to the multitude of His lovingkindnesses.
He made them also to be pitied
Of all those that carried them captive.

Save us, O Jehovah our God,
And gather us from among the nations,
To give thanks unto Thy holy name,
And to triumph in Thy praise.

Blessed be Jehovah, the God of Israel,
From everlasting even to everlasting.
And let all the people say, Amen.
Praise ye Jehovah.

17

WHO CAN SHOW FORTH ALL HIS PRAISE ?

PSALM CVI. is manifestly the continuation of
Psalm cv., but it presents the other and darker
side of the picture.

The inspired recital in Psalm cv. begins with the
call of Abraham and carries us on to the entrance into
Canaan. Psalm cvi. continues the survey from the
Exodus to the Babylonian captivity and subsequent
universal dispersion, and looks on prophetically to the
time when, in faithfulness to the covenant of which
Psalm cv. sings, Jehovah shall " save " His people,
and " gather them from among the nations, to give
thanks unto His holy Name and to triumph in His
praise." [1]

Psalm cv. (as shown in the introductory remarks
to the exposition of that Psalm) deals entirely with
God's unfailing faithfulness to Israel, while Psalm cvi.
sets forth the sad contrast of Israel's continued faithlessness to God.

The keynote of Psalm cv. is found in the words,
" *Remember His marvellous works that He hath done*," [2]
and of Psalm cvi. in the words, " *They soon forgat His
works*." [3]

The contemplation of God's wonderful works in
their deliverance, and the manifold gifts and benefits
He has bestowed upon them, calls forth praise in
Psalm cv. ; but the contemplation of Israel's sins

[1] Ps. cvi. 47. [2] Ps. cv. 5. [3] Ps. cvi. 13.

and failures calls forth the penitential confession in Psalm cvi.

Before entering into an examination of the long national *Vidduj*, or confession, which finds its parallels only in the Old Testament in the prayers of David and in the striking confession in Nehemiah ix., we pause for awhile to consider the introduction, consisting of the first five verses.

Before the Psalmist can proceed to unroll the long record of Israel's sins, rebellions, unbelief, and in-gratitude, he strengthens himself in the thought of God's unfailing mercy and the unchangeableness of His purpose of grace.

A parallel is found in Psalm xxv., where the in-spired writer (who there, as here, personifies and repre-sents the whole godly remnant of the nation)—before pouring out his heart in the petition, " *Remember not the sins of my youth, nor my transgressions* "—prays, " *Remember, O Jehovah, Thy tender mercies and Thy lovingkindnesses, for they have been ever of old* " (or " from eternity "), and therefore can never fail.

It is this thought of Jehovah's faithfulness and superabundant grace which prevails over Israel's mani-fold transgressions and apostasies, which inspires the singer with the call to praise with which the Psalm begins, and with the *Berachah* (blessing) with which it closes.

הַלְלוּיָה—" *Hallelujah.*" This solemn and majestic word—which, alas! is often taken glibly on the lips of those whose souls are not attuned to the heavenly music with which it is charged—is one of the richest and most significant in the inspired vocabulary, and is, so to say, put into the mouths of God's true people by the spirit of inspiration as a means by which they are to stir up *one another* to the blessed exercise of praise and worship. Hallelujah means " *Praise ye Jehovah.*" It is one calling upon another, or others, to engage in this holy task.

Of the Seraphim we read in Isa. vi. that " one cried unto another," *as if to incite one another* in the exercise of crying " Holy, holy, holy, is Jehovah of Hosts : the whole earth is full of His glory." And saints, too, when they meet, are intended and exhorted to consider, and to " provoke " one another, not only unto love and good works among themselves, but unto the higher and more blessed task of rendering true praise and worship to their all-glorious God.

But no one is in a fit condition to say to others, " *Hallelujah*, praise *ye* the Lord ! " if his own heart is not filled with the sense of God's praiseworthiness, so as to say also, " Praise the Lord, O *my* soul ! "

The Hallelujah in this psalm is followed by two short sentences of inspired praise, which must have become very familiar to pious Israelites of old, but which never ceased to stir fresh emotions of gratitude and adoration in the hearts of the spiritually-minded.

" *Hodu la-Yehovah ki tobh, ki l'o'lam chas'do* "— " *O give thanks* " (or " *praisefully acknowledge*," or " *joyfully confess* ") " *unto Jehovah, for He is good ; for His mercy* " (*His* " *lovingkindness* ") " *endureth for ever.*"

This short refrain, consisting in the original of only seven words, and composed probably in the first instance by the sweet Psalmist of Israel himself, formed part of the daily service of praise which accompanied the divinely appointed ritual in the Temple, and in the 16th chapter of the First Book of Chronicles we read of certain Levites, whose chief duty it was to lead the people in the singing of it, and to see to its proper accompaniment by instrumental music.

Ancient Israel never tired of it. Some of the Psalms have this short refrain as the chief burden of their song — as, for instance, the grand old One Hundredth, the climax of which is :

" *For Jehovah is good ;*
His mercy (or ' *lovingkindness* ') *endureth for ever,*
And His faithfulness unto all generations."

One psalm—the 136th—the climax of the Great Hallel—has the refrain not only at the beginning and the end, but the second line—the words *ki l'o'lam chas'ddo*—" For His mercy (or ' lovingkindness ') endureth for ever," is repeated no fewer than twenty-six times.

During the *seventy years'* captivity in Babylon all music ceased in Israel, for how could they sing Jehovah's song " in a strange land " ? [1] But no sooner did a remnant return, and the rebuilding of the House of God commence, than they took up the old refrain again, " *And they sang one to another in praising and giving thanks unto Jehovah, saying, For He is good, for His lovingkindness endureth for ever toward Israel.*" [2]

Now again, during a much longer " captivity," and universal dispersion, the voice of true praise is silent in Israel. But not for ever, for " *Thus saith Jehovah, Yet again there shall be heard in this place whereof ye say it is waste, . . . even in the cities of Judah and in the streets of Jerusalem that are desolate, . . . the voice of joy and the voice of gladness, . . . the voice of them that say, Give thanks to Jehovah of Hosts, for Jehovah is good, for His lovingkindness endureth for ever.*" [3]

And it is meet that this short refrain should occupy so prominent a place in the worship of Jehovah, for it is in itself a summary of all true praise. It sings of

[1] Ps. cxxxvii. 4.   [2] Ezra iii. 11.   [3] Jer. xxxiii. 10, 11.

what God is in Himself, and what He is, and ever shall
be, to His redeemed people. " *Jehovah is good* "—
this is the Old Testament equivalent to the New Testament declaration, " *God is love.*" This is His nature,
this is His essence ; and because He *is* good He delights
in doing good, and therefore " His mercy "—His
graciousness—" His lovingkindness " (as the word חֶסֶד
is more properly rendered) endureth for ever " toward
Israel," and toward all that fear Him.

In the second verse the Psalmist seeks to impress
us with the greatness of the task to which he invites
us in the first verse.

" *Who can utter the mighty acts of Jehovah or shew
forth all His praise ? *"

Here is a challenge thrown down ; who can take it
up ? Who can worthily and adequately set forth His
glory ? Who can declare His mighty deeds, not only
in creation and providence, but, above all, in redemption ?—for the גְּבוּרֹת (*g'bhuroth*—" mighty acts ") of
which the inspired singer here speaks are primarily
" the manifestations of His all-conquering power, which
makes everything subservient to His redemptive
purposes." [1]

Who—to repeat the Psalmist's question—can show
forth *all* His praise ? [2] Well might the sweet Psalmist
himself exclaim, " *Many, O Jehovah my God, are the
wonderful works which Thou hast done, and Thy thoughts
which are to us-ward ; they cannot be set in order unto
Thee : if I would declare and speak of them, they are
more than can be numbered.*" [3]

---

[1] Delitzsch.

[2] תְּהִלָּתוֹ—*t'hillatho*—*i.e.*, the glory of His self-attestation in history
" by those mighty acts of power and grace " which Psalms cv. and cvi.
celebrate.

[3] Ps. xl. 5.

" I am of opinion," observes Calvin, " that there is no man who has ever endeavoured to concentrate all his energies, both physical and mental, in praising God, but will find himself unequal for so lofty a subject, the transcendent grandeur of which overpowers our senses."

Yet the greatness and "transcendent grandeur" of the task must not deter us from attempting it ; and, though we cannot utter one ten-thousandth part of the divine perfections and glory of Him who is "exalted far above all blessing and praise," the exercise is good for our souls ; and He who stoops to listen to the lisping of babes and sucklings when they attempt to utter His praises, will not despise even our poor and feeble attempts to declare His mighty acts, and to show forth His praise if we only do so, not with our lips only, but from our hearts.

The third verse sets forth one very acceptable way by which we may show forth God's praise, and at the same time bring blessedness to ourselves, viz. by living and *acting* worthily of God.

" *Blessed are they that keep* (or, ' *observe* ') *justice,*
And he that doeth righteousness at all times."

The word—*mish'pat*—in the first verse, rendered in the Authorised Version " judgment," stands here for " justice," " right," " rectitude," to which the word—*ts'daqah*—" righteousness "—forms the amplifying parallel. These two words are often found together, and describe the fruit which God expects from His people as the result of the moral training and the care and attention which He has bestowed upon them.

Thus in the parable of the vineyard in Isaiah v. we read, " The vineyard of Jehovah of Hosts is the House

of Israel and the men of Judah His pleasant plant,
and He looked for *mish'pat*—judgment—but behold
oppression; for *ts'daqah*—righteousness—but behold
a cry."[1] " Blessed," indeed, would Israel have been
if they had always conformed to the law of justice
and righteousness, and done righteousness at all times.
It is Israel's terrible failure which weighs so heavily
on the Psalmist's heart, and leads to the long penitential confession " which sets forth in melancholy
detail the converse truth of the misery that follows
breaking the law."

But there is also a prophetic element in this
beatitude, and there is a time coming when a restored
and converted Israel, with the law of God put in their
inward parts, shall stand out prominently as a holy
nation, as a people who " keep justice and do righteousness at all times."

Meanwhile, dear reader, let us enter into this
" blessedness," for though we are not, as Israel of old,
under the law, but under grace, it yet is required of
us that the righteousness of the law shall be fulfilled
in us who walk not after the flesh but after the spirit.
Let us, therefore, observe justice and do righteousness
" at all times," even when it involves loss and sacrifice, and so prove ourselves true followers of Him
" who loveth righteousness and hateth wickedness,"
and who at that day shall give " the crown of
righteousness " to all those who walk in His
footsteps.

The thought of God's faithfulness and everlasting
mercy, which overtops all Israel's sins and trans-

---

[1] There is a play on the sound of the words in the original : " He
looked for *mish'pat* (justice), but behold *mispach*—oppression (or
' shedding ' of blood) ; for *ts'daqah* (righteousness), but behold *ts'aqah*
(a cry).

gressions, inspires the Psalmist with the touching prayer which may well find an echo in our hearts :

" *Remember me, O Jehovah, with the favour that Thou bearest unto Thy people* (or, ' *when Thou favourest Thy people* ').
Oh visit me with Thy salvation,
That I may see the prosperity (or ' *good* ') *of Thy chosen,*
That I may rejoice in the gladness of Thy nation,
That I may glory with Thine inheritance "—

which may be summarised thus : " In the blessing which Thou hast yet in store for Thy people include me, even me also. Oh visit *me* with Thy salvation ! "

There is indeed " something very pathetic," as one has well observed, " in this momentary thought of self. It breathes wistful yearning, absolute confidence in the unrealised deliverance, lowly humility, which bases its claim with God on that of the nation." [1]

The " salvation " and " good," or " prosperity," for which he prays that he himself also may be permitted to share, are primarily, though not exclusively, the national restoration and the prosperity which God has promised His people in their own land. But we may use this prayer also in relation to the greater spiritual things. In the words of a great preacher and saint : " *Remember me, O Lord, with the favour which Thou bearest unto Thy people*—insignificant as I am, do not forget *me*. Think of me with kindness, even as Thou thinkest of Thine elect. I cannot ask more, nor would I seek less. Treat me as the least of Thy saints are treated, and I am content.

" It should be enough for us if we are treated as the rest of the family. This feeling would prevent our wishing to escape trial, persecution, and chastisement :

[1] Maclaren.

these have fallen to the lot of saints, and why should we escape them ? "

It is a sweet prayer, at once humble and aspiring, submissive and expansive—it might be used by a dying thief or a living apostle. " *Oh visit me with Thy salvation.* Bring it home to *me* ; come to my house and to my heart, and give me the salvation which Thou hast prepared and art alone able to bestow."

Note the fourfold designation — " Thy people;" " Thy chosen," " Thy nation," " Thine inheritance." They are all primarily used of Israel, and describe the everlasting, indissoluble relationship which exists between God and them. " *For thou art a holy people unto Jehovah thy God,*" He said to them ; " *Jehovah thy God hath chosen thee to be a people for His own possession above all peoples that are upon the face of the earth.*" [1] " *And ye shall be unto Me a kingdom of priests, and a holy nation.*" [2] " *For Jehovah's portion is His people ; Jacob is the lot of His inheritance.*" [3]

And this was not only true in the past, but is true still. Israel is still God's people—the only people which He has " chosen " as a people out of all the peoples of the earth ; they are not only the " ancient " nation, but the " everlasting " nation, for the gifts and calling of God are " without repentance," or change of mind, on His part ; and Jehovah will not permanently forsake " His inheritance."

But while this is so—and it is not without design that the Psalmist emphasises these indissoluble relations between God and Israel before he proceeds to narrate Israel's manifold sins and rebellions, which might otherwise have led men to think that God has now cast off the people which He hath foreknown— it is also a glorious fact that in and through Christ,

[1] Deut. vii. 6.   [2] Ex. xix. 6.   [3] Deut. xxxii. 9.

millions from among other nations are now brought into the same covenant relationship with the God of Israel. Believers, of whatever nation, " who in time past were no people, are now the people of God."

And we are a " chosen generation "—chosen in Christ " before the foundation of the world, that we should be holy and without blame before Him in love." We are also His " holy nation," for all essential elements which constitute nationality are found in the new brotherhood which Christ has established.

That which constituted Israel a nation was a common origin, descent, language, country, and destiny. Now all these essentials of nationality are found in their truest and deepest sense in the Church of Christ. Like Israel, all believers trace their origin to a direct act of God's creative power : " Jehovah that created thee, O Jacob ; He that formed thee, O Israel." And we have all one common descent—we are born again, not of corruptible seed, but of incorruptible, by the Word of God, which liveth and abideth for ever. God is our Father, and we have the spirit of sonship in our hearts, whereby we cry, " Abba, Father."

And not only are we all the children of God by faith in Christ Jesus, but we, too, can claim Abraham for our father, for " as many as are of faith, the same are Abraham's seed and heirs according to the promise."

And we, too, have one common country—our heavenly fatherland. " Our citizenship," says the Apostle Paul, " is in heaven, whence also we look for a Saviour, the Lord Jesus Christ." On earth we are, like Israel during the dispersion, pilgrims and strangers. We have one language—the language of the Spirit— common to all God's children, which now can only express itself for the most part in " groanings which cannot be uttered," but which by and by shall burst forth in fulness of praise.

And we have one hope of a common destiny—even " that blessed hope "—of seeing Christ, and being for ever with Him and like Him.

In Christ we are also God's inheritance, and it is for a fuller comprehension of this mystery that the Apostle prays in Eph. i. 18 : " Having the eyes of your heart enlightened, that ye may know what is the hope of His calling, and what the riches of the glory of His inheritance in the saints."

18

ISRAEL'S GREAT NATIONAL CONFESSION

WE now come to the body of the Psalm, which, as stated in the introductory remarks, is one long וִדּוּי—*Vidduj*, or penitential confession.

At the close of the preceding Psalm, which records the marvellous works which Jehovah had done for them, we are told the purpose which God had in redeeming them from Egypt and in planting them in the promised land.

> " He brought forth His people with joy,
> And His chosen with singing ;
> And He gave them the lands of the nations,
> That they might keep His statutes and observe His laws." [1]

Now here in Psalm cvi. we are shown how completely they failed to respond to the purpose of God, and how, from the very beginning and all along, their history has been one long story of rebellion, ingratitude, and sin.

> " We have sinned with our fathers ;
> We have committed iniquity ; we have done wickedly."

This is a general confession, which reminds us of Dan. ix. 5, where the same three verbs, חָטָאנוּ הֶעֱוִינוּ הִרְשָׁעְנוּ *chatanu, he'evinu, hir'sha'nu*, are found together.[2] " We have sinned and have committed iniquity (or, ' dealt perversely '), and have done wickedly, and have re-

---

[1] Ps. cv. 43–45.
[2] They occur also, and in the same order, in 1 Kings viii. 47.

belled, even turning aside from Thy precepts and from
Thine ordinances."

In both Scriptures the accumulation of synonyms
for sin " witnesses at once to the gravity and manifold-
ness of the offences, and the earnestness and compre-
hensiveness of the acknowledgement." The Rabbis
may be right in asserting that three kinds and degrees
of sin are set down in the sixth verse of our Psalm in an
ascending scale : " Against oneself, against one's
neighbour, against God ; sins of ignorance, sins of
conscious deliberation, sins of pride and wickedness."

The expression, " We have sinned *with* our fathers,"
is not to be weakened to mean merely that the present
generation had sinned like their ancestors, but gives
expression to the profound sense of national solidarity,
" which speaks in many other places of Scripture, and
rests on very deep facts in the life of nations and their
individual members." [1]   It is equivalent to the confession that not only have we sinned ourselves, but we
are involved in the sins of our fathers and of our nation.

The Psalmist proceeds to set forth in detail the chief
sins of which they were corporately guilty as a people.

The 7th verse sums up their conduct in Egypt,
when the promise of deliverance was brought to them
by Moses, and at the Red Sea :

" *Our fathers understood not* (or, ' *considered not* ')
Thy wonders in Egypt ;
They remembered not the multitude of Thy loving-
     kindnesses,
But were rebellious at the sea, even at the Red Sea."

One great reason of Israel's unbelief and rebellion is
forgetfulness of God's former mercies. If they had
remembered God's " marvellous works " which He had

[1] Maclaren.

already done on their behalf—as they are urged to do in the preceding Psalm—they would not so often have become demoralised by fear, nor disbelieved His word as to what He has ever been ready to do for them. But they "remembered not the multitude of His lovingkindnesses," and so became unbelieving and rebellious.

And Israel is not alone in this sin of forgetfulness. "Every man has experience enough of God's goodness stored away in the chambers of his memory to cure him of distrust, if he would only look at them. But they lie unnoticed, and so fear has sway over him." And fear—itself the child of unbelief—leads to mistrust, and mistrust to rebellion.

Truly, to come back to the context, if God had dealt with them according to their deserts, He would have been justified if He had left their redemption unaccomplished in Egypt, or from miraculously interfering on their behalf at the Red Sea.

" *Nevertheless, He saved them for His Name's sake,*
 That He might make His mighty power to be known."

Here is the blessed secret of it all. He saved and delivered them, and did all that He could for them, not because they deserved it, or because of anything in them, but for His great and glorious Name's sake, the impelling motive being found in His own heart of love and purpose of grace, not only for Israel, but for all nations, who, through the story of His dealings with His chosen but rebellious people, might be brought to trust in His Name, which (as already explained in these pages) stands for Himself—the unchangeable Jehovah, as He has progressively revealed Himself to His people— a God not only infinite in power and wisdom, but in His grace and covenant faithfulness.

And so, instead of consuming them in His wrath, or giving them over into the hands of the pursuing enemy, as they so well deserved, when, in spite of all they had already experienced of His goodness, they fell a-murmuring and rebelled against Him—" He saved," or delivered them, that " He might make His mighty power to be known," and so add everlasting renown to His own blessed and holy Name :

> " *He rebuked the Red Sea also, and it was dried up :*
> *And He led them through the depths as through a wilderness ;*
> *And He saved them from the hand of them that hated them,*
> *And redeemed them from the hand of the enemy.*"

How sublime and wonderful it all is !

On the third day of creation, when the earth which had been *thohu vabhohu* (waste and void) was being shaped and formed as a fit habitation for man, and " the deep stood, as it were, in an attitude of opposition to God's will, that His glory as the God of order should be manifested in the orderly distribution of the elements on this beautiful earth," [1] He only had need to speak, and, as we read in Psalm civ. :

> " *At Thy rebuke they fled* (i.e. *the waters*) ;
> *At the voice of Thy thunder they hasted away ;*
> *The mountains rose—the valleys sank down.*"

" Terrorised by the despotic command of God," [2] as Delitzsch expresses it, the waters started asunder, mountains rose aloft, the dry land with its heights and its low ground appeared. And the same creative voice sufficed to make " a way " for His people " through the sea, and a path through the mighty waters " ; for when the Red Sea formed, as it were, an obstacle to

---

[1] Hengstenberg.　　　　[2] Ps. cix. 6–9.

their progress, " *He rebuked it*," and forthwith it was dried up, and He led them through it as through an evenly spread-out " wilderness," so that " they stumbled not." [1]

And not only so, but when the eager enemy, sure of success, pursued them even into the sea, He commanded:

" *And the waters covered their adversaries ;*
There was not one of them left "—

which is an echo of Ex. xiv. 28 : " And the waters returned, and covered the chariots and the horsemen, even all the host of Pharaoh that went in after them into the sea ; there remained not so much as one of them."

Thus Jehovah wrought a mighty deliverance for His people, and redeemed them from the hand of the enemy.

" *Then* "—momentarily constrained by the display of His mighty power and His gracious interposition on their behalf—" *believed they His words : They sang His praise.*"

But, alas ! neither their faith nor their song was of long duration, for very soon they fell again to murmuring and lusting, and tempted God in the wilderness, so that of the bulk of that particular generation which " saw His work " and experienced so much of His power and goodness, God had to " swear in His wrath that they should not enter into His rest "—though, as we shall see, He always took care to preserve a remnant, so that His purpose of grace concerning the nation should not fail.

[1] Isa. lxiii. 12, 13.

19

THE SIX GREAT NATIONAL SINS IN THE WILDERNESS

IN verses 13 to 34 the Psalmist goes over, in his penitential confession, the outstanding sins in the wilderness of which they were *corporately* guilty as a people.

Six great sins are enumerated in this sad and humiliating list, and the cause of all is traced back in the 13th verse to forgetfulness of God and the marvellous works which He had already wrought for them, and an impatient disinclination to wait His time and way for the further unfolding of His counsel with regard to them.

"*They soon forgat His works.*" The Hebrew literally reads, שְׁכְחוּ מִהֲרוּ—*miharu shakhechu*—"*they made haste*" (or, "*they hasted away*"), "they *forgat.*" Oh, the terrible bias to evil and godlessness in our depraved human nature! We are ever "slow of heart to believe," and reluctant to obey God's word, but ready "to make haste," to forget His word and works, and to *rush* into evil!

The Psalmist has doubtless in his mind, in the 13th verse, the sad fact that it was only on the third day after their miraculous deliverance at the Red Sea, when momentarily overwhelmed by the display of His divine power and goodness, "they believed His words; they sang His praise," that their unthankful, impatient, unbelieving murmurings began anew.

And Israel is not alone in the sin of forgetfulness

and impatient murmuring. Of how many of us God
has to complain in the same way. " We remember
pain and sorrow," to quote the words of another,
" longer than joy and pleasure. It is always difficult
to bridle desires and be still until God discloses His
purposes. We are all apt to try to force His hand
open and to impose our wishes on Him, rather than let
His will mould us."

The first of the six specific great sins in the desert
enumerated in this *Vidduj*, or national confession, is
set forth in the 14th verse :

> " *And they lusted exceedingly* (or, ' *they lusted a lust* ')
>   *in the wilderness,*
> *And tempted God in the desert.*"

The Hebrew idiom, " they lusted a lust," is taken
from Num. xi. 4, and refers to their twice-repeated
murmurings for flesh. By this evil desire to satisfy
their carnal appetite, they " tempted God " in their
hearts, as the Psalmist, in Psalm lxxviii., tells us, for
they despised the provision which He in His wisdom
had ordained for them " by asking food according to
their desire " (or, " their own pleasure ").[1] It was the
expression of unbelief and rebellion :

> " *They spake against God :*
> *They said, Can God prepare a table in the wilderness ?* "

And it was an aggravation of their sin that they lusted
after these things " *in the wilderness,*" for it showed how
little their hearts were set on that Land of Promise to
which they were being led. *There*—in the land flowing
with milk and honey—abundance of meat and corn and
wine, and every other good thing, were promised them
if they truly obeyed God's voice and kept His word.

[1] Ps. lxxviii. 18.

As to the wilderness, they were only intended *to pass through it,* and ought to have been satisfied with the supply of their barest necessities. God, however, in His wisdom and goodness, provided for them even in the desert, not only abundance, but also *the most suitable food,* considering the climate and the circumstances in which they found themselves.

But so little did they enter into God's plan and purpose for them that they were for ever complaining because they could not have their favourite dainties *in the wilderness,* and even murmured at finding the desert " no place of seed, or of figs, or of vines, or of pomegranates " [1]—as if God had intended them to *settle* there !

From bitter experience they had to learn that not the things we covet after, but what God in His wisdom provides for us, are conducive to our real good.

As to the flesh they lusted after.

" *He gave them their desire (or request),*
    And sent leanness (lit., ' *wasting sickness* ' [2]) *into*
        their soul."

It has been well said that some prayers may be " answered in anger and denied in love." God often grants even the wicked the attainment of the objects of their desire, but the very things they lust after become the means of their punishment.

In this case it was so with God's own people ; for " while the flesh was yet between their teeth, ere it was chewed,"

    " *The anger of God went up against them,*
        And slew of the fattest of them,
        And smote down the young men of Israel."

[1] Num. xx. 5.
[2] רָזוֹן *razon*—" consumption," as Delitzsch renders it.

And the name of that place was called Kibroth-hatta-avah,[1] because there they buried the " people that lusted."

And those " graves of lust " in the wilderness are object lessons and warnings to us, dear Christian reader, " to the intent that we should not lust after evil things, as they also lusted."

The second great sin in the wilderness was the insurrection against their divinely-appointed leaders.

> " *They envied* (or, *were jealous*) *against Moses,*
> *Against Aaron, the holy one of Jehovah.*"

The inspired singer has Numbers xvi. and xvii. in his mind, and rightly presents the rising under Korah, Dathan, and Abiram as a movement which gave expression to the disaffection of the whole people, for behind the seditious leaders there were " two hundred and fifty princes of the congregation called to the assembly (*i.e.* those who formed, so to say, the council of the nation), men of renown " ; and, after the terrible visitation on the ringleaders, " all the congregation murmured against Moses and against Aaron, saying, Ye have killed the people of the Lord." [2]   This was rebellion against Jehovah as well as great ingratitude to Moses, to whom, under God, they owed so much. The expression יְהֹוָה קְדֹשׁ—*q'dosh Yehovah*—" the holy one of Jehovah," used here of Aaron, is an echo of the words of Moses to the mutineers.   They hypo-critically professed to stand up for the rights of the congregation, saying to Moses and Aaron, " *Ye take too much upon you, seeing all the congregation are holy. . . . Wherefore, then, lift ye up yourselves above the assembly of Jehovah* "—as if Moses and Aaron had taken this honour unto themselves.   But Moses answered :

---

[1] Num. xi. 33, 34 ; Ps. lxxviii. 31.   [2] Num. xvi. 2–41.

" *Jehovah will show who are His, and who is holy* " ;
and this had particular reference to the high-priesthood
to which Aaron was consecrated.

The real cause of the insurrection, as far as the
ringleaders were concerned, was envy, or *jealousy*,
as the word (קָנָא—*qana*) primarily signifies ; but, as
another has well observed, " Envy often masquerades
as the champion of the rights of the community,
when it only wishes to grasp these for itself. These
aristocratic democrats cared nothing for the pre-
rogatives of the nation, though they talked about
them ; they wanted to pull down Aaron, not to lift
up Israel."

In like manner did the " princes of Israel "—the
Scribes and Pharisees—speak some fifteen centuries
later to Him who is the true Priest and King, chosen
and appointed of God before the foundation of the
world, and who, not only according to His office (as
in the case of Aaron) but *in His character*, is the " Holy
One." " All God's people are holy," they said in
effect. " We are Abraham's seed, and have never yet
been in bondage to any man ; we need no Redeemer,
or any one to make us free—whom makest Thou
Thyself ? "—while in their case, too, the real cause of
their opposition to Him was envy and the fear that if
they " let Him thus alone all men will believe on Him,"
and their own influence and power with the people
would be gone.

The terrible end of the whole rebellious company is
briefly described in verses 17, 18.   There was a double
punishment.

> " *The earth opened and swallowed up Dathan,*
> *And covered the company of Abiram :*
> *And a fire was kindled in their company ;*
> *The flame burned up the wicked.*"

The latter form of punishment, as we know from Num. xvi. 35, overtook " the 250 men that offered the incense." As in the case of Nadab and Abihu, having presumptuously " offered strange fire " before Jehovah, they were devoured by the fire of His holy wrath,[1] the whole serving as an object lesson and warning of the terrible fate which will overtake those who rise up against Jehovah and against His holy ones, or who presumptuously try to approach Him by any other way than the one He Himself has appointed.

The third great national sin in the wilderness of which mention is made in the *Vidduj*, or penitential confession, is the worship of the golden calf.

" *They made a calf in Horeb,*
And worshipped a molten image :
And they changed their glory
For the likeness of an ox that eateth grass."

This section of the poetic narration has the sad story of Exodus xxxii., and its rehearsal in Deut. ix. 8–12, for its basis. " In Horeb," where they had such wonderful manifestations of His majesty and power, and so soon after they had heard the very voice of God out of the fire saying, " *I am Jehovah thy God : . . . thou shalt have no other gods beside Me* "—and where they had so solemnly pledged themselves with the words : " All that Jehovah hath spoken will we do, and be obedient "—they fell into this gross idolatry.

There is a tone of inspired contempt in the Psalmist's voice as he thinks, not only of the *sin,* but of the *folly*

[1] Korah is not mentioned, and this is in keeping with the historical account in Num. xvii. and Deut. xi. From Num. xxvi. 10, however, it would appear that Korah himself perished with the rest of the rebels, though in the wonderful mercy of God " the sons of Korah died not."

of it. " They made *a calf*," he says—a term everywhere used in contempt. " They would gladly have
made an ox ; but they were not able to get this length,
so contemptible was the whole undertaking." [1]

This would be shame and folly enough for heathen
who had never known God, but think of *Israel* bartering
away " their glory " for such a senseless, stupid thing
as this ! For that which lifted this peculiar people
out of the depths of moral and spiritual degradation
into which they had sunk with the rest of mankind,
and set them high above all the nations, was the self-
revelation in their midst of the true and living God.
To them He made known His glory—that is, the
glorious attributes of His character, the Divine perfections of His being. And He was to be " *their*
glory " ; " *for this is your wisdom and your understanding in the sight of the peoples* "—as Moses impresses
upon them. " *For what great nation is there that hath
God so nigh unto them as Jehovah our God is whensoever
we call upon Him ?* " [2]

And this ever " blessed God," the Creator and
Sustainer of all things, whose glory is above the heavens,
they " exchanged for the image of an ox that eateth
grass " ! And neither the sin nor the folly of it is
lessened by the excuse which they might have advanced
that the calf was not intended as a substitute, but only
as a *representation* of Jehovah, or, at any rate, of some
of His attributes. For did not the same Divine voice
which proclaimed to them in words of thunder, " Thou
shalt have no other gods beside Me," also say : " *Thou
shalt not make to thyself a graven image, nor any likeness
of anything that is in heaven above, or that is in the earth
beneath. . . . Thou shalt not bow down thyself unto
them, nor serve them.*"

[1] Hengstenberg.   [2] Deut. iv. 6, 7 (R.V.).

And how *foolish* to seek to represent the infinite, eternal, unchangeable Jehovah, who is Spirit, by any material object, or by the likeness of any creature ! " To whom, then, will ye liken Me, or shall I be equal, saith the Holy One " [1]—is His own challenge to those who seek to justify idolatry on the ground that these material objects which they set up for men's " veneration " are intended only as " symbols " and " aids " to the worship of the true God. Besides, history and experience supply proof enough that visible representations of God and Christ, perhaps honestly intended in the first instance to be only sacred " symbols " and " helps " to devotion, have, sooner or later, become themselves the object of worship.

But, to return to the more direct context. The cause of their sins and apostasies is again (and for the third time in this Psalm) traced to their forgetfulness of what God had been to and done for them.

" *They forgat God their Saviour,*
Who hath done great things in Egypt,
Wondrous works in the land of Ham,
And terrible things by the Red Sea."

[1] Isa. xl. 25. " After the same fashion, the Ritualists must need set up their symbols and multiply them exceedingly. Spiritual worship they are unable to apprehend ; their worship is sensuous in the highest degree, and appeals to eye and ear and nose. Oh, the folly of man to block up their own way to acceptable worship and to make the path of spiritual religion, which is hard to our nature, harder still through the stumbling-blocks which they cast into it. We have heard the richness of Popish paraphernalia much extolled, but an idolatrous image when made of gold is not one jot the less abomination than it would have been had it been made of dross or dung : the beauty of art cannot conceal the deformity of sin. We are told also of the suggestiveness of their symbols ; but what of that when God forbids the use of them ? Vain also is it to plead that such worship is *hearty.* So much the worse. Heartiness in forbidden actions is only an increase of transgression."—C. H. SPURGEON.

Not only " remembered they not," but soon forgat
(verses 7–13) what God did for them in Egypt, but by
the " terrible things " which He did at the Red Sea in
the overthrow of the Egyptians, and in finally delivering them out of their hands He showed Himself in a
particular manner to be " *their Saviour.*" Then it was
that they, momentarily, at least, " believed His word
and sang His praise," [1] saying :

" *Jehovah is my strength and song,*
And He is become my salvation."

And yet after all that, and with the accumulated
proofs of His presence, power, and grace, they " forgat
God their Saviour," and they turned aside quickly out
of the way which He commanded them, and made
them a golden calf. Yea, they changed the glory of
the incorruptible God for the likeness of an ox that
eateth grass. [2] How very great this sin of idolatry
(which was the primary cause of their ultimate national
ruin) was in God's sight, may be inferred from the stern

---

[1] Ex. xv. 2.

[2] The " calf " or " ox " form of the image has been pretty generally
taken to be due to Egyptian influences. But, according to Professor
George Rawlinson, " the Egyptian calf-worship, or rather bull-worship,
was not a worship of images, but of *living animals*. A sacred bull
called Apis was worshipped at Memphis, and another called Mnevis
at Heliopolis, both being regarded as actual incarnate deities. Had
Egyptian ideas been in the ascendant it would have been natural
to select a living bull, which might have gone before the people
literally." He suggests that the molten calf points back to an
older idolatry, such as is glanced at in Josh. xxiv. 14, when the
Israelites are warned to put away the gods which their fathers
served on the other side of the flood, *i.e.* the Euphrates. Certainly
the bull-form was more distinctive of the Babylonian and Assyrian
than of the Egyptian worship. It is asserted, however, by other
authorities that, apart from the living bull, the Egyptians also
worshipped a golden, or gilded bull — the image, or portraiture,
of Apis.

and terrible resolve which He had formed utterly to exterminate them, had not Moses averted His wrath by his earnest pleading and intercession on their behalf :

" *Therefore He said He would destroy* (or, ' *annihilate* ') *them*
Had not Moses, His chosen, stood before Him in the breach,
To turn away His wrath, that He should not destroy."

The metaphor here used is found also in other scriptures. It is taken from a besieged city, in the walls of which the enemy has at last succeeded in making a breach and is about to enter, with a view to destroy, unless some valiant warrior throws himself into the gap to drive him back, prepared even to fill up the breach with his own body. Thus Moses acted in the supreme crisis as the champion on behalf of the people, ready, if need be, to encounter the wrath of God on their behalf. And the weapon with which he succeeded in turning away God's anger from them was intercession.

" *Moses besought Jehovah, his God, and said, Why, O Jehovah, doth Thy wrath work up against Thy people that Thou hast brought forth out of the land of Egypt with Thy great power, and with a mighty hand ? . . . Turn from Thy fierce wrath and repent of this evil against Thy people.*"

And not only did he thus plead with God on their behalf, but he was ready to offer himself as a sacrifice for them.

" *Moses returned unto Jehovah, and said : Oh, this people have sinned a great sin, and have made them gods of gold ; yet now if Thou wilt forgive their sin— ; and if not, blot me, I pray Thee, out of Thy book which Thou hast written.'* "[1] And in this respect Moses comes nearer to our Lord Jesus Christ than any other man in the history of Israel, except, perhaps, the Apostle Paul, who also not only pleaded earnestly with God for Israel " that they might be saved," but was willing to be himself anathema from Christ, for his brethren, his kinsmen according to the flesh.

But Moses in particular, who, so to say, rushed into the breach as Israel's champion in that hour of danger, reminds us of Him, who from the foundation of the world was the appointed Mediator between God and man, the Prophet " like unto," and yet greater than Moses—the One who did " stand in the gap "[2] and endured all God's righteous anger against sin on our behalf—who His own self bare our sins in His body upon the tree, and now lives for evermore to make intercession for us.

The fourth principal sin in the wilderness was their unbelief and demoralisation in consequence of the evil report about the land brought by the spies :

" *They despised the pleasant land,*
They believed not His word,
But murmured in their tents,
And hearkened not unto the voice of Jehovah."

Almost every sentence in this narrative is taken by the inspired singer from the historical accounts in the Pentateuch, and particularly from Numbers xiii. and xiv. The expression, " They despised," is an echo of Num. xiv. 31 : " *The land which ye despised.*" And what kind of a land was it that " they despised " and refused to enter ? It was *erets hem'dah*—a pleasant, or

[1] Ex. xxxii. 11-14, 31, 32.   [2] Ezek. xxii. 30.

delightsome, land—a description of Palestine which is found also in Jer. iii. 19 and Zech. vii. 14 : " A good and large land, flowing with milk and honey " [1]—as God Himself has assured them in advance—" A land of brooks of water, of fountains and springs flowing forth in valleys and hills ; a land of wheat and barley, and vines and fig-trees, and pomegranates, of olive oil and honey " [2]—yea, " the glory of all lands," as Ezekiel designates it.[3] And this land they " despised " by refusing, at God's command, to go up to possess it.

And the reason was that " They believed not His word " of promise, many times repeated, that He would assuredly give them the land. They believed rather the word of the ten unfaithful spies, who terrified them with the stories of the strongly fortified cities and the giants whom they saw there, forgetting, or disbelieving, the word of Jehovah : " Say *not* in thine heart these nations are more than I—how can I dispossess them ? *Thou shalt not be afraid of them ;* thou shalt remember what Jehovah thy God did unto Pharaoh, and unto all Egypt " ; and again, " *Thou shalt not be affrighted of them,* for Jehovah thy God is in the midst of thee, a great God and a terrible. And Jehovah thy God will cast out those nations before thee " [4]—in spite of fortifications and giants.

But when Joshua and Caleb reminded them of these promises, saying : " If Jehovah delight in us, then He will bring us into this land, and give it unto us " [5]—" they hearkened not unto the voice of Jehovah," but " murmured in their tents," and were

[1] Ex. iii. 8.   [2] Deut. viii. 7–10.
[3] Ezek. xx. 6–15.   [4] Deut. vii. 17–24.
[5] Num. xiv. 8–10.

ready in their demoralisation even to stone the two
faithful witnesses.

> " *Therefore He sware unto them,*[1]
> *That He would overthrow them in the wilderness,*
> *And that He would overthrow their seed* [2] *among the
>   nations,*
> *And scatter them in the lands* "—

a fearful and terrible oath and sentence, which verified
itself in the fact that the carcases of the whole of that
unbelieving generation did fall in the wilderness—an
object-lesson and warning to us, dear Christian reader,
to give diligent heed that we fall not after the same example of disobedience ; or " lest, haply, a promise being
left us of entering into God's rest, any one of you should
seem to have come short of it " (Heb. iv. 1–11, R.V.).

The threat of the dispersion of their seed among
the nations, and that He would scatter them in the
lands, is founded on the two great threatening chapters,
viz. Leviticus xxvi. and Deuteronomy xxviii., and is
rightly brought into this connection by the Psalmist,
who views the exile as being the climax of the punishment of Israel's national sins, which began already
at the Red Sea and in the wilderness.

The fifth great sin in the wilderness was their
participation in the abominable Moabitish worship of
Baal-peor :

> " *They joined themselves also to Baal-peor*
> *And ate the sacrifices of the dead.*
> *And they provoked Him by their doings,*
> *And a plague broke in upon them.*"

[1] The Hebrew is *va-yisa yado*—lit., " He lifted up His hand "—
the gesture or attitude in taking an oath.

[2] According to Hitzig and Delitzsch, *u-l'hapil*—to overthrow, or
" make them fall," in the 27th verse, is a scribal error, for *u-l'haphitz*,
" and to disperse them." (See Ezek. xx. 23.)

The word *va-yitsam'du*, translated "they joined themselves," which is brought over from the historic account in Num. xxv. 3, literally means, "to be fastened," or *yoked* together. Having thrown off the yoke of Jehovah they "yoked themselves" to this particularly unclean idol,[1] whose worship was associated with lascivious profligacy, becoming, so to say, one with him "in a quasi-physical union."

The sacrifices of the dead do not refer to practices of necromancy, as some have supposed, but means the sacrifices which were offered "*to the dead*" idol, who is thus contrasted with Jehovah the living God. The Psalmist has Num. xxv. 2 in his mind, where we read that "*they (the profligate daughters of Moab) called the people unto the sacrifices of their gods, and the people did eat and bowed down to their gods.*"

Again we detect a tone of contempt in the Psalmist's voice, who, as we have seen in his references to the worship of the golden calf, wants to impress us not only with the *sin*, but with the *folly* of turning away from God.

In Horeb they made them a calf, and exchanged "their glory" for the likeness of an ox that eateth grass, and now in Shittim, in the land of Moab, they forsook the Holy One of Israel, "the living God," and Creator and Sustainer of all things, who hath made the earth by His power, and hath established the world by His wisdom, and by His understanding stretched out the heavens,[2] and yoked themselves—to what? To Baalpeor, a "*dead*" idol, who could neither speak, nor see, nor

---

[1] "Baal-peor," literally "Lord of Peor," was the name given to the Moabitish idol Kamosh or Chemosh (the Moabitish god of war only in that country, from one of the places where he was worshipped) namely, Mount Peor (Num. xxiii. 28), at the foot of which Israel lay encamped. The profligacy described in Numbers xxv. was a regular, if not essential, part of the worship of this "god."

[2] Jer. x. 10–13.

hear, nor smell, nor touch, nor walk—and whose worship had such a terribly debasing effect on his votaries !

And this same folly is committed by sinners *now*. " Men usually make a profit, or think they do, on their barter," observes another writer ; " but what do they gain who exchange God for an idol ? " And this is true, not only of any material idol of gold, or silver, or wood, or stone, but of the idols of the intellect or of the heart which are exchanged for faith in the living God, the Father of our Lord Jesus Christ, and worshipped by the majority of modern men and women in these most civilised countries. These, too, " eat the sacrifices of the dead," which can never satisfy.

But to return to our context. Every sin brought its retributive punishment, and in this case " *the plague broke in upon them*," and those who died of the plague were twenty and four thousand, as the historic narrator in Num. xxv. 9 records.[1] Even then the anger of the Lord would still have burned against them and consumed many more of the people, had not another champion, so to say, entered into the " breach " (as Moses did after the sin of the golden calf) and appeased the wrath of God—this time not by intercession and the offer to sacrifice himself for the people, but by the execution of a public exemplary act of punishment on two notable transgressors.

" *Phinehas stood up and executed judgment,*
    And it was reckoned unto him for righteousness unto
        all generations (or, *to generation after generation*
        for ever)."

[1] The judicial retribution inflicted, according to the command of Moses, by the judges of Israel, " slaying every one his man," is called by the Psalmist a " plague," as in Num. xxv. 9. But it is probable, as has been suggested, that the judges were not duly obedient to the command of Moses, and consequently a plague broke out from the Lord upon the people.

The expression *va-te-chashebh lo lits'daqah* — " it was reckoned unto him for righteousness "—is used elsewhere only of Abraham in Gen. xv. 6 ; but here it is not the " justifying righteousness " which is meant. That can never be the reward of any work, but must be laid hold of by faith, as God's gift in and through Christ. But there is such a thing as God Himself bearing testimony to the righteousness of a man's character and conduct. Phinehas' " work of righteousness " sprang from his faith in God, and was the expression of his holy zeal for His glory ; or, to quote the words of another, " It was an act which had its origin in the faithfulness which had its root in faith, and which, for the sake of this, its ultimate ground, gained him the acceptation of a righteous man, inasmuch as it proved him to be such." [1]

Phinehas' reward was the permanent bestowal of the priesthood by God Himself upon him and his descendants, " from generation to generation, for ever "— that is, that there should be no other human priest, nor an order of priesthood of the Aaronic type, except those belonging to his line.[2] Which promise was fulfilled.

The sixth great sin of which they were as a people corporately guilty in the wilderness was the strife against Moses and Aaron at the waters of Meribah,

[1] Delitzsch.

[2] " Phinehas' priesthood is called ' everlasting,' not in his person, but in his posterity, whose sons were successively high priests till the captivity of Babylon (1 Chron. vi. 4–16), and at the release from the captivity Ezra, the priest and scribe, was of his line (Ezra vii. 1–6), and it continued in that line until, or very near, the approach of our High Priest (Christ), who is of the order of Melchizedek."

in the fortieth year of their wilderness wanderings, as recorded in Num. xx. 2–13 :

" *They angered Him also at the waters of strife,*
So that it went ill with Moses for their sakes :
For they rebelled against His Spirit,
And he spoke unadvisedly (or *rashly*) *with his lips.*"

As a matter of chronology, this sin at Meribah-Kadesh preceded the events of which the Psalmist had plaintively sung in verses 28–31, viz. the sin and punishment associated with Baal-peor ; but he brings it up in this order probably because he regards it as forming a climax (not as regards the order of time, but in magnitude of guilt) to the series of national transgressions in the wilderness. For in this sin at Meribah they not only angered God, but succeeded at last in dragging down with them their noble leader Moses, who, wearied out by their provocations and rebellions, gave way momentarily to impatience and unbelief, and was in consequence of it himself excluded, " for their sakes," from entering the Promised Land. " That," as another writer observes, " was in some respects the masterpiece and triumph of the nation's sin."

In this short strophe the inspired singer again echoes words and expressions from the historical narrative in Numbers, and its rehearsal in Deuteronomy. Thus the line, " *It went ill with Moses for their sakes* " (or, " *on their account* "), has for its basis the words of Moses himself in Deut. i. 37 : " *Jehovah was angry with me for your sakes.*" The expression, " *They rebelled against His Spirit,*" refers not to the spirit of Moses, as some have interpreted, but to the Holy Spirit of God ; and the word הִמְרוּ—*him'ru*—" they rebelled," is a direct echo of the word which Moses

addressed to them on that occasion : " Hear now, ye
rebels "—*hammorim.* This word about rebelling against
His Spirit reminds us also of the solemn passage in
Isa. lxiii. 10 : " *But they rebelled,*[1] *and grieved His
Holy Spirit ; therefore He was turned to be their enemy,
and Himself fought against them* " *;* and of the admonition to Christians in the New Testament : " Grieve
not the Holy Spirit by (or ' in ') whom ye were sealed
unto the day of redemption." [2]

The words which Moses spake " unadvisedly " or
" rashly " with his lips are those recorded in Num. xx.
11 : " *Hear now, ye rebels ; shall we bring you forth
water out of this rock ?* " which, together with the smiting
of the rock twice (when, according to God's command,
he was not to smite at all this time, but only to speak
to the rock), was the expression of impatience, tinged
with unbelief.

This may seem to us a small sin compared with the
great transgressions of the people, but it must be
remembered that it was *Moses* who committted it—
Moses who stood in such a near relationship to God as
no other man except Christ, and who was Israel's law-
giver and God's representative before the people.
Hence the sentence, which may seem to us severe :
" *Because ye believed not in Me, to sanctify Me in the
eyes of the children of Israel, ye shall not bring this assembly
into the land which I have given them* " [3]—from which
we may learn the solemn truth that the fuller our
knowledge of God, and the nearer our relationship to
Him, the more exceedingly sinful does our sin become
in His sight—a truth which may in a sense be regarded
also as the key to the whole history of the Jewish
nation, and the explanation of the reason why they

[1] The same Hebrew word as in our Psalm.
[2] Eph. iv. 30, R.V.   [3] Num. xx. 12.

have suffered more than any other people. "You only have I known of all the families of the earth," He says, "therefore will I visit you for all your iniquities,"[1] for Jehovah is "a jealous God," who judgeth the sins of His own people with greater severity than He does the sins of those who do not stand in spiritual or covenant relationship to Him. Let us, therefore, be ever watchful, dear Christian reader, and pray without ceasing, "Hold Thou up my goings in Thy paths, that my footsteps slip not." "Hold Thou me up, and I shall be safe." "Keep my heart, O Lord, and set a watch before my mouth, that, however great the provocation, I speak not ' unadvisedly with my lips.' "

To return for a moment to this brief strophe in our Psalm, which sings of the last, and in some respects the greatest, of Israel's sins in the wilderness. We are reminded here that Moses, Israel's great law-giver and mediator of the old covenant, who in many ways is so striking a type of Christ, the Mediator of the New Covenant, *presents also points of contrast*—both in his character and mission—through which the moral supremacy and greater glory of our Lord Jesus Christ shine forth. To touch only on this one point : "Moses," we read, "was very meek" above all men that were upon the face of the earth,[2] and was thus a type of Him whose outstanding characteristic was that "He was meek and lowly of heart"; but in the end, in an unguarded moment, when severely tried, Moses' meekness and patience gave way, for "when they rebelled against His Spirit he spake unadvisedly with his lips." But our Lord Jesus, the Prophet "like unto," yet greater than Moses, endured the contradiction of sinners against Himself, even unto the end, and when He was reviled, reviled not again, but even under the greatest

[1] Amos iii. 2.   [2] Num. xii. 3.

provocation manifested a divine spirit of long-suffering and forgiveness.

We shall see when we come (D.V.) to deal with the last section of this Psalm how Jehovah's grace and faithfulness abound toward Israel in spite of all their sins and rebellions. Meanwhile, let us ponder on the solemn lessons contained in the section of the Psalm which we have been considering, and remember that " these things "—viz. Israel's sins and failures in the wilderness, and the judgments which overtook them— " were our examples " (or, more literally, " *types*," solemn object-lessons to us) " *to the intent we should not lust after evil things, as they also lusted. Neither be ye idolaters, as were some of them ; as it is written, The people sat down to eat and drink, and rose up to play. Neither let us commit fornication, as some of them committed, and fell in one day three and twenty thousand. Neither let us tempt the Lord, as some of them tempted, and perished by the serpents. Neither murmur ye, as some of them murmured, and perished by the destroyer. Now these things happened unto them by way of examples (or as types) ; and they were written for our admonition, upon whom the ends of the ages are come* " (1 Cor. x. 7–12).

20

THE APOSTASY IN THE LAND AND THE
PUNISHMENT WHICH FOLLOWED

FROM the sad story of the nation's sins and rebellions in the wilderness (verses 13–34), and the
punishments which overtook them, the Psalmist proceeds in this sorrowful Confession to speak of Israel's
disobedience and progressive apostasy after they
entered Canaan.

He dwells particularly on the two outstanding sins
of which they were guilty, viz. disobedience to the
command to extirpate the idolatrous inhabitants of
the land, and their adoption of their bloody, soul-
destroying worship.

> " *They did not destroy the peoples*
> *As Jehovah commanded them,*
> *But mingled themselves with the nations,*
> *And learned their works,*
> *And served their idols,*
> *Which became a snare unto them.*"

God's commands and warnings on this subject were
explicit, and oft repeated : " *I will deliver the inhabitants*
of the land into your hand ; and thou shalt drive them
out before thee. . . . They shall not dwell in thy land,
lest they make thee sin against Me ; for if thou serve
their gods it will surely be a snare unto thee."

Again : " *Take heed to thyself, lest thou make a*
covenant with the inhabitants of the land whither thou
goest, lest it be for a snare in the midst of thee, but ye

shall break down their altars and dash in pieces their pillars, and ye shall cut down their asherim, . . . lest thou make a covenant with the inhabitants of the land, and they play the harlot after their gods, and sacrifice unto their gods." [1]

But they disobeyed God's commands, and the very thing they were solemnly warned against came to pass.

The command to utterly destroy the Canaanites has occasioned a good deal of quibbling on the part of unbelievers, who, instead of laying to heart the solemn warning to the ungodly contained in this sentence of doom against these peoples, set themselves up as judges of God's character, and tell us that it is inconsistent with the attribute of mercy for such a command to have been given to Israel.

The simple believer, on the other hand, remembering the marvellous long-suffering which God exercised toward these Canaanitish nations, and how for many centuries He had been waiting and restraining His anger because " the iniquity of the Amorite was not yet quite full," [2] can not only exclaim, " *Great and marvellous are Thy works, Lord God Almighty ; just and true are Thy ways, Thou King of nations* " ; but they can even see also His love and concern for humanity as a whole in this stern decree against the degenerate Canaanite, who, even in the universal corruption of the ancient world, stood out as notorious for his cruelties and abominations.[3]

It is in accord with fact, as borne witness to both by Scripture and history, that the command to destroy the Canaanites was with a view to the salvation of the rest of mankind.

By the time the God of glory appeared to our father

---

[1] Ex. xxiii. 31–33, xxxiv. 11–17.   [2] Gen. xv. 16.
[3] See *The Shepherd of Israel and His Scattered Flock*, pp. 107, 108.

Abraham, moral darkness already covered the earth, and gross darkness the peoples ; and during the four centuries of Israel's sojourn in Egypt, not only was the " Amorite " filling up more and more the cup of his iniquity, but the whole Gentile world was sinking deeper and deeper into idolatry, and all the moral and physical degradation which it occasions—and there was the danger that the knowledge of the true and living God, and all truth and virtue, would disappear from the earth.

Then God in His great mercy interposed. He chose one small naturally stiff-necked people, to whom He made Himself known, and whom He took under His special training, with a view to the bringing back a lost world to Himself—the source of life, and light, and blessedness. It was, so to say, a matter of life and death to the whole of mankind that this tree which God was planting for the eventual healing of all the nations should not be corrupted from without, nor stunted in its growth by adverse influences. The ground, therefore, had to be purified, and the festering mass of moral corruption altogether removed from the land.

This—apart from the deserved judgment on a people whose cup of iniquity was " full," and whose day of grace was past—was God's intention in the command utterly to extirpate the Canaanite from the land. But they disobeyed God's command—not from feelings of compassion, but " from want of holy zeal and from slothfulness " ; not from want of inclination, but because they were deficient in strength on account of their unbelief, and in consequence of their guilt.[1] Hence the humiliating record in the Book of Judges, which the Psalmist doubtless has in his mind : " *Judah*

[1] Hengstenberg.

*could not drive out the inhabitants of the valley, because
they had chariots of iron."* " *The children of Benjamin
did not drive out the Jebusites that inhabited Jerusalem."*
" *Manasseh did not drive out the inhabitants of Beth-shean
and its towns."* " *Ephraim drove not out the Canaanite
that dwelt in Geser, but the Canaanite would dwell in
that land."* And so on with all the tribes. The most
disappointing record is that of the Asherites, for they
not only *suffered the Canaanites to dwell among them,
but* " *the Asherites dwelt among the Canaanites,* the
inhabitants of the land ; for they did not drive them
out."

And the cause of failure in every instance was not
with God, but in their unbelief and disobedience.
The consequence was, that that which the command
was intended to prevent came to pass. These corrupt
inhabitants of the land became a מוֹקֵשׁ—*moqesh—lit.*,
" a bait," " a lure," " a *snare,"* laid for them by the
great adversary, whose chief aim has been, and is,
to frustrate the purpose of God in the election and call
of Israel, viz. that through them all the nations
should be brought back to God. Thus the solemn
warnings of Moses and Joshua came to pass : " *If ye
at all go back (from God's command) and cleave unto the
remnant of these nations, even these that remain among
you, and make marriages with them, and go in unto them,
and they to you, know for a certainty that Jehovah, your
God, will no more drive these nations from out of your
sight ; but they shall be a snare and a trap unto you, and
a scourge in your sides, and thorns in your eyes, until ye
perish from off this good land, which Jehovah, your God,
hath given you."* [1] And what a terrible humiliating
picture is presented to us in this brief summary of
the progressive apostasy and degeneration of the

[1] Josh. xxiii. 12, 13.

mass of the people after they took possession of the land.

"*They mingled*" (or "mixed themselves up") "*with the nations*" (or "heathen," as the word *Goyim* ought, perhaps, to be rendered here), "*and learned their ways.*"

They probably intended at first to have only what they regarded as harmless social intercourse with these Canaanites, but gradually the "mixing," or "mingling," became closer, and, as we read in Judg. iii. 6, "They took their daughters to be their wives, and gave their own daughters to their sons"—the very thing they were specifically forbidden to do. Then they took to imitating, and even diligently to "learn" their abominable idolatries and devilish practices: "*Yea, they sacrificed their sons and their daughters unto demons,*"[1] who delighted in it, just because it is most hateful in the sight of Jehovah.

"*And shed innocent blood,*
Even the blood of their sons and of their daughters,
Whom they sacrificed unto the idols of Canaan;
And the land was polluted with blood.
Thus were they defiled with their works,
And played the harlot in their doings"—

i.e., they became morally defiled themselves with their abominations and spiritual whoredom, and they polluted also the land on which they were placed, which was His, and which He designed that it should be known as the "holy land."

What a striking commentary all this is on the

---

[1] שֵׁדִים—*Shedim*—of uncertain etymology—"devils" or "demons"; the false gods of the heathen, who were regarded as inimical to man and greatly dreaded. See the Exposition of Deuteronomy, xxxii. 16, 17, in Part I., p. 64.

theory of evolution, by which all modern rationalistic writers attempt to explain the history of Israel! To quote a paragraph of my own from elsewhere :

"Modern so-called 'progressive' Rabbis — confirmed and supported by many 'modern' Christian theologians, who also no longer believe in a Divine revelation—speak boastfully as if the Jew had discovered or *evolved* the belief in One God. 'This,' says one of the greatest of modern Jewish lights (viz., that the Jewish people 'created Monotheism out of itself ') ' is Israel's imperishable merit.' But the very opposite is the truth. Not only did Israel not create the belief in one true and living God ' out of itself,' but history testifies to the fact that Israel was naturally as prone to idolatry as any of the other Semitic peoples to whom they are related ; and when left to themselves they could not even *retain* the knowledge of the living God after it had been divinely communicated to them. And if the light of the knowledge of God *was* maintained in their midst, the fact is to be ascribed, not to the ' monotheistic genius ' of the Jewish people, but to Divine acts and interpositions, in judgments and in mercy, of Israel's God. Instead of claiming ' imperishable merit,' as is done by modern Rabbis, Israel's true prophets and psalmists confess with broken hearts that ' to us belongeth confusion of face, to our kings, to our princes, and to our fathers ' (Dan. ix. 8) : for though the God of glory revealed Himself in our midst, and dealt with us as with no other nation, ' though He commanded the clouds from above, and opened the doors of heaven, and rained down manna upon them to eat,' and showed them many other great and wonderful signs, ' their hearts were not right with Him,' and they continuously ' turned back and dealt unfaithfully, like their fathers ;

they were turned aside like a deceitful bow. For they provoked Him to anger with their high places, and moved Him to jealousy with their graven images.' " [1]

But to return to our context. God's feelings in relation to it all, and the punishments which it brought upon them, are briefly set forth in verses 40–43.

" *Therefore was the wrath of Jehovah kindled against His people,*
And He abhorred His inheritance."

Still they were " His people " and " His inheritance," for the covenant relationship, in spite of all, was not dissolved. But this fact—that it was *His* people that had fallen into these depths of abominations—stirred up His holy wrath and righteous indignation all the more. " The feeling described in verse 40 is like to that of a husband who still loves his guilty wife, and yet, when he thinks of her lewdness, feels his whole nature rising in righteous anger at her, so that the very sight of her affects his soul. How far the Divine wrath can burn against those whom He yet loves in His heart, it is hard to say ; but certainly Israel pushed the experiment to the extreme." [2]

The expression of His abhorrence was the punishment He subjected them to :

" *And He gave them into the hand of the nations,*"

with whom, in spite of Divine warnings, they had " mingled," and whose abominable " works " and vile practices they had " learned." " *And they that hated them* "—for there can never be any real love and affinity between a Canaanite and an Israelite—" *ruled over them.*" And what kind of a rule it was under

---

[1] From *The Shepherd of Israel and His Scattered Flock.*
[2] C. H. Spurgeon.

which they were brought for their iniquity we are told in the 42nd verse :

" Their enemies also oppressed them ;
    And they were brought into subjection under their hand."

Yet He did not *entirely* forget or forsake them, and at the least sign of repentance He interposed on their behalf.

" Many times did He deliver them ;
    But they were rebellious in their counsel " (or " self-will ")—

i.e., they went their own stiff-necked way. " God's counsel was to make Israel free and glorious, but they leaned upon themselves, following their own intentions," [1] therefore they *" were brought low in "* (*or " through ")* *" their iniquity."*

This is the record of their behaviour and experience after they took possession of Canaan, and more especially that which characterised the period of the Judges. It reminds us of the similar solemn national confession in Neh. ix. 26–31 (R.V.) :

Nevertheless they were disobedient, and rebelled against Thee,
And cast Thy law behind their back, and slew Thy prophets
Which testified against them to turn them again unto Thee,
And they wrought great provocations.
Therefore Thou deliveredst them into the hand of their
        adversaries,
Who distressed them :
And in the time of their trouble, when they cried unto Thee,
Thou heardest from heaven ; and according to Thy manifold
        mercies
Thou gavest them saviours who saved them out of the hand
        of their adversaries.

[1] Delitzsch.

But after they had rest, they did evil again before Thee :
Therefore Thou leftest them in the hand of their enemies,
So that they had the domination over them : yet when they
    returned,
And cried unto Thee, Thou heardest from heaven ;
And many times didst Thou deliver them according to Thy
    mercies ;
And testifiedst against them, that Thou mightest bring them
    again
Unto Thy law : yet they dealt proudly, and hearkened not unto
Thy commandments, but sinned against Thy judgments (which
    if a man do, he shall live in them), and withdrew the shoulder,
And hardened their neck, and would not hear.
Yet many times didst Thou bear with them, and testifiedst
    against them
By Thy Spirit through Thy prophets : yet would they not give
    ear :
Therefore gavest Thou them into the hands of the peoples of
    the lands.
Nevertheless in Thy manifold mercies Thou didst not make a
    full end of them, nor forsake them, for Thou art a gracious
    and merciful God.[1]

Thus their whole history in the land is summed up
by the inspired writers as alternating periods of sin,
punishment, and deliverance recurring in constantly
repeated cycles, " in which the mystery of human
obstinacy is set over against that of divine long-
suffering ; and one knows not whether to wonder
most at the incurable levity which learned nothing
from experience, or the inexhaustible long-suffering
which wearied not in giving wasted gifts." [2]

Before proceeding to the exposition of the last five
verses of this Psalm, which form its climax, I pause to
make one or two observations of a practical nature.

I.—How striking and wonderful are these solemn
confessions ! We may search in vain through the
literature of all the other nations for any parallel to

[1] Nehemiah ix. 26–31.   [2] Maclaren.

such national self-indictment. " Surely," observes one,
" never but in Israel has patriotism chosen a nation's
sins for the theme of song, or, in celebrating its victories
written but one name, the name of Jehovah, on its
trophies." The reason is that " never but in Israel "
did *inspired prophets and psalmists* write the nation's
history, and their fervent " patriotism " had for its
basis, not national pride or self-glory, as is the case
among other nations—or the sentiment which expresses
itself in the maxim, " My country, right or wrong "—
but *righteousness, justice,* and *truth.*

Not to flatter the people, or foster self-vanity, was
the aim of Israel's inspired historians and poets, but
to expound and apply the great truth, amply confirmed from their own history, that it is righteousness
alone which " exalteth a nation, but sin is a reproach
to any people " ; [1] and that disregard of God and disobedience to His commands is not only an offence
against His Divine Majesty and grievous in His sight,
but is certain, sooner or later, to bring misery and ruin
on ourselves.

Let us, then, learn a lesson from this inspired
national *Vidduj* (or confession) in *true* patriotism, and
remember that not only of individuals, but of communities and nations, the inspired declaration holds
true : " *He that covereth his transgressions shall not
prosper ; but whoso confesseth and forsaketh them shall
obtain mercy.*" [2]

II.—Then, secondly, how do these confessions and
self-accusations on the part of Israel affect you individually, my dear Christian reader ?   Are you ready-
as are so many, to cast stones at the Jews, and say :
" Oh, what a wicked and stubborn people ! How they
deserve all the punishments that have come upon

[1] Prov. xix. 34.   [2] Prov. xxviii. 13.

them ! " If so, then the Divine intention in these
inspired records is missed, as far as you are concerned.
No, they were intended as a mirror in which we may
see *ourselves*—the natural perversity of *our* hearts,
the evil tendencies of our nature—so that, putting no
confidence in self, we may wholly confide in His mercy,
and watch unto prayer, that *we* may be kept from
provoking God in like manner.

We have been reminded, when dealing with Israel's
sins and the punishments which came upon them in the
wilderness, that " these things happened unto them
by way of example " (or, more literally, " as types "),
" and they were written for our admonition, upon
whom the ends of the ages are come." [1] The same is
true, also, of Israel's history after they entered the
Promised Land.   Still the record is put down " for our
admonition " ; and would to God that Christians laid
it more to heart ! But, alas ! the professing Church
of Christ has paid no heed to the warnings of Jewish
history, and, in spite of the fuller light of the New
Testament, has fallen into the same sins which brought
about the fall of Israel.

God's people in this dispensation have no command to " destroy," or in anywise to use violence
against individuals or communities who are opposed
to Christ and His Gospel, even though they may be as
morally corrupt as the Canaanites, this being the " Day
of Grace," " the acceptable year of Jehovah," during
which He bears in His infinite long-suffering with the
apostate nations, until *their* cup of iniquity be " full,"
when *He Himself*, in the person of the Messiah, will
execute vengeance, the right of which belongeth to
Him alone.   Meanwhile " He commandeth men that
they should all everywhere repent," [2] and commissions

[1] 1 Cor. x. 11.   [2] Acts xvii. 30 (R.V.).

His servants to carry the glad tidings of *free grace* to all who will believe His Gospel.

But while the particular command about destroying the Canaanites cannot now be applied to the Church, the Jews, " mingling themselves with the nations and learning their works," find their parallel in the Church's mixing itself up with the world, and conforming to its maxims and ways. Christ " died for our sins, that He might deliver us out of this present evil world, according to the will of our God and Father." And the oft-reiterated commands and exhortations in the New Testament are : " *Be ye separate, saith the Lord* " ; *Be not unequally yoked together with unbelievers* " ; " *Love not the world, neither the things that are in the world* " ; " *Be not fashioned according to this age, but be ye transformed by the renewing of your mind* "—for only so could the Church maintain its true life in God, and bear effective witness for Him in the world.

But, alas ! instead of continuing in the path of faith and obedience, and walking apart in purity with her heavenly Bridegroom " outside the camp," the professing Church very soon, and only too readily, began to respond to the blandishments of the world, and became more and more contaminated, both in doctrine and practice, until it degenerated into the paganised " Christendom " which is before us.

And even in evangelical circles, and among those who are the children of God, is there not too often a " mingling " with the world, an eager pursuit of its pleasures and ambitions, an imitation of its " works," and assimilation with its ways ?

The gross forms of idolatry, such as the Jews learned from the Canaanites, are now out of fashion ; but there are other idols than those made of wood or stone, and the false gods which are worshipped by the modern

civilised world—the names of which I will not enumerate—and to which Christians are too often tempted to
pay homage, are not less opposed to the worship of
the one true and living God, and not less hurtful to the
souls of men than was the worship of Baal or Moloch.

" We stand astonished, doubtless, at this horrid,
barbarous, and unnatural impiety of offering children
by fire to a Moloch," writes Bishop Horne ; " but how
little is it considered that children brought up in the
way of ignorance, error, vanity, folly, and vice, are
more effectually sacrificed to the great adversary of
mankind ! "

Or, as an old German commentator expresses it
more fully : " Among us such sacrifices take place by
careless bringing up of children, when parents encourage them, for example, in pride and other sins,
offer them to the god of the world, and carefully inculcate the maxims of the world, and fill them with
love of vanity and show."

It is to *Christians* in the New Testament that the
exhortation is addressed : " Little children, keep yourselves from idols." [1]

[1] 1 John v. 21.

21

" NEVERTHELESS " : JEHOVAH ABIDETH FAITHFUL

BUT to return from what may seem a digression to the more direct context of our Psalm. In verses 44–46 the Psalmist's prophetic range of vision widens, from the time of the Judges to *the history of the whole of the succeeding age down to the present time* ; " for the whole history of Israel has essentially the same fundamental character, viz., that Israel's unfaithfulness does not annul God's faithfulness. That verifies itself even now." [1]

" *Nevertheless He regarded* " (or " *saw* ") " *their distress When He heard their cry ; And He remembered for them His covenant, And repented according to the multitude of His loving-kindnesses. He made them also to be pitied Of all those that carried them captive.*"

" Nevertheless "—this word, though not perhaps the most literal translation of the Hebrew conjunctive letter *vav*, for which it stands, and which, as far as verbal accuracy is concerned, ought perhaps to be rendered " and," or " but," or " yet "—does none the less best express in English the true force of the original.

" Nevertheless "—this may in a sense be regarded as the key-thought to the whole of this great scripture.

The preceding Psalm (cv.) rehearses, as we saw, God's " marvellous works " for this peculiar people—

[1] Delitzsch.

their election and call out of His free grace; the
covenant He made with Abraham; His watchful care
over the patriarchs and their seed during their long
sojourn in Egypt; the display of His power and grace
in their redemption from the land of bondage; and His
shepherd-care over them in the wilderness till He
brought them safely into the Land of Promise.

But what was God's purpose in it all? This we are
told in the last lines of that Psalm:

" *He brought forth His people (from Egypt) with joy,*
His chosen ones with singing,
And He gave them the lands of the nations;
And they took " (or " *inherited* ") " *the labours of the*
  peoples,
That they might keep His statutes
And observe His laws."

But then follows the penitential confession in
Psalm cvi., which sets forth Israel's *failure* and manifold sins and transgressions in the wilderness, and
throughout their chequered history in the land, so that
" *the wrath of Jehovah was kindled against His people,*
and He abhorred His inheritance, and gave them over into
the hand of the nations, so that those that hate them might
bear rule over them."

And we now can carry the story of Israel's sins
and apostasy still farther. After the seventy years'
captivity in Babylon a remnant of all the tribes returned, which in process of time grew considerably
and became a formidable people—though the bulk
of the nation has, ever since the destruction of the first
temple, remained a *diaspora.* There were indeed some
glorious episodes in the history of the restored remnant,
more particularly in the Maccabean period; but in
the main, though cured of the gross forms of outward
idolatry, the moral features of *the great mass of the*

people did not change. The land became more than ever defiled with the sins of the people who dwelt in it, and the climax of Israel's apostasy was reached in the rejection of the Messiah, and in their resisting the Holy Spirit. Then indeed did God pour out His wrath upon them, and He scattered them once more among the nations and dispersed them through the countries, and for nineteen centuries no people on earth has suffered as they have suffered.

But the question may be asked, "What then?" Have the promises which God made to the fathers, and confirmed by oath, failed? Has God for ever cast off the people which He foreknew? The answer to these questions is found in the last verses of our Psalm, which are summed up in the word "Nevertheless." Oh, the infinite grace and marvellous faithfulness of Jehovah! Here truly is an illustration of the Apostle's words, "Where sin abounded grace did *superabound.*" Twice in Psalm cvi. does this word "Nevertheless" occur in the English version—once at the beginning of the long confession, and once at the close.

Already, at the very beginning of their national history, when the offer of deliverance was brought to them in Egypt and when they were at the Red Sea, their character and conduct was such that had God dealt with them according to their deserts, He would have been justified in leaving their redemption unaccomplished :

" *Nevertheless He saved them for His Name's sake,*
  That He might make His mighty power to be known."

This is the secret of it all. All He ever did or ever shall do for Israel as a nation, or for individual sinners of all nations, He does " for the sake of His Name," which, as already explained above, embodies His re-

vealed character as the God of grace and truth, *the
motive power being found, not in them, but in His own
heart of love and in the steadfastness of His purpose,
which He formed from before the foundation of the world.*
It would be derogatory to His character as the God of
truth, if having once entered into a covenant with
them, and given them unconditional promises, He failed
to carry His purpose through.   No ;   "*Jehovah will
not forsake His people for His great Name's sake, because
it hath pleased Jehovah to make you a people unto Himself.*" [1]

Between the first and second "Nevertheless" in
this Psalm stands the whole long confession of Israel's
manifold sins and transgressions in the wilderness and
in the land, to which may now be added the centuries
of unbelief and apostasy of the whole period of the
dispersion, from the time of the destruction of the first
temple to the present day—the whole of which is, I
believe, prophetically included in verses 40–46.   Has
not this made a difference ?   Have not Israel's stubbornness and many provocations, which brought about
their banishment from the land and from His presence,
occasioned the annulment of the covenant relationship
into which He had entered with them ?   In the words
of Psalm lxxvii., "Will Jehovah be favourable no
more ?   Is His lovingkindness clean gone for ever ?
Doth His promise fail for evermore ? "   The answer to
these questions is found in the second "Nevertheless " :

"*Nevertheless He regarded their distress
When He heard their cry ;
And He remembered for them His covenant,
And repented according to the multitude of His loving-
kindnesses* "—

[1] 1 Sam. xii. 22.

prophetic words which are an echo of two scriptures in the Mosaic writings, viz. Exod. ii. 24, 25, where we read : " And God heard their groaning, and God remembered His covenant with Abraham, with Isaac, and with Jacob ; and God saw [1] and God took knowledge of them " ; and Lev. xxvi. 44, 45 : " *And yet for all that* "—after the long catalogue of Israel's sins and apostasies, and consequent punishments, which are set forth in that chapter, which gives a Divine forecast of the whole history of the Jewish people from the beginning to the end—" *And yet for all that, when they are in the land of their enemies, I will not reject them, neither will I abhor them, to destroy them utterly, and to break My covenant with them ; for I am Jehovah their God : but I will for their sakes remember the covenant of their ancestors, whom I brought forth out of the land of Egypt in the sight of the nations, that I might be their God : I am Jehovah.*" Wonderful grace and faithfulness of Jehovah ! He who heard their " groaning " in Egypt will yet again hear their " cry " ; He who " saw," or looked with pity, on their oppression under Pharaoh, still regards them with compassion ; and though they have broken the covenant which He made with them at Sinai, and there is no hope for them whatever on the ground of the law or their own righteousness, " *He remembers for them His covenant,*" which existed long before the covenant of the law, and which He already " remembered " when they were yet in Egypt before the Sinaitic covenant was made—viz., " His covenant with Abraham, with Isaac, and with Jacob," which was not in the nature of a contract

---

[1] רַיַּא—*Vayar*—the same word as rendered " He regarded " in Ps. cvi. 44, which means to " regard *with compassion* " (see Gen. xxix. 32 ; 1 Sam. i. 11). For God to " see," or behold the need, is to help. " Calamities melt away beneath His gaze, like damp stains in sunlight."

between two parties, but of an unconditional promise
to the fulfilment of which He alone is pledged—the
covenant of which this same Psalmist sings at the beginning of Psalm cv., which Jehovah " *remembers for ever,*"
and to which He himself points His people as the
pledge and assurance of His everlasting faithfulness :
" *For the mountains may depart and the hills be removed ;
but My kindness shall not depart from thee, neither shall
the covenant of My peace be removed, saith Jehovah, that
hath mercy on thee.*" [1]   And because He is a God of such
infinite grace and everlasting faithfulness, therefore He
will not always chide, neither will He keep His anger
for ever—however well deserved—but " *repenteth Himself according to the multitude of His lovingkindnesses.*" [2]

And even while given over for their sins into the
hands of their enemies and cruelly oppressed by those
who hate them, He never utterly forgets or forsakes
them, but raises up friends for them, even in the lands
of their oppression ; yea, " *He makes them also to be
pitied of those that carried them captive,*" in accord with
the prayer of Solomon at the dedication of the temple :
" *Forgive Thy people who have sinned against Thee, and
all their transgressions wherein they have transgressed
against Thee, and give them compassion before those who
carried them captive, that they may have compassion on
them ; for they are Thy people, and Thine inheritance,
which Thou broughtest forth out of Egypt.*" [3]

Our long Psalm ends with a prayer and a doxology.

(1) *The Prayer :*

> " *Save us, O Jehovah, our God,
> And gather us from among the nations
> To give thanks unto Thy Holy Name,
> And to triumph in Thy praise.*"

---

[1] Isa. liv. 10.   [2] Compare Deut. xxxii. 36 ; Joel ii. 13, 14.
[3] 1 Kings viii. 50.

This inspired prayer is based on God's own word of promise, oft repeated, and will assuredly be fulfilled. Yea, it is in itself in the nature of a prophecy, for it is because God has revealed His purpose, and promised to do these very things, that Israel's psalmists and prophets find it in their hearts so to pray.

The answer to this cry, " Save us : gather us from among the nations," in which the Psalmist utters the soul of the godly remnant of the people, is found in such definite promises as these : "*Therefore fear thou not, O Jacob My servant, saith Jehovah ; neither be dismayed, O Israel ; for lo, I will save thee from afar, and thy seed from the land of their captivity, and Jacob shall return and shall be quiet and at ease, and none shall make him afraid." " Israel shall be saved in Jehovah with an everlasting salvation. Ye shall not be put to shame nor confounded, world without end."* [1] "*He that scattered Israel will gather him, and keep him, as a shepherd doth his flock.*"

The blessed consequence of Israel's national re-gathering and spiritual salvation will be that they will " *give thanks unto* " (or, more literally, לְהוֹדוֹת—*l'hodoth*— " *make joyful confession* " unto, or *of*) " His Holy Name " —that blessed Name which (as already stated more than once) stands for His glorious *Self* as the God of grace and salvation, and embodies all the Divine perfections of His being, all the glorious attributes of His character, which shine out so resplendently in His dealings with this peculiar people. Yes, Israel's joyful and most blessed task, when saved and gathered, will be to confess that " Holy Name," which shall then be fully known to them in and through their Messiah (who is the embodiment and revealer of the Name, or character of God) ; and they shall not only confess it,

[1] Jer. xxx. 10, 11, xxxi. 10 ; Isa. xlv. 17.

and sanctify it in their own hearts and lives, but they shall " *glory* " in it [1] and make it known among the nations, so that "from the rising of the sun to the going down of the same," the great and glorious and Holy Name of Jehovah shall be hallowed and praised. [2]

The verb—לְהִשְׁתַּבֵּחַ—*l'hishtabe'ach*—in the second line of the 47th verse, which in this form is found only in this one place in the Hebrew Bible, and rendered " triumph," is, as the grammarians will tell us, the reflexive of the *Piel of* שַׁבֵּחַ—*shabe'ach*—and means " to account oneself happy " ; [3] and the line ought therefore to be translated, " In order that we may account, or esteem, ourselves happy in Thy praise," or, " in praising Thee "—for it is life eternal truly to know and confess His Holy Name ; and well may those esteem themselves happy whose blessedness it is to show forth the praises of Jehovah—a God of infinite grace and faithfulness. And into this blessedness Israel shall yet fully enter ; for, in spite of past failure, God's purpose in and through them will yet be accomplished : " *This people have I formed for Myself ; they shall shew forth My praise.*"

(2) *The Doxology :* [4]—

" *Blessed be Jehovah, the God of Israel,*
From everlasting unto everlasting,
And let all the people say, Amen.
Hallelujah."

---

[1] Ps. cv. 1–3.   [2] Ps. cxiii. 3.   [3] See Hebrew of Eccl. iv. 2.

[4] I do not enter into the question as to whether this *Berachah* (" Blessing," or Doxology), which is incorporated in 1 Chron. xvi. 36, and forms also the concluding Doxology of the Fourth Book of the Hebrew Psalter, was an original part of the Psalm (as I am personally strongly inclined to think), or is a liturgical addition of the compiler, as most modern scholars assume. Whatever its inspired origin, its fitness as the climax of response to the whole Psalm is manifest.

" *Blessed be Jehovah* "—the everlasting great " I AM "—the faithful, unchangeable God, who is, and was, and eternally shall be, "the King eternal, immortal, invisible—the *only* God." " *The God of Israel,*" who, in infinite grace and condescension, has entered into indissoluble covenant relationship with this nation, and has thus in a special sense bound up His Holy Name with theirs, in which fact rests their national preservation and ultimate spiritual salvation—" *From everlasting to everlasting* "—in ceaseless, unbroken continuity ; for when earth's dispensations shall have ended, and time shall be no more, Jehovah's praises shall still be proclaimed by the redeemed family through the eternal ages in ever fuller and more perfect strains.

" *And let all the people* "—the whole congregation— " the Israel of God "—those whose blessedness it is to know Jehovah as *their* God—" the people whom He hath chosen for His own inheritance "—" *say Amen.*"

" Martin Luther once said of the Lord's Prayer that it was the greatest martyr on earth, because it was used so frequently without thought and feeling, without reverence and faith. This quaint remark, as true as it is sad, applies perhaps with still greater force to the word ' Amen.'

" Familiar to us from our infancy is the sound of this word, which has found a home wherever the nations have learnt to adore Israel's God and Saviour. It has been adopted, and without translation retained, in all languages in which the Gospel of Jesus, the Son of David, is preached.[1]

[1] In Isa. lxv. 16, the words, " He that blesseth himself in the earth shall bless himself in the God of truth," etc., is literally, " shall bless himself in the God, Amen." Stier observes that we have here an indication that Amen will be one of the very words of the holy language used on earth during the millennium, even as it is now used in the Church.

" It is a *great* word, this word Amen ; and Luther
has said truly, ' As your Amen is, so has been your
prayer.'

" It is a WORD OF VENERABLE HISTORY in ISRAEL
and in the CHURCH.

" It dates as far back as the law of Moses. When
a solemn oath was pronounced by the priest, the response of the person who was adjured consisted of the
word ' Amen.' In like manner the people responded
' Amen,' when, from the heights of Ebal and Gerizim,
the blessings and the curses of the Divine law were
pronounced. Again, at the great festival which David
made when the ark of God was brought from Obed-
Edom, the psalm of praise which Asaph and his
brethren sang concluded with the words, ' Blessed be
the Lord God of Israel for ever and ever. And all the
people said, ' Amen ' " (1 Chron. xvi. 36).[1]

And we, too, dear reader, will conclude with
" Amen," which means " truth," " even so," " so be
it." *Amen*, Lord—let the prayer in the 47th verse
speedily be answered : Save Thy people Israel, and
gather them from among the nations, that through
them Thy way may become known on the earth, Thy
saving health among all the nations ! Yes, *Amen*—
blessed be Thou, Jehovah the God of Israel, from everlasting to everlasting !

And the Psalm ends with the word with which it
also began—" Hallelujah "—which also has become a
universal word in Christendom, and needs no translation, but which in English means :

" Praise ye Jehovah."

---

[1] Adolph Saphir, in *The Lord's Prayer*.

Part 4

"LOOK UNTO THE ROCK FROM
WHENCE YE WERE HEWN": THE
GRACE AND POWER OF GOD AS
MANIFESTED IN THE HISTORY OF
ISRAEL

Isaiah 51

Isaiah 51

HEARKEN to Me, ye that follow after righteousness, ye that seek Jehovah : look unto the rock whence ye were hewn, and to the hole of the pit whence ye were digged. Look unto Abraham your father, and unto Sarah that bare you ; for when he was but one I called him, and I blessed him, and made him many. For Jehovah hath comforted Zion ; He hath comforted all her waste places, and hath made her wilderness like Eden and her desert like the garden of Jehovah ; joy and gladness shall be found therein, thanksgiving, and the voice of melody.

Attend unto Me, O My people ; and give ear unto Me, O My nation : for a law shall go forth from Me, and I will establish My justice for a light of the peoples. My righteousness is near, My salvation is gone forth, and Mine arms shall judge the peoples ; the isles shall wait for Me, and on Mine arm shall they trust. Lift up your eyes to the heavens, and look upon the earth beneath ; for the heavens shall vanish away like smoke, and the earth shall wax old like a garment ; and they that dwell therein shall die in like manner : but My salvation shall be for ever, and My righteousness shall not be abolished.

Hearken unto Me, ye that know righteousness, the people in whose heart is My law ; fear ye not the reproach of men, neither be ye dismayed at their revilings. For the moth shall eat them up like a garment, and the worm shall eat them like wool ; but My righteousness shall be for ever, and My salvation unto all generations.

Awake, awake, put on strength, O arm of Jehovah ; awake, as in the days of old, the generations of ancient times. Is it not thou that didst cut Rahab in pieces, that didst pierce the monster ? Is it not thou that driedst up the sea, the waters of the great deep ? that madest the depths of the sea a way for the redeemed to pass over ? And the ransomed of Jehovah shall return, and come with singing unto Zion ; and everlasting joy shall be upon their heads : they shall obtain gladness and joy ; and sorrow and sighing shall flee away.

I, even I, am He that comforteth you : who art thou, that thou art afraid of man that shall die, and of the son of man that shall be made as grass ; and hast forgotten Jehovah thy Maker, that stretched forth the heavens, and laid the foundations of the earth ; and fearest continually all the day because of the fury of the oppressor, when he maketh ready to destroy ? and where is the fury of the oppressor ? The captive exile shall speedily be loosed ; and he shall not die and go down into the pit, neither shall his bread fail. For I am Jehovah thy God, who stirreth up the sea, so that the waves thereof roar : Jehovah of hosts is His name. And I have put My words in thy mouth, and have covered thee in the shadow of My hand, that I may plant the heavens, and lay the foundàtions of the earth, and say unto Zion, Thou art My people.

Awake, awake, stand up, O Jerusalem, that hast drunk at the hand of Jehovah the cup of His wrath ; thou hast drunken the bowl of the cup of staggering, and drained it. There is none to guide her among all the sons whom she hath brought forth ; neither is there any that taketh her by the hand among all the sons that she hath brought up. These two things are befallen thee ; who shall bemoan thee ? desolation and destruction, and the famine and the sword ; how shall I comfort thee ? Thy sons have fainted, they lie at the head of all the streets, as an antelope in a net ; they are full of the wrath of Jehovah, the rebuke of thy God.

Therefore hear now this, thou afflicted, and drunken, but not with wine : Thus saith thy Lord Jehovah, and thy God that pleadeth the cause of His people. Behold, I have taken out of thy hand the cup of staggering, even the bowl of the cup of my wrath ; thou shalt no more drink it again : and I will put it into the hand of them that afflict thee, that have said to thy soul, Bow down, that we may go over ; and thou hast laid thy back as the ground, and as the street, to them that go over.

22

GOD'S WONDERFUL WORKS IN THE PAST SET FORTH AS THE BASIS OF HOPE FOR THE FUTURE

THE preceding section of Isaiah's prophecy ended with words of warning addressed by the Servant of Jehovah to the godless majority, who, in contrast to the God-fearing remnant who " obey His voice " and are content to walk with Him, even in the " darkness " (verse 10), set up a false light for themselves, and prefer to walk in the sparks, or " burning darts," of their own kindling. The end of these despisers of His word is expressed in the words, " *This shall ye have of My hand* (or, '*from My hand is this to you* '), *ye shall lie down in sorrow.*" [1]

But God's people are not only commanded to trust where they cannot see, sometimes the Lord graciously condescends to show them *the moral reasonableness of faith.* This is the main purpose of the 51st chapter. In it God seeks to strengthen the faith of His own people in the promises which He has given them in relation to the future by a rehearsal of the wonders He did for them in the past.

In the Hebrew Bible this chapter is divided into seven short paragraphs of unequal length. The first paragraph consists of verses 1–3.

" *Hearken to Me, ye that follow after righteousness and that seek Jehovah.*" It is *the godly remnant* of

---

[1] See the exposition of Isa. l. 4–11 in my booklet, *The Obedient Servant of Jehovah and His Counsel to His Followers.*

Israel, who are thus addressed, and whose attention
God claims for the message He would convey to them.

" *Hearken* "—not merely with the outer ear, but
with the inner ear of the heart—the word (שִׁמְעוּ, *shim'u*)
having the sense of giving heed with a view to obey.
It is the same word as is rendered *obey*, or " *obeyeth*,"
in the 10th verse of the 50th chapter.   Those addressed
are described as " *followers* " (or " diligent pursuers "
—*rod'phei*) after " *righteousness*."   This is how the
Apostle Paul characterises the whole of Israel in contrast to the other nations : " *What shall we say, then,*"
he exclaims, " *that the Gentiles who followed not after
righteousness have attained to righteousness, even the
righteousness which is of faith.   But Israel which followed
after righteousness have not attained to the law of righteousness.   Wherefore, because they sought it not by faith,
but, as it were, by the works of the law.*" [1]

How very sad and pathetic ! The people whose
chief aim has been the attainment of righteousness
with a view to fit them for communion with God ;
the people of whom the same apostle himself bears
witness " that they have a zeal for God "—missed the
goal of their strivings because they misunderstood
and misapprehended the nature and object of the law,
and thought that righteousness could be attained by
works and outward observances.

But while this is true of the majority of the nation,
there has always been, thanks be to God, a *remnant*
in Israel who were seekers of righteousness and seekers
of God, not by the law of works, but by the law of
faith ; men who were imbued with the spirit of the
Prophets and the Psalmists, who sought nearness to
God, not on the ground of anything in themselves,
but could pray like Daniel : " *We do not present our*

[1] Rom. ix. 30–32.

God's Wonderful Works 271

supplications before Thee for our righteousness, but for Thy great mercies' sake,[1] or, like David : " *Remember, O Jehovah, Thy tender mercies and Thy lovingkindnesses, for they have been ever of old* (or, ' *from eternity* '). *Remember not the sins of my youth, nor my transgressions ; according to Thy lovingkindness remember Thou me for Thy goodness' sake, O Jehovah.*"[2]

And this will be the case with *all* Israel by and by. They shall not only " follow after," but attain unto, and " know righteousness," when in and through the righteousness of their Messiah all the seed of Israel shall be justified and shall glory,[3] and shall also become known throughout the earth as *doers* of righteousness, in whose very hearts and inward parts God's law shall be written.

Note the parallelism to " *Ye that seek after righteousness* " is " *Ye that seek Jehovah,*" for He is the only source of the righteousness which can make sinful men meet for fellowship with Him, Who is the Holy and Righteous One ; and to Himself, as the living fountain, all who " hunger and thirst after righteousness " must come and drink in order to be satisfied. But, to repeat, it is the godly remnant of Israel—the seekers of Jehovah—who long for His grace and salvation, who are here addressed, for they only, in contrast to the godless majority in the nation, " are in a condition by faith to regard that as possible, and in spirit to behold that as real, which seems impossible to human understanding, because the very opposite is lying before the eye of the senses." [4]

And this is the message which He has for them : " *Look unto the rock whence ye were hewn, and to the hole of the pit whence ye were digged.*" This is explained in the words which immediately follow : " *Look unto*

[1] Dan. ix. 18.   [2] Ps. xxv. 6, 7.   [3] Isa. xlv. 25.   [4] Delitzsch.

Abraham your father and unto Sarah which bare you."
Abraham is, so to say, the rock whence the stones
were hewn of which the House of Jacob is composed ;
Sarah's maternal womb is the hole of the pit (or
" fountain ") from which Israel was brought forth.

Now I beg of you to note, dear reader, that these
words are not addressed to the remnant of Israel with
a view to inculcate in them a spirit of humility as if
they were intended to remind them of their supposed
obscure or mean origin—in which sense one often hears
this scripture misapplied. As to this the Jews have
no occasion to be ashamed or humbled by looking
back on their origin. Many Gentile peoples would be
glad if they could trace their origin so far back to one
man of such nobility of character as Abraham was.
No ; they are directed to look back and ponder, not
on the supposed humbleness, but *on the supernatural
character of their origin,* and on the great wonders
which God wrought for them in the past, so that their
faith may be strengthened in what He says to them
with reference to the future.

All our hopes, whether for Israel, or for the world,
or for ourselves, are based on the grace of God and on
the power of God, and these two foundation attributes
of God's character are nowhere more strikingly displayed than in the beginnings of Israel's history to
which we are pointed back in this chapter. Of the
grace of God we are especially reminded by the two
Hebrew words in the second verse, קְרָאתִיו וַאֲבָרְכֵהוּ—
*q'rathiv v*ᵃ*abhar'khehu.* " *I called him and I blessed
him,*" and the *almighty power* of God as displayed in
the origin of the Jewish nation is forcibly brought
before us in the two words, אֶחָד וָאַרְבֵּהוּ—*echad v'ar'behu*
—" one," or " but one," and I increased him, or
" made him many."

I.—" I called him and I blessed him." In the midst of the darkness which then covered the earth, and the gross darkness which rested on the peoples, the God of glory appeared unto our father Abraham, and " He called him," saying, " *Get thee out of thy country and from thy kindred, and from thy father's house, into a land which I will shew thee.*" Thus Jewish history begins with the miracle of God's self-revelation, and with an act of His sovereign grace and condescension. If God had not in His grace made Himself known to Abraham he would have remained in the darkness of idolatry in which the people around him and his own kindred and father's house lived.

In apocryphal and midrashic literature Abraham is indeed represented as a philosopher and hero, who, as the result of a process of cogitation, arrived at the conclusion that there is but one true God, and then devoted his life to the promulgation of this blessed discovery. But these legendary accounts of Abraham have no more basis of historic fact than the claim of some modern rationalistic Jews and certain Modernist Christian theologians, that the Jews, as a people, *evolved* the belief in one true and living God by " a genius for monotheism " which they are supposed to possess.

Oh no ; it is not by " searching," or by his own cogitations or reasonings, that man can find God. What Scripture records to Abraham's everlasting honour is, that when God made Himself known to him and " called him," he gladly responded to God's call, in spite of the sacrifice which it involved, and the obstacles which were in his way. " By faith," we read, " Abraham, when he was called to go out into a place which he should after receive for an inheritance, obeyed ; and he went forth, not knowing whither he went."

And not only did God call him, but He "*blessed him.*" To be called out of the world's darkness to the knowledge of the living God, and to be brought into such intimate relation with Him as to be called "the friend of God," is itself the greatest of blessings. But in many other ways also did God bless him—both in things of time and in things of eternity ; and He constituted him also the depository of blessing for all nations, in accord with His word of promise when He first called him : "*I will bless thee, . . . and be thou a blessing, . . . and in thee shall all families of the earth be blessed.*" [1]

II.—But not only did He exhibit His sovereign *grace* in the call and blessing of Abraham, but in what He did for and through Abraham and Sarah, He displayed also His *almighty power.*

"I called him," He says—not "alone," as in the Authorised Version, but "one," *i.e.* "*when he was but one* "—" and I increased him." This reminds us of *the miraculous origin of the Jewish nation.*

Think of it, dear reader. When God came to Abraham, saying, "Get thee out of thy country, and from thy kindred, and from thy father's house, . . . and *I will make of thee a great nation,*" Abraham was "one" childless man—and that one, as the writer of the Epistle to the Hebrews reminds us, already, by reason of his age, "as good as dead." And as to Sarah, it is not without design that in the very first mention of her name in the Bible it is immediately emphasised, "*And Sarai was barren* ; she had no child." And not only so, but when the promise of the birth of Isaac was eventually made, Scripture leads us to infer that it was no longer naturally possible for Sarah to bear a child. But when to nature the fulfilment of the promise

[1] Gen. xii. 2, 3.

seemed quite impossible, and Sarah herself *laughed* at the possibility of it, God came to Abraham, saying, " Wherefore did Sarah laugh, saying, Shall I of a surety bear a child which am old ? Is anything too hard (or ' too wonderful ') for Jehovah ? " [1]

And because there is nothing too wonderful for Jehovah, and God wanted to teach the whole of mankind through the history of Israel that He is *the God of the impossible*, who quickeneth the dead and calleth things that are not as though they were ; and because Abraham, though taking well into account the natural impossibilities of the situation, " considering his own body now as good as dead, and the deadness of Sarah's womb," [2] yet " staggered not at the promise through unbelief, but was strong in faith, giving glory to God, being fully persuaded that what He had promised He was able also to fulfil—*therefore sprang there even of one, and him as good as dead, so many as the stars of the sky in multitude, and as the sand which is by the seashore innumerable.*"

Now do we really believe this, dear reader ? Do we believe in the supernatural origin of Israel's history— in the miracle of God's grace and power to which we are pointed back in the first two verses of this chapter ? for only then shall we truly believe in the promise in relation to the future which immediately follows.

Note the connection : " *Look unto Abraham your father, and to Sarah that bore you ; for when he was but one I called him, and I blessed him, and increased him— for Jehovah hath comforted Zion ; He hath comforted all her waste places, and hath made her wilderness like Eden, and her desert like the garden of Jehovah.*"

" *Jehovah* "—the same wonder-working God of infinite grace and almighty power, who did for Abra-

[1] Gen. xviii. 13, 14.   [2] Rom. iv. 19 (R.V.).

ham and Sarah what seemed naturally impossible, and who in the very beginning of Israel's history made Himself known as the God with whom nothing is too hard or too wonderful—" hath *comforted* Zion." The verbs (*nicham* and *vayasam*—" He hath comforted," " He hath made," or " turned ") in this 3rd verse are *preterites*—a tense frequently used in prophetic scripture of the future, " inasmuch as to the eye of faith and in prophetic visions the future has the reality of a present and the certainty of a completed fact." [1] Yes, so sure and certain are these glorious promises of God in relation to Israel's future that, as far as *His purpose* is concerned, they are viewed as already *accomplished.*

" Zion " is in this prophecy viewed as the counterpart of Sarah ; or, to put it differently, Sarah, in her original barren state, is the type of Zion in her present desolate condition. Viewed naturally, it may seem as unlikely that this " barren woman " Zion, should again be a " joyful mother of children " in her own home or " house ",[2] as it was for Sarah to bear a child when she was already past age ; but Jehovah, who wrought that miracle at the beginning of Israel's history, and who fulfilled his promise to Abraham in spite of natural impossibilities and human impossibilities, and comforted Sarah by the birth of Isaac, shall yet again " comfort Zion."

There is much about the comfort which Israel is yet to experience after their long night of sorrow, in this second part of Isaiah. Its very first words are *nachamu, nachamu*—" Comfort ye, comfort ye, My people, saith your God." Hence the Rabbis have styled this great prophecy " The Book of Consolations."

---

[1] Delitzsch.

[2] Ps. cxiii. 4. See the exposition of this Psalm in *Types, Psalms, and Prophecies.*

The ground of the comfort which God will minister to them is also set forth in the first words of the prologue : " *Speak ye comfortably to* (or, ' *speak ye to the heart* ' *of*) *Jerusalem, and say unto her that her warfare* (or, ' *her appointed time of servitude* ') *is accomplished, her iniquity is pardoned* (or, ' *her debt is paid* '), *that she hath received of the Lord's hand double for all her sins.*" Israel's long night of sorrow and sufferings, which was the direct consequences of her sins, shall then be ended, and " *as one whom his mother comforteth so will I comfort you,*" He says, " and ye shall be comforted in Jerusalem " (Isa. lxvi. 13). And not only will He comfort Zion herself by His return unto her with mercies, and with the sense of His forgiveness and love, and make her joyous and fruitful, but " *He shall comfort all her waste places* (or ' *ruins* ') *and make her wilderness like Eden, and her desert like the garden of Jehovah.*"

How glorious a transformation ! From a state of total barrenness into another Eden, with all its fertility and beauty, and instead of its present condition of utter desolation it shall be like " *the garden of Jehovah,*" as glorious as if it had been directly planted by Himself for His own joy and delight.

And it is both the people and the land which will thus be " comforted " and transformed, for " Zion " stands here, as in so many scriptures, as the name for both, and the promise must be understood literally in relation to the land, and spiritually in relation to the people. For many centuries Jerusalem has lain in ruins ; and Palestine, naturally a fruitful land, has been known pre-eminently " as the land that is desolate." Let it not be forgotten that the long-continued desolation of the land is directly due to the sin of the people. " The land," we read, " shall be desolate because of them that dwell therein, for the

fruit of their doings " (Mic. vii. 13) ; for Palestine
became involved in the sin of Israel, even as creation
became involved in the sin of Adam. But we are
looking forward to the time when, as one of the blessed
results of the glorious redemption which has been
accomplished by our Lord Jesus Christ, " creation
itself shall be delivered from the bondage of corruption
into the liberty of the glory of the children of God."
And so also, when Israel is pardoned and the covenant
relations between God and His people are restored, the
curse which has rested on the land shall be lifted, and
" the wilderness and the solitary place shall be glad,
and the desert shall rejoice and blossom as the rose." [1]
Yea, " He shall comfort all her waste places, and make
her wilderness like Eden and her desert like the garden
of Jehovah."

But what the land in its desolate condition has been
in relation to the people, the people in its condition of
unbelief and apostasy has been in relation to God, viz.
a barren wilderness, a spiritual desert. But this moral
and spiritual wilderness of the people also shall be
transformed. And not only so, but as this same
prophet tells us in the 35th chapter, " Waters shall
break out in the wilderness, and streams in the desert,"
i.e. not only will Israel himself, now a moral wilderness, be quickened and refreshed, but out of him shall
flow rivers of living waters for the spiritual quickening
and refreshment of the world.

And if we want to know when this wonderful transformation will be brought about, and by what means
or power it will be accomplished, the same prophet
tells us in the 32nd chapter : " *Until the Spirit be
poured upon us from on high,*" he says, " *and the wilderness become a fruitful field, and the fruitful field be*

[1] Isa. xxxv. 1.

esteemed a forest." [1] And then, when both the land and the people are thus " comforted " and transformed, "*joy and gladness shall be found therein, thanksgiving and the voice of melody.*" " *For thus saith Jehovah: Yet again there shall be heard in this place, whereof ye say it is waste without man and without beast, even in the cities of Judah and in the streets of Jerusalem. . . . The voice of joy and the voice of gladness, the voice of the bridegroom and the voice of the bride, the voice of them that give thanks to Jehovah of hosts; for Jehovah is good, for His mercy* (or, '*His lovingkindness*') *endureth for ever.*" [2]

And this joy and gladness, and the voice of melody of restored and converted Israel, will reverberate through the universe, and will be the echo and response, so to say, of God's own joy over His restored national prodigal, even as we read in Zephaniah: " *He will rejoice over thee with joy; He will rest in His love* (or, ' *be silent in His love* '—*as if it were too much, or too deep for expression); He will joy over thee with singing.*" [3]

No wonder that the prophet Isaiah—in view of the blessed issues of the conversion and blessing of Israel, not only to Israel himself, but to the world—exclaims in the 49th chapter: " *Sing, O heavens; be joyful, O earth, and break forth into singing, O mountains; for Jehovah hath comforted His people and will have compassion upon His afflicted.*"

Before passing on to the next paragraph, let me add a brief practical word.

By God's grace we, too, my dear Christian reader—whether we be Jews or Gentiles—are included among those who are " followers after righteousness and seekers after God." Yea, though we may not be of Israel after the flesh we are the children of Abraham by faith, and this beautiful scripture, though addressed

[1] Isa. xxxii. 15.   [2] Jer. xxxiii. 10, 11.   [3] Zeph. iii. 17.

primarily to the godly remnant in Israel, has a message for us also. We, too, when tempted to stagger at the promises of God in unbelief because their fulfilment seems to us naturally impossible, or, humanly speaking, improbable, should bring to mind the " works of Jehovah " and meditate " on His wonders of old." Let us remember how in the whole history of Israel, which has been well characterised as " the history of miracle and the miracle of history," He has again and again proved to those who have believed His word and trusted in His holy Name, that He is a God of the impossible — or, according to His own word to Abraham, that there is nothing " too hard " or " wonderful " for Jehovah. As fellow-workers for Israel's salvation, let us exercise strong faith in God and not be daunted by what may seem to us impossibilities.

We look on the Jewish nation now and say, " What a moral and spiritual desert ! " We look on the Promised Land and say, " How barren, how desolate ! " Let us look to the rock whence we were hewn ; to the hole of the pit whence we were digged. Was not Abraham as good as dead ? Was not Sarah naturally barren ?

Yea, have we not experienced the supernatural power of God in our own hearts and lives ? Has He not quickened and transformed our own souls ? And what He has done in the past He will do, only on a more glorious scale, in the future ; and what He has done for us, He can and will do for others.

23

THE BLESSING OF THE NATIONS BOUND UP WITH THE SALVATION OF ISRAEL

THE second of the seven short paragraphs into which our chapter is divided consists of verses 4 to 7. In it we see the blessing which will result to the other nations of the earth from the restoration and conversion of Israel. We are reminded of the words addressed by God to His Servant the Messiah (chapter xlix. 6), that His mission would extend beyond the bounds of Israel to the Gentile nations. "*It is too light a thing that thou shouldst be My Servant to raise up the tribes of Jacob and to restore the preserved of Israel : I will also give Thee for a light to the Gentiles, that Thou mayest be My salvation unto the end of the earth.*"

This second brief paragraph begins also with a call of attention. "Hearken" (*haq'shibhu*)—the word in the original is different than the one with which the chapter begins, but the meaning is much the same. It might perhaps be best rendered "Listen" or "Attend" ; and to mark the importance of the message which He is about to communicate to them, the call is repeated, *ha-azinu*—"Give ear."

This time they are to hear something which concerns not only themselves, but others also ; not only what God will do for them, but what He will do *with* them and *through* them.

"*O My people ; O My nation.*" Here we are reminded of Israel's unique calling and relationship to

God. They are the only people which, *as a nation,* God has chosen as His own peculiar possession out of all the nations of the earth. Hence He speaks to them, and of them, as He does not speak of any other nation. " *You only have I known of all the families of the earth,*" He says through Amos ; [1] or, in the words of Moses, " *Hath God assayed to go and take Him a nation from the midst of another nation, by trials, by signs, and by wonders and by war, and by a mighty hand and an outstretched arm, and by great terrors, according to all that Jehovah your God did for you ?* " [2] Israel is God's *nation,* and it is of them that the Psalmist sings : " *Blessed is the nation whose God is Jehovah ; the people whom He hath chosen for His own inheritance.*" [3] Truly, to quote from another Psalm, " He hath not dealt so with any other nation," nor is there any other people which *corporately as a people* stands in such a covenant relationship to Him.

And be it remembered, dear Christian reader, that Israel's unbelief and rejection of Christ has not broken up this covenant relationship between them and God, " for the gifts and calling of God are without repentance " or " change of mind " on His part ; and though Israel has been faithless and disobedient, *God* abides faithful and " *remembers His covenant for ever, the word which He commanded to a thousand generations— the covenant, namely, which He made with Abraham, and His oath unto Isaac, and confirmed the same unto Jacob for a statute, to Israel for an everlasting covenant.*" [4] It is true that Israel's unbelief and national apostasy has brought about not only their banishment from their land, but from the presence of God, and that as a nation they are at present " Lo-ammi," " not My

---

[1] Amos iii. 2.　　　　[2] Deut. iv. 33, 34.
[3] Ps. xxxiii. 12.　　　　[4] Ps. cv. 8–10.

people." But not utterly and for ever did God cast off His people which He foreknew. "God forbid," or, "far be the thought," the Apostle Paul exclaims; for that would be derogatory to His character as a God of truth and faithfulness. No; Israel is still "His people"; "theirs" are still "the promises"; their rejection is only temporary—"until the fulness of the Gentiles be come in," and then "all Israel shall be saved, even as it is written," *i.e.* in Old Testament prophecy, which he proceeds to quote, and which on the testimony of the Apostle Paul, still contains glorious promises in reference to Israel's future.

Meanwhile their "fall" has been the occasion for God to extend His salvation to the Gentiles, and their temporary "casting away" has brought about "the reconciling of the world," and many millions from among the Gentiles, who formerly were "no people," [1] are now together with the remnant, according to the election of grace, from Israel, "the people of God," and form "a chosen generation (or elect race), a royal priesthood, a holy nation, a people for God's own possession." But the inclusion of Gentile believers within the bounds of promise and of covenant does not affect the purpose of God with *the nation*, nor does the Church displace Israel in the plan of God in relation to the other nations. The mission of the Church is to evangelise the world with a view to the gathering in of *individuals* out of all nations into its fold, but it is reserved for restored and converted Israel as a nation to bring *the nations* to a knowledge of their glorious Messiah and King, and bring *universal* blessing to the world.

But from this not altogether unnecessary digression let us return to our text. "*Hearken unto Me, O My*

[1] 1 Pet ii. 10 (R.V.).

people ; give ear unto Me, O My nation "—and the
message to which they are to pay such particular
attention is contained in the words which follow:
" *For a law from Me shall go forth, and My judgment
(or ' ordinance,' or ' rule ') for a light of the peoples will I
establish (or ' cause to rest ').*" The *Torah* ("law ")
which should thus proceed direct from Him to be
promulgated among the Gentile nations (as the plural,
ammim, " peoples," indicates) is not the old law from
Sinai, but the new law which proceeds from Zion. It
is the new covenant as distinguished from the " old."
It is " the law of faith " (Rom. iii. 27), not binding
upon one race or nation only, but " by the command of
the everlasting God made known to all nations for the
obedience of faith " (Rom. xii. 26). It is " the Gospel
of Redemption," as Delitzsch defines it, which experimentally becomes in us also " the law of the Spirit of
life in Christ Jesus which makes us free from the law of
sin and death."

The term *mishpat*—" judgment " (which stands
here as the equivalent of *Torah* ("law ") is " the new
order of life " established by the Messiah, in which
Israel and the nations are united. This new law
Jehovah says, " *shall go forth from Me,*" for He is the
Author and Source of it, but it is established on earth
through the medium of the Messiah—hence we read
in the 42nd chapter, " *Behold My Servant whom I
uphold, My Chosen, in whom My soul delighteth ; I have
put My Spirit upon Him ; He will bring forth judgment
(mishpat) to the nations. He will not fail nor be discouraged, till He have set judgment in the earth, and the
isles shall wait for His law.*" This expression, " a law
shall proceed from Me," must also be compared with
the great prophecy in the 2nd chapter, where we read
that " in the latter days," when the mountain of

Jehovah's house shall be established on the top of the mountains, and all nations shall flow unto it to be taught of His ways in order that they may walk in His paths, " *Out of Zion shall go forth the law and the word of the Lord from Jerusalem.*"

Here we see the Divine source and earthly centre of the new Messianic " law " which is to bring light and justice to the world. It originates in God ; Messiah is the Mediator of it, but Zion-Israel is the centre where it is " established," and whence its light goes forth to all the nations of the earth. This is God's method of procedure in blessing the world ; He works in and through Israel outwards. This is His revealed purpose from the very beginning. " *In thee,*" He said to Abraham, " *shall all the families of the earth be blessed.*"

A partial fulfilment and foretaste, as it were, of these great Messianic promises the world has already had. All the knowledge of the true and living God, and of His " law " which Gentiles possess, has come to them " out of Zion," and through the instrumentality of men of Israel. It was through individual Jews—to repeat words I used elsewhere—whose hearts were set on fire with love and devotion to Jesus of Nazareth, whom their nation despised and rejected, who went forth into the world, taking their lives in their hands, to preach Him among the Gentiles ; and through the inspired writings of Jewish apostles and evangelists, that individuals from all nations—a multitude which no man can number—have been brought into the knowledge and fellowship of their Messiah. But when God shall have mercy on Israel again ; when, not only *individual Jews*, but the *whole nation*, shall be baptized with the " pentecostal spirit " and burn with the same love and zeal for the glorious Person of their Messiah and for the extension of His Kingdom, which characterised the great apostle to the Gentiles, who in so many respects is the type of His nation—then nations, *as nations*, shall "join themselves to Jehovah," and the day of which the prophets sang, and for which they yearned—the day of universal peace and righteousness, when God's way shall be known in all the world and His saving health among all nations—shall at last break on this earth.

And the time when God's rule shall thus be established is fast hastening; yea, is already at hand—literally, " *Near is My righteousness, gone forth is My salvation.*" The terms *ts'daqah* (" righteousness ") and *y'shu'ah* (" salvation ") are frequently used as synonyms in the second part of Isaiah, for the righteousness which the prophet announces as about to be revealed is not the manifestation of God's character as the Righteous One, and not merely " the faithful fulfilment of the promised deliverance " —as one commentator explains—but His " *justifying righteousness* " which He bestows on us sinful men, and which, when laid hold of by faith, makes them fit to appear in His holy presence.   It can therefore be used as the equivalent of " salvation," though the term *y'shu'ah* (" salvation ") is more comprehensive and includes all that God, out of His free grace, does for sinners.   " *My* righteousness ; *My* salvation," He says, for man cannot originate them, nor supply them for himself, nor can they be bought, but can only be received as a free gift from God.   They come to us in and through the Messiah, whose very name " Jesus " (*Yeshu'ah*) means " God's salvation," and who, " by His knowledge," makes the many righteous.

One thing which is included in the " salvation " of God, which is about to be manifested, is His righteous rule over the nations.   This is expressed in the next

sentence : " *And Mine arms shall judge the peoples.*"
" Mine arms " stand for *Himself* ; He by His own power
and might will judge them.   This is to be understood
in the same sense as chapter ii. 4.   " *He will judge among
(or ' between ') the nations, and rebuke (or ' decide, or
dispense justice,' as Von Orelli renders it) for (or to) many
peoples.*" He will rule, and with His own strong
" arms " administer justice to the nations, but He shall
also " judge " and " rebuke " those among the peoples
who oppose themselves to His righteous rule, or hinder
the universal spread of His righteousness and salvation
throughout the earth.

One of the blessed consequences of this Divine
administration of justice and righteousness will be that
there shall be no more deadly feuds, nor a reliance upon
weapons, but universal peace.   " *They shall beat their
swords into plowshares, and their spears into pruning
hooks ; nation shall not lift up sword against nation,
neither shall they learn war any more.*"

Instead of relying on their own strength, or arma-
ments, or material resources, they shall all look to
Jehovah :   " *On Me shall the islands wait, and in My
arm shall they trust.*"

It is now generally agreed among scholars that the
term אִיִּים—*iyim*—means not necessarily *islands*, but
the distant maritime *coasts*, and is in most cases where
it is used a representative expression for countries—
especially for far countries—in general.   Yes, upon
Jehovah, the living God of Israel, shall the peoples in
all lands, even in the most distant parts, wait, for they
shall discover what individuals among the nations
even now find that with Him is the fountain of life, and
that in His light alone can we see light ; and in the
Almighty " arm," which supports the universe, " shall
they trust."

And here, again, we observe that it is *God in Christ* who will thus be the hope and confidence of all the ends of the earth.   This we see by comparing these words : " *Mine arms shall judge the peoples ; on Me shall the islands wait,*" etc., with chapter xlii. 4, where we read of the Servant of Jehovah, " *He will not fail, nor be discouraged, till He have set judgment in the earth, and the isles shall wait for His law.*"

And this new order of things, and the blessedness resulting from it, shall continue for ever.   This is set forth in the 6th verse : " *Lift up your eyes to the heavens and look upon the earth beneath.*"   There is no sight more glorious than heaven's lofty dome, studded with innumerable bright orbs which, in sublimest, though inaudible, music, proclaim the infinite wisdom and power of God.   And there is nothing also like the heavens and the earth (which stand here, as in many other places in Scripture, for the whole framework of nature) to impress man with the apparent stability of things.   They seem fixed and firm, and there is no visible mark on them of dissolution or decay.   But, though they appear so fixed and permanent, they will vanish and disappear, while God's righteousness and salvation will remain.

And this is not only a figure of speech used here by way of illustration, but a solemn prophetic statement of what will actually take place : " *For the heavens shall vanish away* [1] *like smoke, and the earth shall fall to pieces*

---

[1] The verb נִמְלָחוּ—*nim'lachu*, rendered " vanish away," occurs nowhere else in this form, and there has been much disputation among commentators about it.   Some have tried to derive its meaning from other cognate forms of the same root, all of which have reference to *salting* (from the noun מֶלַח, *melach*—salt).   But it seems clear enough that it is the niphal form of the verb מָלַח—*malach*—" to tear away," " to disperse," or dissipate.   It might thus perhaps be better rendered, " The heavens shall be dispersed in fragments."

like a (disused, worn-out [1]*) garment, and its inhabitants shall in like manner perish.*"

What a terrible announcement this is for those whose hopes are all bound up with the present visible order of things! So terrible, indeed, that they put it from them, or refuse to believe it. " What sign is there," they say, " of any possible change ? Is not nature governed by unchangeable law ? Do not all things continue as they were from the beginning of the creation ? " willfully forgetting the sudden destruction which overtook the world at the Flood, and the other great judgments of God which came upon men " unawares."

But whatever scoffers may say, and whether men are prepared for it or not, " *the Day of the Lord* WILL *come as a thief in the night, in the which the heavens will pass away with great noise, and the elements will be dissolved with fervent heat, and the earth and the works that are therein shall be burned up.*"

But when this fearful cataclysm of nature shall have taken place, and when the heavens and the

---

[1] The Hebrew כְּמוֹ־כֵן—*kemo-khen,* rendered " in like manner " in the English versions, has also been variously rendered by interpreters. The words translated just literally mean " like so " ; and this, or " just so," is the rendering given in the LXX and Vulgate. Delitzsch translates " like this," which he supposes was accompanied with a contemptuous gesture to express " like a mere nothing."

The Jewish commentator, Samuel Luzzatto, makes the phrase to mean " in an instant," strictly the time required to say " khen," and compares it to the German phrase, " *in einem Nu.*"

Most modern writers, however, take כֵּן—*khen*—to be the singular of כִּנִּים—*kinnim*—the word translated " *lice* " in the account of the plagues of Egypt, and explained by later lexicographers to mean a kind of stinging *gnat.* These interpreters all render the sentence, " *and the inhabitants thereof shall die like gnats.*" But, as Delitzsch observes, the singular of *kinnim* (lice or gnats, which though not used in the Bible, is found in the Talmud) would be, not *kin* or *khen,* but *kinnah.* On the whole, I think the rendering given in the English Bible and in the ancient versions preferable.

earth " that now are " shall pass through the fiery ordeal and be, as it were, dissolved, " *My salvation* " —*i.e.* as manifested in those who by His grace have become the subjects of it—" *shall be for ever* " ; " *and My righteousness* "—as displayed in those who have become *partakers of it*—" shall not be abolished "— literally, תְּהָת אֹל—*lo-thechath*—" shall not break up " or " go to ruin," but remain *indestructible*. We are reminded of the beautiful words in chapter liv. 20 : " *For the mountains may depart, and the hills be removed ; but My lovingkindness shall not depart from thee, neither shall the covenant of My peace be removed, saith Jehovah, that hath mercy on thee.*

And not only shall God's redeemed people " abide for ever " when the world and the lust thereof shall have " passed away," [1] but out of the havoc and ruin of the old order of things there shall emerge, as this same prophet Isaiah announces, " the new heavens and the new earth " [2] wherein shall dwell righteousness. " *Wherefore, beloved,*" writes the apostle, " *seeing that ye look for these things, give diligence that ye may be found of Him in peace without spot and blameless in His sight.*" [3]

The third brief paragraph, which consists of only two verses (7 and 8), is an exhortation to God's oppressed and persecuted people not to be afraid of man. This exhortation is based on the glorious promises in the first six verses. " *Hearken unto Me, ye that know righteousness, (the) people in whose heart is My law.*"

For a third time there is a call to earnest attention, addressed to the godly remnant, to what He is about to say, and the message is one of encouragement. The word for " hearken " is the same with which the chapter begins, and means, as already explained, not

<hr />

[1] 1 John ii. 17.   [2] Isa. lxv. 17, lxvi. 22.   [3] 2 Pet. iii. 13, 14.

only to hearken with the outer ear, but to *give heed*, with a view to obey. There is progression of thought in these first eight verses. Instead of " ye that follow " (or " diligently *pursue* ") after righteousness, as in verse 1, it is " ye that *know* righteousness," *i.e.* " know it from your own experience." As Delitzsch correctly explains, not only " as a gift of grace, but also as *conduct* in harmony with the plan of salvation." We are reminded of Hosea v. 3 : " *Then we shall know if we follow on to know Jehovah* " ; or, as the Revised Version renders the words perhaps more correctly, " *And let us know, let us follow on to know,*" for if we are true " seekers " of Jehovah we shall assuredly find Him, and if we are diligent " followers " after righteousness we shall attain to an even deeper experimental knowledge of it.

Another characteristic of God's true people is expressed in the next clause : " *The* (or *thou*) *people with My law in their heart.*"

One of the great promises attached to the new covenant is : " *I will put My law in their inward parts, and in their hearts will I write it,*" so that it shall be the standard and impulse of their life, and that they may become at least in measure like Him, who could say of Himself : " *I delight to do Thy will, O My God ; yea, Thy law is within My heart.*"

In contrast to God's true people are " the wicked," to whom He says :

" *What hast thou to do to declare My statutes, and that thou takest My covenant in thy mouth ?* " [1]

If I may digress from the exposition for a moment, I would ask you, dear reader, to which of these two classes do you belong ? We may not be openly " wicked," but are we mere *professors*, who draw nigh

[1] Ps. l. 16.

to God with their mouth and who honour Him with their lips, while our hearts are removed far from Him,[1] as was the case with the godless majority in Israel ? or are we true subjects of the new covenant, with the law of God written *in our hearts* as the inward spring of our lives and actions, so that " the righteousness of the law is fulfilled in us because we walk not after the flesh, but after the spirit ? "

But to return to our context. The word of encouragement which He has for those who know righteousness, and have His word dwelling in their hearts, is this : " *Fear ye not the reproach of men, nor be dismayed at their revilings.*"

Again and again in this second part of Isaiah does God in His grace seek to strengthen the hearts of His weak and fearful children with these words, " Fear not ; be not dismayed," and sometimes He stoops in His condescension to reason with them, and to show them the groundlessness of their fears, since He, the Almighty Everlasting God, is with them to strengthen, to help, and to deliver them. More particularly are they exhorted not to fear anything that man could do unto them.

The godly remnant, the true Israel, always had and always will have to suffer reproach and persecution from the haters of God and His truth. It is part of their high calling and the distinguishing mark of those who are heirs of God's Kingdom, while to their revilers and persecutors it is " a manifest token " of the judgment of God for which they are reserved. But those who know Jehovah and have His sure word of promise must not be terrified or be discouraged at the taunts and revilings (or literally, " blasphemies ") of the ungodly.

[1] Isa. xxix. 13.

One reason why they are exhorted not to fear them is expressed in the generic name " man " by which they are described.   The word is '*enosh*, which means weak, or sickly, man, and suggests the idea of their frailty and *mortality*.   Delitzsch, Von Orelli, and most other modern scholars are, therefore, justified in rendering the second half of the 7th verse, " *Fear ye not the reproach of mortals*, nor be ye dismayed (or ' alarmed ') at their revilings," for however much they may boast in their might, their short day will soon pass, and their power to do evil come to an end, " *For the moth shall eat them up like a garment, and the worm shall devour them like wool*."

There is a play on the words in the original for " moth " and " worm " ('*ash* and *sas*) which cannot be reproduced, nor can it be stated with absolute certainty what tiny insects are here intended, though '*ash* is now pretty generally understood to stand for " moth," [1] but what the double figure affirms is, that the most *insignificant* instrumentality and the smallest exertion of strength " are sufficient to annihilate the sham greatness and sham power " of the revilers and persecutors of God's people, " and that long before they are actually destroyed they carry the constantly increasing germ of destruction within themselves." [2]

But whilst the enemies of God and of His redeemed people shall perish, " *My righteousness*," He says, " *shall be for ever, and My salvation* "—the righteousness and salvation which are already the portion of those " who know righteousness " and have His law in their hearts, but into the full realisation of which they will enter in the day of His manifestation—shall be *l'dor dorim*—literally, " to an age of ages," *i.e.* to

[1] A Jewish proverb says the *sas* is a brother to the '*ash*.
[2] Delitzsch.

an age which embraces endless ages within itself, or, " to eternity."

Before passing on to the next paragraph let me remind you again, dear Christian reader, that the things which are here spoken to the godly remnant of Israel are written also for *our* learning and encouragement. There is no cause for *us* either to fear " the reproach of mortals," or be dismayed at the sayings and blasphemies of the godless, or indeed at anything that man or time can do, or bring to us. And if we, like the godly at all times, have to endure something for His dear Name's sake, let us take to heart the words of Christ : " *Blessed are ye when men shall reproach you and persecute you, and say all manner of evil against you falsely for My sake. Rejoice and be exceeding glad, for great is your reward in heaven, for so persecuted they the prophets which were before you.*"

24

WHY GOD'S PEOPLE HAVE NO OCCASION TO FEAR: A GLORIOUS VISTA OF THE FUTURE

WE now come to the fourth of the seven short paragraphs into which our chapter is divided. It may be summarised as an impassioned prayer, in which the prophet gives expression to the yearnings of the godly remnant of Israel that the God of their fathers, who wrought such wondrous things for them in the past, may even now interpose on their behalf, and deliver, and save, and bring about the glorious time which, on the ground of His own promises, is prophetically contemplated in the first eight verses of the chapter.

It reminds us of Psalm xliv. There, after the rehearsal of the wonderful works which God did at the beginning of Israel's history—how He drove out the doomed Canaanitish nations and caused His own people to strike root and flourish, and the solemn thankful confession :

" *They got not the land in possession by their own sword,*
Neither did their own arm save them ;
But Thy right hand, and Thine arm, and the light of Thy countenance,
Because Thou wast favourable unto them "—

the Psalmist, as the representative of the remnant of the true Israel, exclaims : " *Thou art my King, O God* "

—or, more literally—" *Thou art He, my King, O God*,"
i.e. " Thou art still the same, Thine arm has lost none
of its might since those ' days of old ' ; and Thou art
' *my* King and *my* God,' for Thy covenant with our
fathers still stands—*command* (i.e. *even now*) *deliverance*
(or *salvation*)—*for Jacob*." So it is here. As I indicated at the very beginning of the exposition of this
chapter, God seeks in this very precious section of
Isaiah's prophecy to strengthen the faith of the godly
remnant of His people in the great promises concerning the future, by reminding them of what He did
for them in the past.

In the first paragraph (verses 1–3) He told them to
" look to the rock whence they were hewn, and to the
hole of the pit whence they were digged," and reminded
them of their miraculous origin—how that, in spite of
the fact that when He called Abraham their father, he
was " *but one*," and that one, by reason of his age, " as
good as dead," He " blessed him and increased him,"
and made of him a mighty nation.

They may well believe, therefore, His promise that
He will yet again " comfort Zion," in spite of her
present barren and desolate condition (even as, in spite
of natural impossibilities, He comforted that " barren
woman " Sarah by the birth of a son in her old age),
and make her wilderness like Eden and her desert like
the garden of Jehovah.

Now, from their supernatural origin *as a people*, we
are taken in the brief paragraph, which we are about to
consider, to the wonders which God wrought for them
in the beginning of their history *as a nation* ; and again
the past is called up with a view to confirm faith and
to create hope in relation to the future.

The paragraph begins with the cry, עוּרִי עוּרִי—*'uri 'uri*
—" *Awake, awake, put on Thy strength* (or, lit., *clothe*

Thyself with might), O arm of Jehovah; awake, as in the days of old, the generations of ancient times"—of which we have not only the written record, but of which " we have heard with our ears, and our fathers have told us "—as the inspired singer prays in the Psalm from which I have already quoted as a parallel to this scripture.

The arm of Jehovah is the emblem of His Divine power. At present it is, as it were, *dormant*, or quiescent, for it is not *visibly* and *manifestly* exercised on behalf of truth and righteousness, and for the help of His oppressed people. But that arm of Jehovah has not grown lifeless, nor has it lost any of its might by reason of age. " *Thou hast (still) a mighty arm; strong is Thy hand and high is Thy right hand,*" as Ethan the Ezrahite sings in another Psalm, in which there is reference to the same mighty deeds of God in Israel's past history as in this chapter in Isaiah.[1] Jehovah needs only to put His power in motion—to rouse, as it were, His arm, and " clothe it with might," out of the fulness of His own omnipotence—and the oppressor of His people shall be smitten down before Him, even " as in the ancient times " when " Thou hast scattered Thine enemies with the arm of Thy strength."

Jehovah's mighty deeds in the past, to which the prophet appeals in this paragraph, and which serve as the basis of hope for the future, are those which He wrought when He brought His people out of Egypt : " *Is it not Thou* (lit., *was it not Thou, yea, Thou*)[2] *that didst cut Rahab in pieces, that didst pierce the dragon?* "

Rahab is an emblematical name for Egypt, and is

---

[1] Ps. lxxxix. 8–13.

[2] אַף הִיא *at hi*—is, as Delitzsch correctly explains, an emphatic repetition—that is to say, a strengthening of the subject, and equivalent to " Thou, yea, Thou."

used also in other scriptures—as, for instance, in Ps. lxxxix. 10 : " *Thou hast broken Rahab in pieces as one that is slain.*" It was probably used by the later inspired writers in an *ironical* sense, to show up Egypt's *empty boastfulness*, and with a view to bring home to the Jews, who were inclined in times of national danger to fly to Egypt for help, that this was to lean on " a broken reed " ; for though Egypt might promise much it could accomplish nothing——the etymological meaning of the word being " *arrogance.*"

This comes out clearly in Isaiah xxx., where the prophet denounces the " rebellious children " who, contrary to the counsel of God, seek, by an alliance with their former oppressors, " to strengthen themselves in the strength of Pharaoh, and to take refuge in the shadow of Egypt," to whom they send ambassadors with costly gifts : " *But they shall be ashamed,*" says the prophet, " *because of a people that cannot profit them, that are not a help nor profit, but a shame and also a reproach ; . . . for Egypt helpeth in vain and to no purpose, therefore have I called her* (i.e. *Egypt*) *Rahab* (i.e. ' *arrogance* '), *that sitteth still* " : or, as Gesenius and Delitzsch translate, " great mouth that sitteth still " [1]—that is, one who is arrogant in her boastfulness, but in the time of need is found to be impotent to render any help.

And not only did God smite proud Egypt and " cut it to pieces " when it held on to Israel and would not let it go, but He pierced " the dragon," or, literally (*tannin*), the sea " monster," i.e. *Pharaoh*, the word being the same as in Ezek. xxix. 3, where Jehovah says : " *Behold I am against thee, Pharaoh, king of Egypt, the great monster* (*tannin*) *that lieth in the midst*

[1] In the Authorised Version the words are misrendered, " Their strength is to sit still."

of the rivers, that saith my river is mine own, and I have made it for myself." But this proud *monster* of the Nile was " wounded," or " pierced through," when he dared in his pride lift himself up against God, saying : " Who is Jehovah, that I should hearken unto His voice to let Israel go ? " [1]

In the 10th verse we are reminded of the mighty acts of God for His people which followed the Exodus from Egypt : " *Was it not Thou—yea, Thou,*" the prophet proceeds, " *that driedst up the sea, the waters of the great deep ; that madest the depth of the sea a way for the redeemed to pass over ?* " Yes, when there was nothing before them but the sea and the Egyptians behind, and there seemed no way of escape from the pursuing host, God stretched forth His strong arm and made " *a way in the sea, and a path in the deep waters,*" that Israel, and all men through them, might learn that with Jehovah nothing is impossible, and that He can *create* ways where there are none, and that He is able to deliver His people, it matters not how imminent may be the danger.

Now note, because Jehovah of the Exodus is still the same, and His almighty power is still available for the deliverance of His people, and for the accomplishment of His purposes, " *Therefore* (or ' *and* ') *the ransomed of Jehovah shall return and come with singing unto Zion, and everlasting joy shall be upon their heads : they shall obtain* (or ' *attain unto* ') *gladness and joy, and sorrow and sighing shall flee away.*" The look into the future is cleared and strengthened, as Delitzsch observes, by the look which the prophet had just cast into the past.

With one or two insignificant variations in the original, this 11th verse is a repetition of the last verse

[1] Ex. v. 2.

of chapter xxxv. The prophet loves, as it were, to rest the eye of his prophetic vision on that glorious scene of the " redeemed " and " ransomed " multitudes—redeemed not only outwardly from the power of their enemies and from their long bondage, but redeemed, or " ransomed," also with the greater *inward* spiritual redemption from all their sins and iniquities—streaming back from all the lands of their dispersion to their loved Zion, filling the air with their glad songs of praise, even as, after the redemption from Egypt and the overthrow of Pharaoh and his host in the Red Sea, they sang that sublime song of joy and triumph recorded in the 15th chapter of Exodus, saying :

" *I will sing unto Jehovah, for He hath triumphed*
    gloriously ;
The horse and his rider hath He thrown into the sea.
Jehovah is my strength and my song,
And He is become my salvation.
This is my God, and I will praise Him ;
My father's God, and I will exalt Him. . . .
Thy right hand, O Jehovah, is glorious in power ;
Thy right hand, O Jehovah, dashes in pieces the enemy
. . . Who is like unto Thee, O Jehovah, among the
    gods ?
Who is like Thee, glorious in holiness,
Fearful in praises, doing wonders ? . . .
Thou in Thy lovingkindness hast led the people that
    Thou hast redeemed ;
Thou hast guided them in Thy strength to Thy holy
    habitation."

A foretaste and foreshadowing, in a very limited degree, of what is set forth in this prophecy we have presented to us in what took place after the seventy years' captivity in Babylon. For when Jehovah then brought back the little remnant that were returning to Zion, "*We were*," says the Psalmist, "*like unto them that dream. Then was our mouth filled with laughter, and our tongue with singing. Then said they among the nations, Jehovah hath done great things for them ; Jehovah hath done great things for us, whereof we are glad.*"

But that joy and gladness, not unmixed with tears,[1] which accompanied the restoration of the remnant from Babylon, were but transitory, for that restoration was followed, after a chequered period of national existence in the land, by the universal dispersion consequent on their rejection of the Messiah, and the long night of sorrow and weeping which has lasted nearly two millenniums. No ; there is another restoration, or " return," of scattered Israel foretold by all the prophets.

Not of a remnant only, but of the whole people ; not from Babylon, or any one country or district only, but " out of the north country and from all the countries " whither they had been driven,[2] after which " they shall no more be plucked out of their land " [3] ; a restoration to be followed by the still more glorious event of their conversion, when as a nation they shall look upon Him whom they have pierced, and mourn— a universal mourning which shall end in " everlasting joy," after the greater than Joseph shall have made Himself known to His brethren. For then they shall indeed " *obtain* (or ' *attain unto* ') *gladness and joy* " as a permanent possession, and " sorrow and sighing shall flee away," never to return.

And the joy and blessedness of returned and redeemed Israel in literal Zion will be a type and reflection also of the even fuller joy and greater blessedness of the ransomed of the Lord out of every nation and

[1] Ezra iii. 12.   [2] Jer. xxiii. 8.   [3] Amos. ix. 15.

people and tongue—which will then be safely gathered unto Him in the heavenly Zion, " the Jerusalem that is above," of which the literal Jerusalem will, during the millennial period, be, as it were, the earthly vestibule.

Our wanderings too, dear Christian reader, shall then be at an end, and there, in His immediate presence, we shall enter into the " fulness of joy " and " drink of the river of His pleasures," which never runs dry, but continues to flow " for evermore."

The fifth paragraph in our chapter consists of verses 12 to 16, and it may be viewed, first, as Jehovah's reply to the impassioned prayer of the prophet as the representative of the godly remnant in verses 9 and 10. To the cry, " Was it not Thou, even Thou, who didst work such marvellous deliverance for us in days past ? " God's answer in the 12th verse is " *I* (*even*) *I* "—I am still the same everlasting, self-existing, unchangeable God, and " *I am He that comforteth you* " in your present condition of bondage and sorrow with My word of promise, which can never fail. " *Who art thou, that thou art afraid of man that shall die, and the son of man that shall be made as grass ?* " Is it possible that " *thou* "—with Jehovah as thy comforter, and with the great and precious promises which He has given thee, that He will strengthen and help and deliver thee—shouldest feel thyself so helpless and forsaken, that thou art afraid ?

There is a double reason for the groundlessness of Zion's fear indicated in this verse. The first is found in the words " *I, I am He* "—think of Me, Jehovah— the same who wrought marvellous deliverances for you in the past as thy Protector ; and the second is, think of those of whom thou art afraid. They are described by the generic names of אֱנוֹשׁ—'*enosh* and אָדָם—" *Adam.*" Now, as already explained in my

notes on the 7th verse, 'enosh means not only " man,"
but weak, sickly, mortal man ; and in this verse the
etymological import of the word is rendered more
prominent by the addition of the word יָמוּת—yamuth—
" who shall die " ; and the " son of man," who, as
the very word implies, belongs to the " earth," and is
frail and transitory, and " shall be made " (literally,
yinnathen—" shall be given ") " as grass," which
withers when once the breath of Jehovah is blown
upon it.[1]

And it is not only foolish and unreasonable for
Zion to fear, but sinful ; for fear is the offspring of
unbelief and the result of forgetfulness of God.   This
is set forth in the 13th verse : " And hast forgotten
Jehovah thy Maker, that stretched forth the heavens and
laid the foundations of the earth, and fearest continually
all the day because of the fury of the oppressor when he
maketh ready (or ' as he aims ') to destroy."

How wonderful is the grace of God which expresses
itself even in this rebuke !   For He seeks at the same
time to drive out their fear, and create confidence by
reminding them of His all-sufficient power to save.
You fear because you forget Me, and only look round
and about, and see the enemy making ready to destroy.
But look up, and remember that " I am with thee "—
I, " Jehovah "—the covenant-keeping, faithful God
who will never fail thee ; " thy Maker "—who is surely
able to protect thee.   And if you want still further
proof of My almighty power, look to the heavens above
and the earth beneath you—" that stretcheth forth the
heavens and layeth the foundations of the earth."   The
verbs noteh (" stretcheth ") and yosed (" layeth ") are
both in the participial form, and express the continuous
active display of His omnipotence in the universe.

[1] Chap. xl. 6-8.

For, to use words of my own from elsewhere,[1]
" He not only once for all in the beginning created the
heavens and the earth, and appointed certain ' laws '
to regulate their motions without troubling Himself
further about them, or about man, who is admittedly
the goal and climax of His creative work on earth.
No ; ' My Father worketh hitherto,' said our Lord
Jesus, ' and I work ' ; and this is equally true in
the sphere of creation, providence and redemption.
According to the Biblical view, as a Bible scholar well
observes : " God stretches out the heavens every day
afresh, and every day He lays the foundation of the
earth, which, if His power did not uphold it, would
move out of its orbit and fall into ruin.' " [2]

Truly, with such an omnipotent Protector at hand,
it is foolish and sinful to fear. And this, let me add,
is true, not only of Zion, but of you and of me, dear
Christian reader, who have this same Almighty God
of Israel as *our* Saviour and friend, and His unfailing
great and precious promises to rest upon.

But to return to our immediate context. The
question with which the 13th verse closes : " *And
where is now the fury of the oppressor* (or ' *tormentor* ') ? "
" looks," as Delitzsch truly observes, " into the future,"
and beholds the final deliverance of God's people and
the sudden disappearance of the oppressor. The
danger with which Zion is threatened is real and
imminent ; for it is not, as the Authorised Version
reads, " as if " the oppressor were ready to destroy,
which may imply that the danger was only apparent.
There is no " if " expressed in the text at all ; but,
on the contrary, as properly rendered in the Revised

[1] See exposition of Zechariah xii. in *Visions and Prophecies of
Zechariah.* Reprinted 1972 by Kregel Publications
[2] Hengstenberg.

Version, " when " (or " as ") he makes ready (or
" aims ") " to destroy " ; for there is no doubt of the
readiness and determination of the oppressor. But,
somehow, the hand that is stretched out to give the
annihilating blow is stayed, or withered, or the arrow
that is so carefully adjusted on the string,[1] and so
skilfully aimed with a view to the destruction of God's
people, is diverted, or rebounds on the oppressor, who
is himself swept away, so that not a trace of him is to
be seen ; while the people which, in his mind and
purpose was devoted to destruction, remains.

There are many striking instances in the past history
of Israel to exemplify this truth. Pharaoh at the
very beginning of their existence as a people, " made
ready to destroy " when he issued his decree that all
their male children should be drowned ; and again
when, in defiance of God, who by His mighty power
had brought them forth out of Egypt, he said :

> " *I will pursue, I will overtake,*
> *I will divide the spoil :*
> *My desire shall be satisfied upon them ;*
> *I will draw my sword ;*
> *My hand shall destroy them* " (Ex. xv. 9).

With the sea in front and the pursuing host behind, was there probability of their being delivered ?
But where was in the end the fury of the Egyptian
oppressor ? Israel passed through the ordeal, not only
of the Nile, but of the Red Sea, in safety ; but Egypt
was smitten and Pharaoh and his host were drowned.

To choose one other instance. Sennacherib, with
his mighty host outside the walls of Jerusalem, " made

---

[1] The verb כֹּונֵן—*konen*—translated here " maketh ready," is specially used in reference to the preparation of the bow for shooting by the
adjustment of the arrow on the string. See Ps. vii. 13, xi. 2, xxi. 13.

ready to destroy," and arrogantly defied Jehovah, saying, " *Who are they among all the gods of these countries, that have delivered their country out of my hand, that Jehovah should deliver Jerusalem out of my hand ?* " But where in the end was the fury of the Assyrian oppressor ?

Suddenly, when his hand was lifted up to give the final blow, " the Angel of Jehovah went forth and smote in the camp of the Assyrians a hundred and four score and five thousand."

" *Like the leaves of the forest when summer is green,*
That host with their banners at sunset were seen ;
Like the leaves of the forest when autumn hath blown,
That host on the morrow lay withered and strown.

For the angel of death spread his wings on the blast,
And breathed in the face of the foe as he passed ;
And the eyes of the sleepers waxed deadly and chill,
And their hearts but once heaved and for ever grew still."

And so again and again God has shown that, when in His favour and under His protection, there is really no need for His people to fear, however great and imminent the danger which threatens.

In our chapter it is perhaps Babylon who is in the foreground of the prophet's range of vision as the oppressor " who made ready to destroy " ; but Zion's captives there need not fear, for Jehovah's eyes are upon them, as well as upon their enemies, and His word to them is : " *I am with thee, saith Jehovah, to save thee ; for I will make a full end of all the nations whither I have scattered thee, but I will not make a full end of thee.*" [1] And where in the end was Babylon with all its fury ? Yea, what became of all the other great nations of antiquity—Medo-Persia, Greece, and

[1] Jer. xxx. 11.

Rome, who each in turn " made ready to destroy " ?
Because they brought themselves under God's curse
for their cruelty to His people, they crumbled away
and disappeared, while the Jews still remain. And
the same will be found to be true also in more modern
times. Certain it is that no nation has lifted up its
hand in readiness to destroy this " peculiar " people,
which has not itself been smitten.

And this will yet be demonstrated on a grander
scale in the future, for though Babylon may be the
foreground in this prophecy of Isaiah, it looks on, as
already shown, to the time of the end, and the final
deliverance of Israel and the overthrow of their enemies.
Israel's sufferings are not yet ended. On the testimony
of prophetic Scripture there is yet a climax of tribulation which is spoken of pre-eminently as " the day of
Jacob's trouble " ; [1] there is yet a final gathering of
the nations against them, and the manifestation of
greater hatred, than even they have yet experienced.
But when the confederated Gentile hosts are marshalled
under the Antichrist and the war-cry is raised, " *Come,
let us destroy them from being a nation, that the name of
Israel be no more held in remembrance,*"[2] one more
blow, and the Jewish nation will be no more, Jehovah
shall again say to the remnant which " shall be saved
out of it " : [3] " *And where is now the fury of the oppressor ?* " For it shall come to pass that suddenly " *the
multitude of all the nations that fight against Ariel, even
all that fight against her, and her stronghold, and that
distress her, shall be as a dream, or vision in the night.
And it shall be when a hungry man dreameth, and behold
he eateth ; but he awaketh, and his soul is empty ; or
when a thirsty man dreameth, and behold he drinketh :
but he waketh, and behold, he is faint and his soul hath*

[1] Jer. xxx. 7. [2] Ps. lxxxiii. 4. [3] Jer. xxx. 7.

appetite : so shall the multitude of all nations be that fight against Mount Zion." [1]

The sudden deliverance of the exiled captives whom the oppressor " made ready to destroy," and who to all appearance were doomed to die, is graphically depicted in the 14th and 15th verses :

" *The captive exile* (or, literally, ' *he that is bowed down* ') *is speedily loosed and does not die (to go down) into the pit, neither doth his bread fail* "—in spite of the determinate fury of the oppressor and his readiness to destroy—" *for I am Jehovah, who stirreth up* [2] *the sea that the waves thereof roar : Jehovah of hosts is His name* "—*i.e.* the Almighty, who has all the forces of nature at His command, and at whose wrath earth trembles, and the sea is terrified and roars, and whose indignation the nations are not able to abide,[3] and who is therefore well able to deliver His people, however mighty the foe and however imminent the danger.

The 16th verse takes us to the eschatological climax of the prophecy. It sums up also the purpose of God in the election and preservation of Israel : " *And I have put My words in thy mouth.*" This is one of the chief privileges in the high calling of Israel. " *What advantage, then, hath the Jew ?* " asks the Apostle, " *or what profit is there in circumcision?* " And his own

[1] Isa. xxix. 7, 8.

[2] The verb רֹגַע—*roga'* (the participle of רָגַע—*raga'*—rendered in the A.V. " divideth," and in the R.V. " stirreth up," has been explained by commentators in two directly opposite senses—that of " stilling " and that of " agitating." As far as the word itself is concerned, either rendering is possible, and the first has in its favour the frequent use of the derivative conjugations in the sense of quieting, or being quiet. The other, however, seems to be required by the context, for the word וַיֶּהֱמוּ—*vayehemu*—must indicate a consequence (so that they roar) and not an antecedent (when they roar).

[3] Jer. x. 10.

answer is : " *Much every way ; first of all, that they were intrusted with the oracles of God.*" [1]

" *He shewed His word unto Jacob,*" sings the inspired Psalmist in like manner, " *His statutes and His ordinances unto Israel.*

" *He hath not dealt so with any nation :*

" *And as for His ordinances, they have not known them. Hallelujah !* " [2]

Yes, remember, dear Christian reader, that all that God has spoken, from the call of Abraham to this day, He has spoken through Jewish lips. Of course, this high privilege involved a very solemn responsibility, for the inestimable treasure of God's self-revelation in their midst was " committed," or " intrusted," to them —not for themselves only, but that it might be diffused throughout the earth—a trust which has so far only been partially acknowledged and discharged by them.

" *I have put My words in thy mouth* "—not only to be committed to writing and preserved in a book, but that it may remain also as a word of *living testimony* in their mouths. This, indeed, is the pledge of His everlasting covenant with them as a people. " *As for Me,*" He says, " *this is My covenant with thee, saith Jehovah ; My Spirit that is upon thee, and My words which I have put in thy mouth, shall not depart out of thy mouth, nor out of the mouth of thy seed, nor out of the mouth of thy seed's seed, saith Jehovah, from henceforth and for ever.*" [3] And because they stand thus as a people everlastingly related to Him, and are the appointed custodians of His words, He preserves them, so that, in spite of all the attempts on the part of the nations to destroy them, they still remain. " *I have covered thee,*" He says, " *in the shadow of My hand.*"

It is important to note that what is here stated of

[1] Rom. iii. 1, 2.　　　[2] Ps. cxlvii. 19, 20.　　　[3] Isa. lix. 21.

redeemed Israel, is in chapter xlix. 2 said of the perfect
Servant of Jehovah, the Messiah, who is " Israel's
inmost centre and highest head," and in whom the purpose which God had in the call and election of Israel,
viz. that in and through them all the nations of
the earth should be blessed—is brought to the fullest
realisation.

But in the plan of God the mission of the Messiah is
never entirely dissociated from Israel. At first it is
the godly remnant—those who are of faith in Israel,
who in union with Him make known His words which
He has put in their mouths ; but eventually it is the
whole saved nation, with Messiah in their midst, which
becomes the medium of His salvation unto the ends of
the earth. Hence some things spoken of the Messiah
in some passages of the second part of Isaiah are in
other places applied to the true Israel, who are, as it
were, the body of which He is the Head.

The glorious " eschatological climax " of which I
spoke is reached in the second half of this 16th verse :
" *That I may plant the heavens and lay the foundations
of the earth, and say unto Zion, Thou art My people.*"

The reference, as all commentators admit, is to the
last times. The Jewish Targum paraphrases : " To
restore the people of whom it is said they will be as the
stars of heaven ; and to perfect the church of which it
is said they will be as numerous as the dust of the earth."
The allegorising Christian commentators, who look
upon this scripture as fulfilled in the first coming of
Christ, explain it as setting forth " a completion of the
theocracy and a new arrangement of the condition of the
world " ; or, in the words of Dr. J. N. Alexander, " the
reproduction of the church in a new form, by what we
usually call the change of dispensations." But, as
Franz Delitzsch observes, " The prophecy speaks of a

new heaven and a new earth, in something more than a figurative sense, as a new creation of God."

In the 5th verse of this chapter there is a prophecy (as we have seen) of the passing away of the heavens and the earth that " now are " at the Epiphany of God our Saviour. " *For the heavens,*" we read, " *shall vanish away like smoke, and the earth shall fall to pieces like a disused, worn-out garment, and its inhabitants in like manner shall perish.*"

But out of the wreck and confusion of the old order of things shall emerge " the new heavens and the new earth, wherein shall dwell righteousness " and salvation for evermore ; and as a means and preparation for this glorious consummation, Zion is to be restored and taken back to His favour. The Lo-ammi period of Israel's sorrow and suffering consequent upon their sin will be ended, and He will say unto Zion, *Ammi attah*—" Thou art My people."

And this is not the only scripture in which the new creation is linked with the future blessing of Israel. Thus we read in chapter lxv. 17, 18, of this same prophecy : " *Behold, I create new heavens and a new earth ; and the former things shall not be remembered nor come into mind. But be glad and rejoice for ever in that which I create ; for behold, I create Jerusalem a rejoicing and her people a joy, and I will rejoice in Jerusalem and joy in My people ; and there shall be heard in her no more the voice of weeping and the voice of crying.*"

And again in chapters lxvi. 22 : " *For as the new heavens and the new earth which I will make shall remain before Me, saith Jehovah, so shall your seed and your name remain.*"

25

A FINAL WORD OF COMFORT AND OF WARN-
ING: THE "CUP OF STAGGERING" TO BE
TAKEN FROM ISRAEL AND GIVEN TO
ISRAEL'S FOES

THERE remain yet two brief paragraphs in our chapter for us to consider in this exposition. From the " eschatological climax " and the height of the prophetic Pisgah which we had reached in the preceding verses, where we obtained a glimpse of the glorious future which extends to the new heavens and the new earth wherein shall dwell righteousness and peace for evermore, we are in these last verses of the chapter suddenly brought down to the valley of shame and humiliation of the actual present condition of the land and the people, which are the appointed centre and medium whence this future glory is to radiate among all nations, even unto the ends of the earth.

The fourth brief paragraph in this chapter (verses 9–11) began with the cry, " *Awake, awake, put on strength, O arm of Jehovah: awake, as in the days of old, the generations of ancient times.*" There the prophet, as the representative and embodiment, so to say, of the godly remnant in the nation, addresses God in this impassioned prayer, that He may once again make His arm bare and manifestly interpose for the deliver-ance of His people, even as He did so gloriously again and again in the early days of their history. This

prayer is followed by the glorious promises in verses
11–17, in which we are reminded that Jehovah *is* still
the same as when He cut Rahab in pieces, and pierced
the monster of the Nile, and brought His people out of
Egypt. Therefore " the redeemed of Jehovah shall
(yet again) return and come to Zion with songs and everlasting joy upon their heads."

But during the time—and it embraces the whole
period of Gentile domination—that the arm of Jehovah
has apparently, and to human sight, been dormant, as
far as visible manifest interposition is concerned,
" Jerusalem " (which stands here not only for the
city, but also for the people of which she is, so to say,
the mother) has been lying in an unconscious condition in the dust, overcome, " not with wine," or with
natural sleep, but as one stupefied by some poisonous
draught.

And as, in order that the purpose of God may be
realised and the glorious promises be fulfilled, it is
necessary for Jerusalem to rise from her present degradation to her appointed position, and, by responding
to God's call, fit herself for the accomplishment of her
mission of diffusing the light of Jehovah among all
nations, the prophet, who had in verse 7 uttered the
prayer, " Awake, awake, put on strength, O arm of
Jehovah," now turns to the people with the cry :
" *Hith'oreri, hith'oreri!* "—" *Awake, awake* (or lit.,
Rouse thyself! rouse thyself!), *stand up, O Jerusalem,
thou that hast drunk at the hand of Jehovah the cup of His
wrath, the goblet cup of reeling* (or ' *staggering* ') *thou hast
drunk up and drained.*"

The figure of the intoxicating cup filled with the
" wine of staggering " [1] which God administers to those
who exhaust His long-suffering, is a familiar one in

[1] Ps. lx. 3.

Scripture. The primary passage in which it is fully developed is Ps. lxxv. 8 :

" *For in the hand of Jehovah is a cup, and the wine
     foameth ;
It is full of mixture, and He poureth of the same ;
Surely the dregs thereof all the wicked of the earth shall
     drain them and drink them.*"

This figure is " filled in on a more and more terrible scale " in the prophets,[1] and is in Jeremiah xxv. embodied in a symbolical act : " *For thus saith Jehovah the God of Israel unto me, Take this cup of wine of wrath at My hand and cause all the nations to drink it. . . . And they shall drink it and reel to and fro, and be mad because of the sword that I will send among them.*"

But the cup out of which the Jewish nation has had to drink is extra large and broad, for the description in the original of our passage—*qubba'ath kos*—is not merely a pleonastic expression equivalent to " *goblet-cup*," or " bowl of the cup," as rendered in the Revised Version,[2] but is used, as Delitzsch properly explains, to *give greater prominence to its swelling sides.* And this large goblet, filled to the brim with mixture of the fury of the wrath of God, poor Israel has not only had to drink, but to *drain to its very dregs.*

How terribly and literally true this prophetic description has proved, Jewish history testifies. As I have shown in the first part of this book (see pp. 75–81).

And the terrible record of Israel's sufferings is not ended yet. Indeed, it would almost seem as if they were made to drink the bitterest dregs of the cup at

---

[1] See Jer. xlix. 12, li. 7 ; Lam. iv. 21; Obad. v. 16; Ezek. xxiii. 32–34.

[2] The A.V. has followed the explanation of some of the Rabbinic commentators, which made קֻבַּעַת—*qubba'ath*—to mean " dregs."

the present time, for the sufferings which millions of
Jews in Central and Eastern Europe have been passing
through these past few years, surpass even those which
they endured in the darkest of the Middle Ages.

There is a tone of lamentation in the prophet's
voice as he proceeds to depict the helpless condition of
Jerusalem in her unconscious stupefaction : " *There
is none to guide her among all the sons whom she brought
forth ; neither is there one that taketh her by the hand
among all the sons that she hath brought up* "—a description; not so much of unnatural abandonment, as
of weakness. It is not that no one of her children *will*,
but that none of them *can* help her. " The consciousness of the punishment that their sins had deserved,
and the greatness of the sufferings that the punishment had brought, pressed heavily upon all, that not
one showed the requisite courage to rise upon her
behalf, so as to make her fate more tolerable and to
ward off the worst calamities." [1]   " *These two things
are befallen thee ; who shall bemoan thee ?* (or, ' *who shall
console thee ?* '[2]); *desolation and destruction* (or,
' *devastation and ruin* '), *and the famine and the sword.*"

Some have found a difficulty in this verse, since the
prophet says : " Two *things* have befallen thee," and
then proceeds to enumerate four. But the *two things*
are probably to be understood as two kinds, or
" families " of evil,[3] viz., devastation and ruin of the
city and land, and famine and the sword to the people.
And so great and terrible are the calamities that have
come upon her that even the inspired prophet, speaking in the name of God, is at a loss as to how or where-

[1] Delitzsch.
[2] ינּוד, *yanud*—from נוד—*nud*, to move, be agitated, also to shake the head as an expression of pity—hence to console, comfort.
[3] See Jer. xv. 3.

with to comfort her. The two last words in the 19th verse—*mi an-achamekh*, literally translated, mean " *Who I will comfort thee* "; and the Jewish Targum and one or two Christian commentators have rendered it : " *Who ? I myself will comfort thee.*" But I think the English versions : " *How,*" or " *By whom shall I comfort thee ?* " give the true sense. We are reminded of Lam. ii. 13 : " *What shall I testify of thee ? What shall I liken to thee, O daughter of Jerusalem ? What shall I compare to thee, O virgin daughter of Zion ? For thy breach is great, like the sea—who can heal thee ?* "

The figure of Zion or Jerusalem as the mother, and the people of Israel as her sons, is carried over also to the 20th verse, which gives the reason why, in her helplessness, " there was none to guide her among all the sons whom she brought forth," or to strengthen her, by taking hold of her hand, " among all the sons whom she hath brought up."

" *Thy sons have fainted* "—'*ulphu*—literally, " are covered over," " wrapped round," " veiled,"—an idiom describing a condition of unconsciousness ; " *they lie* (like dead corpses) at the head of all the streets " (*i.e.* in all public places); they lie—*k'tho mikhmar*—literally, as rendered in the Revised Version, " *as an antelope in a net,*" or, " like a netted antelope," *i.e.*, which has been taken in a hunter's net, and lies there exhausted after having almost strangled itself by ineffectual attempts to release itself.[1]

The climax in this picture of humiliation and wretchedness is reached in the last two clauses of the 20th verse : " *They lie,*" we read, " *as those who are full* (or *drunk*) *with the wrath of Jehovah, the rebuke of thy God.*" Ah ! this is the cause of it all, and constitutes the most poignant element in the bitter cup of Israel's

[1] Delitzsch.

sufferings. " It is the punishment decreed by God," as another writer observes, " which has pierced their very heart and got them completely in its power." Yes, let it be remembered, especially by scattered, suffering Israel, that what has happened to them is primarily the cause of God's wrath provoked, " till there was no remedy " [1] by manifold sins and apostasy. It was the hiding of His face which is the cause of all this misery ; it was the withdrawal of His divine protection which made them an easy prey to their Gentile oppressors, so that " *All that found them devoured them ; and their adversaries said, We offend not, because they have sinned against Jehovah, the hope of their fathers.*" [2]

But God will not always chide, neither will He cause His anger to burn for ever. Not utterly and for ever has He cast off the people that He foreknew. Even when making them drink of the staggering cup of His fury, He does not repudiate His covenant relationship to them. It is " the rebuke of *thy* God," He says, " which is the cause of thy present misery," and in this everlasting and indissoluble relationship between them and Jehovah, expressed in the words " *thy* God," rests the hope of Israel.

Still He is their God in a sense which is not true of any other nation, *as a nation*, and soon His anger will be turned away from them, and He will comfort them.[3] " *For a small moment,*" He says, through this same prophet Isaiah, " *I have forsaken thee, but with great mercies will I gather thee. In overflowing wrath I hid My face from thee for a moment, but with everlasting lovingkindness will I have mercy on thee, saith Jehovah thy Redeemer.*" [4]

And not only will He return with mercies to Zion,

[1] 2 Chron. xxxvi. 16. [2] Jer. l. 7.
[3] Isa. xii. 1. [4] Isa. liv. 7, 8.

He is going to direct His fury against those who
oppressed and humiliated them. The last three verses
of the chapter, while full of promise to Israel, contain
very solemn words of warning against those who have
mixed themselves up in God's controversy with His
own people : " *Therefore hear now this, thou afflicted
and drunken, but not with wine. Thus saith the Lord
Jehovah, and thy God that pleadeth the cause of His
people, behold I have taken out of thy hand the cup of
staggering, even the bowl of the cup of My wrath ; thou
shalt no more drink it again.*" Observe the glorious
majesty of the threefold Name which is expressed as
the certain basis of the promise—אֲדֹנַיִךְ יְהֹוָה וֵאלֹהַיִךְ—
'*adonaiykh Yehovah velohaiykh*—" Thy *Lord, Jehovah,
and thy God.*"

The word translated " Lord " is in the plural, and
is the only instance where it is so used of God. It is
intended, as already observed, to express the majesty
of God, but may also, as the name *Elohim*, rendered in
the English Bible " God," which is always in the plural,
contain the hint of the blessed truth more fully unfolded
in the New Testament, that Jehovah the God of Israel
is *Triune* in His essence and being. And this almighty,
everlasting, faithful Jehovah is " *Thy* Lord and *thy*
God," and this itself is an ocean of blessedness for God's
people.

The expression, " *yaribh 'ammo* " (rendered, " that
pleadeth the cause of His people "), is a very precious
and comforting one. It is an *attributive* clause, signifying " He that conducts the cause of His people," as
their advocate, defender, and avenger.

He is this in relation to Israel as a nation, and soon
He will once more " thoroughly plead their cause," [1]
and will do with their oppressors as He did with Assyria,

[1] Jer. l. 34.

Babylon, and the other powers of antiquity. But it is also true in relation to the individual believer, and He ever " stands at the right hand of the needy to save him from them that judge (or ' condemn ') his soul." [1]

Hence the triumphant challenge in Isa. l. 8 : " *He is near that justifieth me ; who will contend with me ?* [2] *Let us stand up together : who is mine adversary ? Let him come near to me.*" Or, in the words of the apostle, " *Who shall lay anything to the charge of God's elect ? It is God that justifieth. Who is he that condemneth ? It is Christ that died ; yea, rather, that is risen again, who is even at the right hand of God, who also maketh intercession for us.*" [3]

But to come back to our context : " *Behold,*" He says, " *I have taken out of thy hand the cup of staggering, even the bowl of the cup of My wrath ; thou shalt no more drink it again.*" This glorious promise contains also yet another proof that the prophecy we have been considering was not fulfilled in the return of the small remnant from Babylon, but must refer to the future. For after the return from Babylon, and in consequence of their rejection of the Messiah, Israel has had to drink out of the bitter cup of suffering more deeply than before, and the transitory joy of the small remnant on their first going back was followed after a time by the universal dispersion and the long night of sorrow and weeping, which has lasted already nearly two thousand years. No, as we have had occasion to note again and again, this prophecy looks beyond the partial restoration from Babylon to the final and universal restoration, when " *the ransomed of Jehovah shall return*

[1] Ps. cix. 31.
[2] The word is *yaribh*, the same as in Isa. li. 22, rendered " plead," or " pleadeth."
[3] Rom. viii. 33, 34.

and come with singing unto Zion, and everlasting joy shall be upon their heads ; they shall obtain gladness and joy, and sorrow and sighing shall flee away."

We come now to the last verse. Not only will pardoned and restored Israel " no more " for ever taste again of the cup of God's wrath, but, " *I will put it,*" He say's, " *into the hand of them that afflict thee* (lit., ' *thy tormentors* '), *that have said to thy soul, Bow down, that we may go over ; and thou hast laid thy back as the ground and as the street to them that go over.*"

Pride and cruelty have been the characteristics of the oppressors of God's people, and many have been not only the " afflictions," or " torments," but the *humiliations* which Israel in " captivity " and dispersion has had to endure—afflictions and humiliations which no other nation could have outlived, and which aimed not only at the breaking of their bodies, but the crushing of their " soul." But it is no matter of indifference to God as to how " the dearly-beloved of His soul," which was given over for a time on account of her sin into the hand of her enemies, was being treated by the Gentile world-powers, and immediately His purpose in the punishment of His own people is accomplished He will turn His wrath upon the nations who have thus treated them.

The 23rd verse reminds of the last words in chapter xlix. : " *Thus saith Jehovah, Even the captives of the mighty shall be taken away, and the prey of the terrible shall be delivered ; for I will contend with him that contendeth with thee, and I will save thy children. And I will feed them that oppress thee with their own flesh ; and they shall be drunken with their own blood as with sweet wine : and all flesh shall know that I, Jehovah, am thy Saviour and thy Redeemer, the Mighty One of Jacob.*"